The Singer-Songwriter Handbook

The Singer-Songwriter Handbook

JUSTIN A. WILLIAMS AND
KATHERINE WILLIAMS

Bloomsbury Academic
An imprint of Bloomsbury Publishing Inc
BLOOMSBURY
NEW YORK • LONDON • OXFORD • NEW DELHI • SYDNEY

Bloomsbury Academic
An imprint of Bloomsbury Publishing Inc

1385 Broadway
New York
NY 10018
USA

50 Bedford Square
London
WC1B 3DP
UK

www.bloomsbury.com

BLOOMSBURY and the Diana logo are trademarks of Bloomsbury Publishing Plc

First published 2017

Library of Congress Cataloging-in-Publication Data
A catalog record for this book is available from the Library of Congress.

ISBN: HB: 978-1-6289-2030-7
PB: 978-1-6289-2029-1
ePub: 978-1-6289-2032-1
ePDF: 978-1-6289-2031-4

Cover image © Benoit Daoust

Typeset by Fakenham Prepress Solutions, Fakenham, Norfolk NR21 8NN
Printed and bound in the United States of America

CONTENTS

LIST OF FIGURES

ACKNOWLEDGMENTS

As happens so frequently, this research project was prompted by the energy and enthusiasm of the next generation of musicians. The passion and dedication of emerging singer-songwriters, both those who train informally and those who follow established programmes at universities and colleges, is inspiring. In particular, Katherine would like to thank her Music Production students at Leeds College of Music (cohorts of 2011–13), and her performance students at Plymouth University (2014–16), particularly those involved in the Words and Music Festival workshops and performances in spring 2015. Justin would like to thank the enthusiastic and creative students at Anglia Ruskin University (2010–12) and Bristol University (2012–16), in particular those students who push communication and creativity to their limits.

This volume was vastly oversubscribed in terms of potential contributors, and we are grateful to all individuals who couldn't be included for their interest and time, and for their contribution to the practise and pedagogy in this arena. We would like to thank all contributors to this volume, which include several leading singer-songwriters, pedagogues, and academics. Every author has been timely, good-humored, professional, and a pleasure to work with. We would like to thank our institutions, the University of Bristol and Plymouth University, for providing research support for the volume.

Staff at Bloomsbury Academic have been a constant source of support for this volume. Commissioning Editor in Popular Music and Sound Studies Ally-Jane Grossan initially commissioned the Singer-Songwriter Handbook. Her enthusiasm for the project was infectious. Ally-Jane recently left Bloomsbury for pastures new, and her successor Leah Babb-Rosenfeld transitioned smoothly into the role, and has done an effective and efficient job of the final stages.

Given that they were the inspiration for this we'd like to dedicate this book to the next generation of singer-songwriters. Be they university or college students, or musicians striking it out on their own, the future is in their hands. We hope they continue keep the tradition of the singer-songwriter alive and evolving.

LIST OF CONTRIBUTORS

Alexandra Apolloni is the Program Coordinator at the UCLA Center for the Study of Women. She holds a PhD in Musicology from UCLA and was the recipient of a 2012 AMS-50 Fellowship. Her writing has appeared or is forthcoming in a number of scholarly and non-academic publications, including the *Journal of Popular Music Studies*, *Women & Music*, and *The Toast*. She is currently working on a book about young women and voice in 1960s Britain.

Nadav Appel holds a PhD in cultural studies from Bar-Ilan University and lectures at Bar-Ilan University, Open University of Israel, and Sapir Academic College. His studies investigate various aesthetic, cultural, and philosophical aspects of contemporary popular music.

Simon Barber is a Research Fellow in the Birmingham Centre for Media and Cultural Research at Birmingham City University, where he researches, writes, and lectures about songwriting, popular music, the music industries, and jazz. He is also the producer and co-presenter of the popular podcast, Sodajerker On Songwriting.

Richard James Burgess is currently CEO for the American Association of Independent Music (A2IM) and previously head of business at Smithsonian Folkways Recordings. Dr. Burgess has earned many gold, platinum, and multi-platinum albums as a studio musician, recording artist, producer, manager, and label owner. He is known for his pioneering work with synthesizers, computers, sampling, early house music, as the inventor of the SDSV drum synthesizer, and for coining the terms EDM and New Romantic. Other books include *The Art of Music Production: The Theory and Practice, 4th Edition* (Oxford University Press, 2013), and *The History of Music Production* (Oxford University Press, 2013).

Lisa Busby, a Scottish artist based in London, is a composer, vocalist, DJ, and a Lecturer in Music at Goldsmiths, University of London. She performs and composes with numerous bands exploring the fringes of song, and how popular forms can be set in new and unusual contexts; and as a solo artist with particular interests in using playback media as instruments, text-based score, installation, and site-specific performance.

Dane Chalfin is a vocal and performance coach working with charting and developing artists internationally. He is also Associate Professor – Vocal Coaching and Rehabilitation and Principal Lecturer in performance and Artistry at Leeds College of music as well as President of the British Voice Association (2015–16).

Claire Coleman is a musician, musicologist, and music educator whose professional interests center on the place and uses of popular music in contemporary culture, and in facilitating meaningful community music interactions. Her doctoral dissertation examines nostalgia in indie folk music.

Andrew Hillhouse is a musician, working primarily in folk, traditional, and choral musics, and is currently Executive Director and Artistic Director at the Harrison Festival Society. He received his PhD in Ethnomusicology from University of Toronto in 2013 on touring as social practice.

Emma Hooper is a musician, author, and academic. She teaches Commercial Music at Bath Spa University, researches gender and pop, plays solo and with others, and her novel Etta and Otto and Russell and James (2015) was published in 18 languages. Her forthcoming novel *A Long Sound, A Low Sound* will be out early 2018 (Penguin Books).

Juliane Jones is a sought-after singer-songwriter and ethnomusicologist, who specializes in popular and East Asian music. After a Fulbright Fellowship to study Chinese Music at the Shanghai Conservatory and completing her PhD on Chinese Kunqu composition, Juliane founded Ragged Silk, a cross-cultural music collective that performs on stages around the world.

Seth Lakeman, a West Country folk singer, songwriter and multi-instrumentalist, has successfully steered English folk into the mainstream over the last decade with high-energy performances and a series of best-selling albums. His previous albums include Mercury-nominated *Kitty Jay* and the gold-selling *Freedom Field,* which features the song "King & Country" and the Top 20 "Word of Mouth."

Mark Marrington is an academic whose current research interests are focused on the musicology of record production and issues relating to music technology and mediation. He has held teaching positions at Leeds College of Music and the University of Leeds and is currently a Senior Lecturer in Music Production at York St. John University.

Zack Moir is a Lecturer in Popular Music at Edinburgh Napier University, and The University of the Highlands and Islands. He has a strong research interest in popular music education and music in higher education, and is one of the editors of the *Routledge Research Companion to Popular Music Education.*

Samuel Nicholls is a Senior Lecturer in Music at Leeds Beckett University, and works with local and national organizations to promote artist and music industry development pathways through a number of events and programs. Sam has previously toured extensively with the band ¡Forward, Russia!, released platinum selling albums with his record label Dance To The Radio, and works as a live music promoter, studio producer, and more.

David Scott is singer-songwriter with the long-established orch-pop group The Pearlfishers, a BBC Radio Scotland broadcaster, and a community music practitioner. He is a Senior Lecturer at the University of the West of Scotland leading on the MA Music framework, songwriting, and creative projects.

Jo Collinson Scott is a lecturer in commercial music at the University of the West of Scotland, where she helped develop the MA Music: Songwriting degree. She is a practicing songwriter and performer who has toured internationally and worked with artists such as David Byrne, Vashti Bunyan, and Teenage Fanclub.

Mark Simos is Associate Professor in Berklee College of Music's Songwriting Department, where over the past decade he has created innovative curricula for songwriting, guitar techniques for songwriters, songwriting collaboration, and tune composition—documenting key elements of his approach in his book *Songwriting Strategies: A 360° Approach* (Berklee Press/Hal Leonard, 2014). He is an acclaimed songwriter, as well as a tune composer, fiddler, and accompanist for Celtic and American traditional music, with more than 150 songs and instrumentals recorded by prominent roots, Americana, and bluegrass artists, including Alison Krauss and Union Station, Ricky Skaggs, and the Del McCoury Band.

Rob Toulson is Professor of Commercial Music at the University of Westminster. He is a successful music producer and developer of innovative iPhone apps related to commercial music production.

Sija Tsai writes on popular music and Canadian music history. She has contributed to *Canadian Folk Music*, *Musicultures*, and CHRY FM. She currently resides in Toronto.

Lee Bob Watson is a singer-songwriter and producer from Northern California. His most recent work is with Lee Bob & The Truth, a rock 'n' roll band.

Justin A. Williams is Senior Lecturer in Music at the University of Bristol. He is author of the book *Rhymin' and Stealin': Musical Borrowing in Hip-hop,* editor of the *Cambridge Companion to Hip-hop*, and co-editor of the *Cambridge Companion to the Singer-Songwriter.*

Katherine Williams is Lecturer in Music at Plymouth University, U. K., where she also leads the performance pathway. She is author of *Rufus Wainwright*, and co-editor of the *Cambridge Companion to the Singer-Songwriter*.

Editors' Introduction

Justin A. Williams and Katherine Williams

How do songwriters hone their craft? What gives them inspiration? How does one expand on already-learned stylistic possibilities? How does one teach songwriting? How did the term "singer-songwriter" come about? How has it embraced new digital techniques of composition? How does someone monetize their music in the twenty-first century?

As many of the contributors to this volume have pointed out, the term "singer-songwriter" evokes particular imagery: a singer on stage, often playing an acoustic guitar, singing about their own life experiences. There is an intimacy involved, perhaps the hushed environment of a coffee house or small bar. Their lives are laid bare for us, in the music, and in their confessional "warts and all," often unpolished, singing style (think Bob Dylan or Joni Mitchell).

The notion of this style of singer-songwriter has its origins in the 1960s folk revival, and was capitalized on by figures such as David Geffen whose Asylum records housed Jackson Browne, Joni Mitchell, Bob Dylan, Tom Waits, Linda Ronstadt, Warren Zevon, and Judee Sill in the early 1970s. This particular notion of the singer-songwriter, as Lisa Busby notes in Chapter 8, does not allow for the digital and post-digital approaches to creativity that have become so widespread in the twenty-first century. Artists such as James Blake, FKA twigs, Thom Yorke, and others are utilizing technology and other influences to create new forms of intimate expression. The deeper that one investigates the figure of the singer-songwriter, the more that one begins to see how much more complicated it is on the surface than that man or woman pouring their heart out on stage with an acoustic guitar.

This project began as a complementary volume to our *Cambridge Companion to the Singer-Songwriter* (2016). While observing the vast quantity of artists engaging with singer-songwriter practices, we identified a pedagogical desire and shortage of texts that dealt with the figure of the singer-songwriter. The *Cambridge Companion* looked at historical figures from seventeenth-century England like Thomas D'Urfey, and artists such as Kanye West who write and perform their own material but are rarely placed in a "singer-songwriter" category. Contributors also dealt with the issue of authorship, considering artists like Adele who collaborate and co-write their music, yet still convey a sense of personal intimacy aligned with the singer-songwriter.

While that volume was intended to provide a history and academic frames for studying the phenomenon, this volume aims to be a more practical, hands-on tool for educators and singer-songwriters alike. Many of the chapters provide ideas or activities for people to experiment with or build into their songwriting and practice routines. Many of the contributors work at universities in songwriting or popular music programs, and other artists (such as Waitress for the Bees, Seth Lakeman, and Lee Bob Watson) share their experiences from their successful professional careers as singer-songwriters. This book provides some context, and case studies of famous singer-songwriters, but is primarily intended as a resource for those learning, or teaching, songwriting and performance. Above all, we hope that this book goes some distance to providing answers to the questions posed at the start of the Introduction.

The first section of the book, entitled Songwriting, is divided into more acoustic-based and electronic-based ideas around songwriting, though the two necessarily overlap. The first chapter, by Nadav Appel, frames the entire book in setting up a standard "disposition" associated with the singer-songwriter. He highlights the group of mostly white, Anglo-American musicians who achieved critical and commercial success in the early 1970s, such as Joni Mitchell, James Taylor, Neil Young, and Carole King, and the musical style associated with them. These artists and the industrial categorization emerge from the 1960s folk revival, and many characteristics that we still associate with singer-songwriters such as autobiographical expression and connection with the listener. In Chapter 2, Mark Simos provides a sandbox for singer-songwriters to play with and experiment with, in the interest of developing active strategies and working outside of comfort zones. Chapter 3 focuses on the pedagogy of popular music in higher education, specifically the case in U.K. universities. In Chapter 4, Simon Barber uses his experience as one half of the songwriting team Sodajerker, and their podcast series *Sodajerker on Songwriting,* to share songwriter thoughts on generating ideas, songwriting routines as well as collaboration and co-writing. Barber uses insight from Mann and Weil, Lamont Dozier, Neil Sedaka, Jimmy Webb, Guy Chambers, KT Tunstall and many others to identify tropes and common methodologies. Lee Bob Watson, the front man behind Lee Bob and the Truth, reflects in Chapter 5 about the necessary items to be a singer-songwriter, in his estimation: a river, a bible, and a broken heart.

The second half of the first part of the book shifts to techniques associated with digital music production. Chapters 6 and 7 deal with the digital audio workstation, and in Chapter 8 Lisa Busby looks at techniques which encompass the post-digital climate—techniques like microsampling—and the work of Radiohead, Animal Collective, Björk, Matmos, and Aphex

Twin. She considers numerous musical examples of digital programming while suggesting exercises for songwriters in order to experiment with such techniques.

Part Two is focused on singer-songwriter performance. Veteran vocal and performance coach Dane Chalfin discusses stagecraft for these performers in Chapter 9. In Chapter 10, Andrew Hillhouse and Sija Tsai discuss the folk festival circuit, and in particular the history of the Mariposa Folk Festival in Ontario Canada which has been a key site for singer-songwriter activity since its founding in 1961. Singer-songwriter Seth Lakeman, in interview with Katherine Williams, discusses some of his past career and opportunities in the music business. He also gives advice on songwriting, and on marketing oneself.

Part Three focuses on aspects of the music industry, and offers guidance through the economic realities of being a professional singer-songwriter. Sam Nicholls discusses revenue streams beyond traditional label models such as online crowdfunding. Jo Collinson Scott and David Scott discuss the concept of "esteem," in particular creative esteem and self-esteem, and the role of professionalism in the career. In Chapter 14, Emma Hooper (as the artist Waitress for the Bees) provides knowledge from her twenty years of experience as a singer-songwriter to discuss how to make the most out of your gigs, and hopefully never play a bad one again.

The fourth section of the book provides specific examples of singer-songwriters and scenes in their contexts. Chapter 15 deals with authorship and authority in the case of the contested authorship of "Sister Morphine," made famous by the British singer-songwriter Marianne Faithfull. In comparing three versions of the song from 1969, 1979, and 1989, Alexandra Apolloni notes the use of Faithfull's voice to claim authorship, reflecting the singer's journey from folk-pop ingénue to a mature singer-songwriter speaking from lived personal experience. Chapter 16 poses the idea of the singer-songwriter as bowerbird, able to gather items from the past and collect them to new purposes. Claire Coleman considers three contemporary indie folk artists, Bon Iver, Joanna Newsom, and Sufjan Stevens, and discusses their bricolage of past aesthetics into something new. In the final chapter of the volume, Juliane Jones provides a snapshot of prominent open mic nights for singer-songwriters in Nashville, New York City, and Shanghai. Her chapter illustrates how important these nights are as a creative space to experiment with ideas and present material to peers, and how laden with cultural value certain venues can be to singer-songwriters. In a sense, we come full circle with the type of singer-songwriter one initially thinks of when hearing the term: a singer with guitar, sharing emotive material from the songwriter's inner world. But, as Jones writes in her final suggestion to budding singer-songwriters, budding singer-songwriters should "Make your own path." We hope that this book not only helps singer-songwriters in the twenty-first century to think about the historical and ideological origins of the persona, but also inspires new ideas, new frames of thinking that ever expand the boundaries of artistic creativity.

PART ONE A

Songwriting

CHAPTER 1

The singer-songwriter disposition[1]

Nadav Appel

In a literal sense, a "singer-songwriter" is a person who writes and performs their own songs. In popular music studies and rock criticism, the term is often used in a narrower sense in order to refer to a group of mostly white, Anglo-American musicians who achieved critical and commercial success in the early 1970s, such as Joni Mitchell, James Taylor, Neil Young, and Carole King, and to the musical style associated with them. Though there is no consensual definition of what a singer-songwriter is supposed to sound like, the aesthetic characteristics that are usually attributed to singer-songwriters are the use of acoustic instruments (the acoustic guitar being the most emblematic), a direct, allegedly "unmediated" style of performance, and an emphasis on lyrical content that is often described as "poetic," "personal," and "confessional."[2] In addition, as Roy Shuker notes, "the concept of singer-songwriter continues to have strong connotations of greater *authenticity* and 'true' *auteurship*."[3]

The singer-songwriter style is often said to have evolved from the 1960s folk revival and folk-rock movement. However, utilizing Simon Frith's tripartite structure of musical experience as determined by three overlapping grids—the art discourse, the folk discourse, and the pop discourse[4]—it appears that this traditional conception of the singer-songwriter draws not only from the folk world's preference for simplicity and forthrightness, but also from commercial pop's "torch song" sentimentality (going back to pre-rock traditions such as the Tin Pan Alley crooners)[5] alongside classical music's cult of the individual genius-composer.

While the folk and pop elements of the singer-songwriter are stylistic—they determine *how* a singer-songwriter sounds and performs—the art element is ideological, as it determines *what* a singer-songwriter is and *who* is deserving of this title. This chapter will be mostly concerned with the stylistic elements, as the romantic conceptions of authenticity and auteurship in popular music have already been heavily scrutinized, critiqued, deconstructed, and reconstructed in many other sources.[6] The pertinent question is what sort of critical, analytical, and practical use is left for the concept of the singer-songwriter in our "post-authentic" age? What remains, other than a possibly outdated and somewhat unfashionable historical style, once we free the singer-songwriter from the clutches of tradition and rockist orthodoxy?

A good place to start is Tim Wise's suggestion that "singer-songwriter" denotes not a genre but "a format which can occur in a variety of genres, styles and historical periods."[7] Following Wise, this chapter will argue that the concept of the singer-songwriter still carries with it remarkable value, for scholars and performers alike, if we approach it as neither a genre nor a format but a *performative disposition*, one that is evident in the works of many contemporary musicians who would not be conventionally identified as singer-songwriters. The term "performative disposition" refers to a defined, relatively stable set of aesthetic and rhetorical principles that can be tactically deployed by musicians working in different styles and genres, whether throughout their entire career, over the course of a whole album, or just in a single performance or recording. You can think of it as a sort of an artistic persona, as long as you remember not that it is a durable, continuous identity but rather that it exists only in its performance.

An implicit assumption that often dominates discussions about singer-songwriters is that, since the performer ("singer") and the author ("songwriter") are one, then the work itself necessarily reflects an actual personal truth about the musician who wrote and performed it. As Wise points out, "the term [singer-songwriter] broadly signifies a certain seriousness of personal expression."[8] However, once we understand the "singer-songwriter" as a performative disposition, it is solely the *performance* of such truth which should matter (that is, unless one is conducting a biographical study of the artist). This applies to audiences and performers alike. When Bob Dylan was interrogated about the autobiographical elements in his work, his reply was:

> A lot of people thought that song [Idiot Wind], that album *Blood on the Tracks*, pertained to me. Because it seemed to at the time. It didn't pertain to me ... I didn't really think I was giving away too much; I thought that it *seemed* so personal that people would think it was about so-and-so who was close to me. It wasn't ... I didn't feel that one was too personal, but I felt it *seemed* too personal. Which might be the same thing.[9]

It is not by chance that Dylan made this specific point in regard to *Blood on the Tracks*—this was, according to David R. Shumway, his first album that actually fit the "singer-songwriter" label.[10] In other words, this was the first album where Dylan fully embraced the performative disposition associated with singer-songwriters, and his words make it clear that this has nothing to do with the actual biographical fidelity of the album's contents. Consequently, if we accept his suggestion that it does not really matter whether a song really is personal or just seems personal, then what we have to determine is what it is that Dylan—and many other musicians—did, and still do, in order to make some of their songs seem so personal. What is it about their performative disposition that enables or even encourages their audience to experience their songs as conveying some sort of a personal truth?

The singer-songwriter disposition rests on four central principles: first, *the foregrounding of the ordinary human voice*, as opposed to vocal or instrumental virtuosity. Second, *the fabrication of a sonic environment which connotes intimacy*, as opposed to spectacle. Third, *the indication of a direct relation to the individual listener*, as opposed to a generalized appeal to a mass audience. And fourth, *the connotation of an air of sincerity*, as opposed to irony or cynicism.

These four principles, which comprise the singer-songwriter disposition, are presented here as binary opposites in order to simplify the presentation of the scheme. It is important to remember that binary opposites are ideal constructions and are never wholly representative of the complexity and hybridity of the real world. Nevertheless, they are useful as an analytical tool. Turning first to the works of one of the most quintessential singer-songwriters of the "classic" era, the Canadian musician Joni Mitchell, we can hear an example of how the singer-songwriter disposition is traditionally performed.

"The Last Time I Saw Richard"—the final track on Mitchell's most critically acclaimed album, *Blue* (1971)—opens with a solo acoustic grand piano playing the song's harmonic progression for almost a minute until Mitchell's untreated vocals come in, close-miked and mixed upfront. This stark sonic environment remains unchanged for the rest of the song, lending a naturalistic effect to the recording, as if Mitchell is simply playing her piano at home, singing to herself—or to us. Even without paying attention to the words that Mitchell sings, it is enough to be familiar with the auditory conventions on which the song's arrangement and production are based in order to identify its connotations of domesticity and intimacy.[11]

The song's lyrics are written in the first person, and the way that the narrator recalls a specific conversation with a specific person ("Richard") at a specific time (1968) and place (a café in Detroit) encourages the listener to make a connection between the lyrical "I" and Mitchell's autobiographical "I." She seems to be describing real world events that had actually happened to her. As the song was allegedly written about her ex-husband, Chuck, it is possible that Mitchell really is describing real world events.[12] However, the question of autobiographical truth is only of secondary importance here. What is paramount is the *performance* of autobiographical truth, the way that Mitchell adapts a performative disposition that lends the feeling of self-disclosure. It is this air of sincerity that led many rock critics to dub musicians such as Mitchell "confessional."[13]

Just as important as the content of the lyrics is the way that Mitchell sings them. Mitchell uses a conversational tone, as if relating a story to the listener, and she plays freely with the song's meter. She either crams too many syllables into the lines or uses not enough syllables while drawing them out with melismatic embellishments. This is a formal way to signify that we should pay attention to what she has to say, that the precision of the lyrics is too important to be constrained or compromised by the structure of the song.

An additional vocal technique that Mitchell uses at certain points—for example, while singing the phrase "all romantics meet the same fate someday"—involves raising the pitch of her singing while lowering its dynamics. This is rather unusual because typically in popular music styles the vocal dynamics tend to increase when the pitch gets higher, which lends the singing a dramatic, emotive effect (listen to the rest of the song: Mitchell does it herself later on). Decreasing the dynamics while raising the pitch, on the other hand, achieves a sort of a hushed, intimate quality, creating the impression that the vocalist is singing at a close proximity to the listener.

It is in the incorporation of all the aforementioned elements—the "intimate" arrangement which is centered around Mitchell's voice, the confessional nature of the lyrics, the very specific techniques of singing and performing, utilized in a precise manner in order to achieve their typical effects—that we can hear what is practically a textbook example of a performance of the singer-songwriter disposition.[14]

The singer-songwriter as a distinct musical style, personified by artists such as Mitchell, reached its peak in the early 1970s. It went out of critical favor, at least in the Anglophone world, in the second half of the decade, more or less simultaneously with (and possibly as a result of) the two great musical revolutions of punk and disco. Thus, critical writing on the subject often limits itself to an identification of singer-songwriters with either the original artists that achieved fame under this title or later musicians who mostly followed a similar musical style.

Scholarly attempts in the last decade to understand contemporary singer-songwriters have been quite scarce. Ian Biddle did some very interesting work from a gender and class perspective on what he calls "the new male singer/songwriter," concentrating on four white male musicians who achieved considerable prominence in the indie music scene during the 2000s: José González, Sufjan Stevens, Devendra Banhart, and Damien Rice. Biddle characterizes their work by "a kind of openness to vulnerability, a commitment to social and sexual intimacy, and a tendency to want to avoid the overt spectacularization of masculinity."[15] The traits and aspects that Biddle attributes to these artists are indeed a typical result of the deployment of the singer-songwriter disposition, and Biddle's study is essential for thinking about the social and political implications inherent in certain types of aesthetic, stylistic, and performative choices.

Concurrently, it is also important to widen the scope of our analysis beyond artists such as the ones investigated by Biddle who already conform to the classical image of the singer-songwriter as a white, acoustic guitar-wielding troubadour. Limiting ourselves to the aesthetic palette identified with traditional singer-songwriters runs the risk of reifying the singer-songwriter disposition on the basis of a contingent aesthetic form (and its underlying racialized and gendered stereotype) that was most often used to perform it when it initially achieved mainstream popularity. In other words, the historical fact that the singer-songwriter disposition first became popular when it was performed with acoustic instruments and recorded with a naturalistic production does not mean that this is the only way to perform it. The basic question that we have to answer is pragmatic and empirical: what means do musicians use in order to produce certain effects? The singer-songwriter disposition should be understood, in this context, as one of the many tools in the contemporary musician's toolkit, a tool that can be deployed whenever its effects—proximity, vulnerability, sincerity, intimacy, and emotional honesty—are required to serve a specific work.

A promising direction for understanding the singer-songwriter disposition is suggested in Ronald D. Lankford Jr.'s study of female singer-songwriters in the 1990s. "While adapting many of the traditional trappings of the singer-songwriter style," writes Lankford about musicians such as PJ Harvey, Courtney Love, and Tori Amos, "these women also pushed hard against old boundaries."[16] Indeed, one of the interesting things about contemporary performances of the singer-songwriter disposition is the way in which they respond to changes in cultural and musical standards and practices and the conventional meanings associated with them.

One important facet of these changes is that the association between acoustic instruments and a sense of intimacy and proximity that was widely accepted in the 1960s and 1970s seems to have faded in the last fifteen years. This is probably a result of the increasing ease of use and access to electronic and digital means of music production, which inevitably led to rising audience familiarity with their sound. Thus, as Simon Zagorski-Thomas notes, while Bob Dylan's move to electric instrumentation in 1965 proved to be quite controversial with portions of his audience, the use of synthesizers and drum loop samples by the English musician David Gray on his 2000 album *White Ladder* sustained the feelings of honesty and unmediated communication associated with his music, even leading the music critic Tyler Jacobson to declare that Gray still "sounds like a guy playing his acoustic guitar."[17] There is no need to stress that Jacobson is well aware in his review that Gray is *not* playing his acoustic guitar. What Jacobson means is that even though Gray is utilizing a host of electronic instrumentation, he still manages to evoke the *effects* associated with the classical guitar playing singer-songwriter.

Listening to hip-hop artist Kanye West's "Love Lockdown," the lead single from his 2008 album *808s & Heartbreak*, it would be quite hard to make a case for West sounding like a guy playing his acoustic guitar. The track's arrangement, though quite stark, is based mainly around electronic instrumentation. The only discernible acoustic instruments are the Taiko drums that accompany the angry, slightly histrionic choruses which stand in contrast to the melancholic verses. However, any electronic music aficionado would recognize the bass sound in the verses as originating from the Roland TR-808 drum machine which is used on the song and throughout the album (and referred toion the album's title). Introduced to the market in 1980, the TR-808 has been used in countless soul, hip-hop and house classics.[18] It does not sound like an acoustic guitar, of course, but its contemporary associations with simplicity, DIY, and a "back to basics" attitude allow it to play, in hip-hop and electronic music culture, a similar role to the one that the acoustic guitar serves in rock-oriented productions.[19]

The uncluttered, minimalist arrangement, revolving mainly around the TR-808 bass beat, contributes to the construction of a singer-songwriter disposition, as West's vocals are performed against a bare and mostly unadorned sonic environment. The lyrics are in the first person, and the vocoder effect certainly draws attention to West's voice and the lyrical content. However, it is the vocals themselves—distorted and digitally manipulated to the point of hardly sounding human—that, at first listen, seem as far removed as can be from the traditional singer-songwriter vocals. Is it still possible to strike a sincere, "confessional" pose while sounding like a cyborg?

To answer this question we have to remember, as Nick Prior points out, that the "warm," intimate vocals associated with the classical crooners and singer-songwriters were also mediated by a certain technology, the electric microphone.[20] There is nothing inherently direct or unmediated that is present in "warm" recorded voices while lacking from the "roboticized" voice produced by vocoders and digital voice manipulators. Again, it is a question of shifting cultural conventions. As Joseph Auner illustrates, the employment of the vocoder during the delivery of "confessional" or "personal" material can already be identified in certain songs recorded during the late 1990s by Radiohead and Moby.[21] In the last decade, the use of cyborgian vocalities has become quite common among performers who attempt to convey emotional honesty and intimacy, as can also be heard in the works of musicians such as Bon Iver and James Blake. In a sense, the digital manipulation of the voice renders it naked and vulnerable by severing the link with its embodied source, stripping it of gendered and racial connotations. As Prior puts it, "the vocoder de-aligns the voice's 'grain' from its gender."[22] Thus, paradoxically enough, the machinic voice is able to function as pure subjective expression, unencumbered by the contingent constraints of one's own body.

We have previously characterized the singer-songwriter disposition as foregrounding the ordinary human voice in opposition to vocal or instrumental virtuosity. Indeed, a common criticism that is raised against the use of auto-tuned vocals is that they constitute a sort of "cheating," that the singer's natural voice is not as good as it sounds on record. It is certainly debatable how well Kanye West can sing in tune without the help of digital voice manipulation, but at the same time it is entirely irrelevant for the singer-songwriter disposition, as the aim is not virtuosity but expression. If the disposition aims to foreground the ordinary voice, then digital processing allows the voice to shed any sign of remarkableness. To paraphrase Roland Barthes, the digitalized voice is "singing degree zero."[23]

Of course, not all contemporary uses of the singer-songwriter disposition are based on vocoderized vocals. In the song "Lights On" (2014), British musician FKA twigs deploys both electronic and acoustic instrumentation to construct a stark, abstract soundscape which is heavily occupied by her close-miked vocals. The sense of proximity constructed by the production is reflected in the lyrical content, which ponders both the perils and the pleasures of emotional and physical intimacy. In "Bad Religion" (2012), Frank Ocean mournfully croons a dialogue—mostly a monologue—between "himself" and a taxi driver inside the driver's vehicle. The arrangement simulates the claustrophobic surroundings of the interior of a taxi cab by using sparse instrumentation—a church organ, a string section, and the occasional snare drum and handclaps—while the soulful vocal delivery and lyrical content reinforce the sense of proximity between Ocean and his addressee, whether that be the taxi driver or the actual listener.

Compared with Kanye West, the means by which FKA twigs and Frank Ocean perform the singer-songwriter disposition are relatively closer to the style employed by the traditional singer-songwriters. Nevertheless, their use of eclectic instrumentation, their reliance on digital production, and the influence of soul and hip-hop phrasings on their singing serve to remind us that the singer-songwriter disposition was always wider and more inclusive than what the "white guy with acoustic guitar" stereotype made it to be.

A more complicated case is presented on the song "Oblivion" (2012) by the Canadian artist Grimes (née Claire Boucher). This track negotiates and pushes the boundaries of the accepted conventions of the singer-songwriter disposition farther than any other song discussed in this chapter. The sonic environment is composed of an insistent, repetitive faux-retro synthesizer *ostinato*, a driving electronic beat, and Grimes's multi-tracked vocals. The lyrics, written in the first person, deal with Grimes's feelings following a sexual assault that she suffered. In a 2012 interview with *Spin* magazine,

Grimes revealed that her motivation in recording the song was both to divulge her feelings and to transform them into something empowering:

> I can't censor myself; it's really important for me to say how I feel. I needed to put out this song. I needed to make this song. I took one of the most shattering experiences of my life and turned it into something I can build a career on and that allows me to travel the world.[24]

How do Grimes's intentions manifest themselves in the song? Her vocal mannerisms and the repetitive, minimalistic nature of the melodic synth vamp tap into the singer-songwriter disposition, constructing an initial intimate sonic arena where Grimes can confess her feelings. Take note that she uses in her singing the same "pitch raising-dynamics falling" trick that we identified in Joni Mitchell's song, which has the effect of simulating proximity between the singer and the listener. At the same time, the propulsive, syncopated rhythm, carried on by a snare backbeat, like a throwback to 1950s rock 'n' roll music, carries the listener out of the self-scrutinizing singer-songwriter disposition and enables us also to experience the song as a joyful dance track. Thus, by juxtaposing the singer-songwriter disposition with the conventions of dance music, Grimes manages to construct a track that is confessional and uplifting, harrowing and empowering at the same time.

In summary, the concept of the singer-songwriter disposition introduced in this chapter is meant to serve as a practical concept for application in the analysis and production of contemporary popular music. Most of the artists who were discussed are not usually labeled singer-songwriters. This is also related to the fact that most of them are not white males—this issue merits a different discussion[25]—but it is also because their aesthetic palette and means of performance and production are quite different from those of popular musicians that have been historically associated with the term. Still, if we regard the singer-songwriter not as an identity or as a fixed style but as a performative disposition, we can see how it is still regularly employed, in original, creative, and occasionally surprising ways, by a variety of artists working in many different genres. Locating the uses of the singer-songwriter disposition in their work enables us to add an additional layer to our understanding of how popular music is written, recorded, performed, and experienced in the twenty-first century.

Notes

1 A draft version of this chapter was presented at the 18th International Conference of the International Association for the Study of Popular Music (IASPM) at the University of Campinas, Brazil. The author would like

to thank the session participants for their helpful remarks, and Bar-Ilan University and IASPM for helping to fund travel to the conference.

2 Roy Shuker, *Popular Music: The Key Concepts*, 2nd edn (London and New York: Routledge, 2005), 248–9; Richard Crawford and Larry Hamberlin, *An Introduction to America's Music*, 2nd edn (New York: W. W. Norton & Co., 2013), 474; Duncan Wheeler and Lucy O'Brien, "The Cultural and Gender Politics of Enunciation: Locating the Singer-Songwriter within and beyond Male Anglo-American Contexts," *Journal of World Popular Music* 1 (2014): 229.

3 Shuker, *Popular Music*, 249 (emphasis in original).

4 Simon Frith, *Performing Rites: On the Value of Popular Music* (Cambridge, MA: Harvard University Press, 1996), 28–44.

5 On the affinity between the classical singer-songwriter style and Tin Pan Alley sentimentality see Larry David Smith, *Elvis Costello, Joni Mitchell, and the Torch Song Tradition* (Westport and London: Praeger, 2004).

6 Sarah Thornton, *Club Cultures: Music, Media and Subcultural Capital* (Hanover and London: University Press of New England, 1996), 26–86; Allan Moore, "Authenticity as Authentication," *Popular Music* 21 (2002): 209–23; Hugh Barker and Yuval Taylor, *Faking It: The Quest for Authenticity in Popular Music* (New York: W. W. Norton & Co., 2007).

7 Tim Wise, "Singer-Songwriter," in *Continuum Encyclopedia of Popular Music of the World*, Vol. 8, ed. David Horn (New York: Continuum, 2012), 433.

8 Ibid., 430.

9 Bill Flanagan, *Written in My Soul: Conversations with Rock's Great Songwriters* (Chicago: Contemporary Books, 1987), 96–7 (emphasis in original).

10 David R. Shumway, "The Emergence of the Singer-Songwriter," in *The Cambridge Companion to the Singer-Songwriter*, eds. Katherine Williams and Justin A. Williams (Cambridge: Cambridge University Press, 2016), 11.

11 For a more detailed discussion of the utilization of specific recording techniques in order to construct a sense of intimacy and proximity, see Nicola Dibben, "Vocal Performance and the Projection of Emotional Authenticity," in *The Ashgate Research Companion to Popular Musicology*, ed. Derek B. Scott (Farnham and Burlington: Ashgate, 2009), 319–21.

12 Michelle Mercer, *Will You Take Me as I Am: Joni Mitchell's* Blue *Period* (New York: Free Press, 2009), 111.

13 For example, *AllMusic*'s single-sentence summary of Mitchell's biography describes her as "[a] confessional singer/songwriter regarded as one of the finest of her generation." According to *Rolling Stone*, Mitchell's *Blue* represents "the zenith of confessional songwriting." Jason Ankeny, "Joni Mitchell," *AllMusic*, http://www.allmusic.com/artist/joni-mitchell-mn0000270491 (accessed February 5, 2016); Jim Macnie, "Joni Mitchell: Biography," *Rolling Stone*, http://www.rollingstone.com/music/artists/joni-mitchell/biography (accessed February 5, 2016).

14 Shumway's examples of what he terms the "confessional mode" or

"confessional stance" in Mitchell's and James Taylor's music are excellent illustrations of additional early employments of the singer-songwriter disposition. Shumway, "Emergence of the Singer-Songwriter," 15–16.

15 Ian Biddle, "'The Singsong of Undead Labor': Gender Nostalgia and the Vocal Fantasy of Intimacy in the 'New' Male Singer/Songwriter," in *Oh Boy!: Masculinities and Popular Music*, ed. Freya Jarman-Ivens (New York and London: Routledge, 2007), 125.

16 Ronald D. Lankford Jr., *Women Singer-Songwriters in Rock: A Populist Rebellion in the 1990s* (Lanham, Toronto, and Plymouth: The Scarecrow Press, 2010), xii.

17 Simon Zagorski-Thomas, "The Stadium in Your Bedroom: Functional Staging, Authenticity and the Audience-Led Aesthetic in Record Production," *Popular Music* 29 (2010): 258; Tyler Jacobson, David Gray: "*White Ladder*," *Hybrid Magazine*, http://www.hybridmagazine.com/reviews/1100/dgray.shtml (accessed August 11, 2015).

18 Paul Théberge, *Any Sound You Can Imagine: Making Music/Consuming Technology* (Middletown: Wesleyan University Press, 1997), 196–8.

19 The "sparse texture and sense of longing and nostalgia" produced by West's use of the TR-808 is also noted in Lori Burns, Alyssa Woods, and Marc Lafrance, "Sampling and Storytelling: Kanye West's Vocal and Sonic Narratives," in *The Cambridge Companion to the Singer-Songwriter*, eds. Katherine Williams and Justin A. Williams (Cambridge: Cambridge University Press, 2016), 160.

20 Nick Prior, "Software Sequencers and Cyborg Singers: Popular Music in the Digital Hypermodern," *New Formations* 66 (2009): 93.

21 Joseph Auner, "'Sing It for Me': Posthuman Ventriloquism in Recent Popular Music," *Journal of the Royal Musical Association* 128 (2003): 111–22.

22 Prior, "Softare Sequences and Cyborg Singers," 93.

23 Roland Barthes, *Writing Degree Zero*, trans. Annette Lavers and Colin Smith (London: Jonathan Cape, 1967).

24 Jessica Hopper, "Grimes Comes Clean: Synth-Pop Provocateur on Her Big Year," *Spin*, December 6, 2012, http://www.spin.com/articles/grimes-interview-2012-big-year (accessed June 24, 2015).

25 Some interesting thoughts on this subject are presented in Wheeler and O'Brien, "Politics of Enunciation," 228–48. It should be noted, though, that for a genre that places a significant stress on the concept of authenticity—traditionally the domain of heterosexual males in popular music—there is a relatively large number of acclaimed female singer-songwriters.

CHAPTER 2

The performing songwriter's dilemma: Principles and practices[1]

Mark Simos

The performing songwriter's creative tasks

A scenario. Picture, if you will, a young songwriter sitting alone at her apartment window: guitar on lap, notebook and pen at hand, ready to write a song. She begins plunking out chords, humming wordless scraps of melody; then starts mumbling inchoate half-words and nonsense syllables, thinking all the while about last night's fight with her annoying boyfriend. Later that week, at the local club, she stands alone on stage, singing her new song for a few dedicated fans and a crowd of noisy office workers laughing at the bar.

This seemingly casual scenario evokes a common popular image of the performing singer-songwriter: writing about her personal experience, as a solo artistic endeavor, accompanying herself as she sings her own songs. Yet there are hidden complexities in this daunting assemblage of creative tasks—at once immeasurably ancient, yet in their juxtaposition distinctively contemporary. These tasks combine—and to an extent, conflate—a set of skills that, in other musical cultures, and in other Euro-American musical eras and genres, have typically been partitioned across distinct creative roles.

Simply writing a great song has always been hard; it is hard even to explain all the reasons why it *is* hard. One reason is songwriting's hybrid nature. We readily acknowledge pedagogies for arts of words (fiction, poetry), and for composing or improvising music; while the songwriter's art, combining both elements, strikes many admirers—and practitioners—as somehow beyond pedagogy.

Yet our heroine faces challenges beyond just mastering that elusive alchemy of words and music required to craft a great song. She will need to hone vocal and instrumental chops, stagecraft, and presence, to put her song across compellingly in performance, and later in recording. (She'll also need a plethora of business, social media, and professional skills: to build her fan base, book a tour, or negotiate a record contract—aspects beyond the scope of this chapter.) Amidst these multiple pressures, she must find her way to work of originality and authenticity—reflecting her true and distinctive voice. No pressure, though!

360° songwriting. As a teacher for the past decade in Berklee College of Music's long-established Songwriting Department, I share with my faculty colleagues some faith that there are workable ways to teach and advance the art of songwriting. Based on my own experience as a songwriter, and my work with student writers of diverse backgrounds and styles, I developed an approach, 360° songwriting, described in my book *Songwriting Strategies: A 360° Approach* (Berklee Press/Hal Leonard, 2014).

Founded on a spirit of self-challenge in both creative work and skill development, 360° songwriting offers a detailed model of alternative songwriting processes, but does not prescribe a single preferred process. Instead, songwriters learn to write "from all directions," with a comprehensive set of cross-training exercises focused on core facets of songwriting: rhythm, lyrics, melody, and harmony. Individual songwriters work with these facets in distinct and diverse ways; but most settle on limited repertoires of preferred strategies. By iteratively experimenting with varying processes and sequences—e.g., writing both from lyrics first and from melody first—songwriters can move beyond habitual creative practices, to expand their range and versatility in songwriting.

Composition vs. performance skills. Many student writers I work with aspire to be *performing* songwriters: writing songs primarily for their own performance, and performing primarily their own songs. I have explored ways to extend the 360° cross-training approach beyond core songwriting skills to the broader set of skills demanded of performing songwriters. Yet working with these writers, observing their creative struggles and challenges, I have come to realize that the interactions of songwriting and performance skills are not easily compartmentalized.

For comparison, consider an aspiring musical theater performer, expected to excel at singing, dancing, and acting. These performance-oriented skills require separate training, yet their interactions are somewhat limited. Being a good singer won't directly help you to be a good dancer; but it won't get too much in your way either. Now imagine a performer who must also write the book and compose the lyrics and music for the songs in their show. This is a fairer analogy to the span of creative tasks—both *compositional* and *performance-oriented* in nature—expected of the performing songwriter.

Though the respective skills of songwriting and performance are qualitatively different, they interweave in complex and subtle, at times counter-intuitive ways. Some of these are direct and unsurprising correlations; it's fairly clear how your limitations in one creative area could restrict you in other areas. For example, limited guitar skills naturally restrict the kinds of chord progression you might hear, play, and incorporate in your songs. Comparable dynamics would apply with other aspects such as vocal skills.

Harder to understand and address is a complementary dynamic: for *strengths* in one creative area can also work *against* progress in other areas. In particular, high levels of skill in vocal or instrumental technique, or in stage performance, can actually make it harder to work on certain aspects of songwriting: a curious sort of inverse relationship of composition and performance skills, where strength does not always build on strength.

These issues can be more difficult to address than known limitations. For most of us, it is easier to forgive our weaknesses than to stop leaning on our strengths, to come to terms with how what we do well can hold us back. In critique, it is tricky for songwriters or listeners to identify problems in songs that are responses to high levels of performance skills; those very skills can obscure the problems. Once identified, these problems can be devilishly hard to work on in revision, and can restrict new writing and broader artistic choices as well. Improving individual skills may even intensify these conflicts. Because songwriting and performance are both central to their overall artistic role, negotiating the distinct yet interwoven nature of these skills, and their interactions, can be said to constitute a quintessential *performing songwriter's dilemma*.

If limitations *and* strengths can get in the way, what are effective ways to fully develop one's artistry as a performing songwriter? Obviously, I do not advocate avoiding or neglecting work on the separate aspects of vocal skills, instrumental chops, or musical knowledge. Yet in working only in isolated fashion on songwriting and performance skills, constraining interactions may remain largely invisible. Working on skills in tandem—in complete songs in performance—may feel more holistic, but also leave subtle interactions entangled and unexamined. How can we experience and engage with these interactions more directly?

Scope of the chapter. This chapter offers practical strategies for tackling these distinctive dynamics: the creative and *un*creative tensions of the performing songwriter's dilemma. I offer concepts and supporting metaphors to explain these dynamics, using specific interactions of songwriting and vocal skills as a detailed example. I then present practices and exercises that extend a cross-training approach to working with these interactions. I evolved these concepts and exercises through reflecting on my own practice as a songwriter, co-writer, and performer; through discussions with fellow faculty; and most importantly, in mentoring many talented, hard-working (and patient!) student songwriters. I gratefully acknowledge all these contributions.

Individual songwriters can apply these techniques in several areas: critique and revision; self-challenges for new creative work; and in negotiating broader rhythms of artistic development. Concepts and exercises are described in non-technical terms, to be accessible not only to students in formal programs of study but to any songwriter, aspiring or experienced, desiring to further develop his or her skills. Though some concepts may seem theoretical in tone, I have found it essential to present them directly to songwriters, to motivate exercises that otherwise can yield frustrating or dissatisfying initial creative results. A grasp of these underlying principles also empowers songwriters to adapt, tailor, and extend exercises and challenges in ways most appropriate for them.

My focus in this chapter is on interference dynamics most relevant to performing songwriters in particular. The principles involved, and variations of the techniques, certainly apply to other profiles of songwriters, and to creative artists across the spectrum: producer/writers, staff or project writers, or those identifying most as performers. I suspect that similar principles are used by artists and teachers in many forms and media, and would welcome perspectives from other disciplines.

Teachers in either academic or less formal settings should also find these materials useful. However, I do not have the scope here to address many issues of curriculum design and pedagogy raised by the approach. And while I hope these concepts could provide useful questions for more scholarly research, I have not surveyed the academic literature for related work. For now, this chapter should serve as a songwriter's and songwriting teacher's report from the field.

Creative work as process and sequence

To understand the interplay of composition and performance dynamics, it's helpful to consider creative work as a sequence of activities, steps, or stages. We create a song, for example, through successive stages of composition, critique and revision, arrangement, performance, production, and recording. You may find it helpful to visualize this sequence of creative activities as a stream, where decisions made in one stage flow "downstream" to influence subsequent stages. Contrasting aesthetic concerns shift to the foreground in successive stages.

Each creative stage requires distinct if overlapping skills, which songwriters develop to varying degrees and at different paces. As we reconcile imbalances in skill levels at various stages, we tend to favor or rely more heavily on the activities of our greatest strengths. This creates asymmetrical dynamics, depending on whether our areas of strength come earlier or later in the sequence:

- *Narrowing*. Strong songwriting skills, relative to performance skills, can generally have positive effects: that is, if we write songs that are challenging for us to perform, we push ourselves in turn to further develop performance skills. The risk for performing songwriters in this configuration is a tendency to narrow or "pinch" their range as songwriters, due to the expectation of performing their songs. These sorts of problems therefore show up particularly in the *range* of songs we write.
- *Compensating*. Conversely, with stronger performance skills, we often compensate or "cheat" by mis-applying skills earlier in the process, masking compositional issues with which we need to engage. As these unaddressed issues ripple through to later stages, they become progressively harder to identify and revise. These dynamics therefore tend to show up particularly in critique and revision of existing songs.

Interactions of songwriting and vocal concerns

To clarify these dynamics, let's look in detail at interactions between songwriting and one specific aspect of performance: vocal skills. This is an illustrative example, as these interactions and their effects can be very clearly heard in vocal melody. Analogous interactions apply to other skills, such as instrumental ability, level of harmonic knowledge, stage performance, etc.

Some songwriters are talented and/or highly trained vocalists, others less skilled, or shy and tentative about their singing. Not skills or limitations alone, but also self-perceptions and attitudes—toward risk-taking, perfectionism, vulnerability—come into play. But while there is no single standard, vocal limitations vs. strengths—whether actual or perceived—do create contrasting dynamics. Roughly speaking: limitations constrict; strengths encourage overuse. We need varying strategies to address these different kinds of problem.

Of course, many songwriters with modest or quirky vocal abilities have written great songs, and even songs with great melodies. Performing songwriters, though, feel the pressure of their dual focus. Thus, whether or not they identify as strong vocalists, they instinctively write for and around their own voices. Songwriters tend to settle on such vocal and melodic habits early in developing their writing process, and can shape them over time into an evocative style that feels highly personal and authentic. This makes such habits particularly resistant to change in revision; while in the long term, they limit the kinds of melodies, and the kinds of songs, you write.

To identify such habits and their effects on your own songwriting, a good first step is to listen back critically to vocal melodies of a number of your songs.

Vocal limitations. If you are less confident in your vocal skills, your song melodies may display some of the following attributes (exemplifying a "narrowing" dynamic as described above):

- staying in comfortable (perhaps emotionally safe) ranges;
- hovering within a restricted gamut of a few pitches;
- hitting the same peaks or valleys in melodic contour repeatedly within a phrase or section;
- lingering and chiming on repeated pitches for long strings of syllables;
- over-using chord tones in the melody for support from harmonic accompaniment.

Features such as narrowed melodic range are not always flaws; for example, a simpler melodic setting might complement a dense, imagery-laden lyric. Thus, critiques based on style- or genre-specific bromides—e.g., "make the chorus melody higher than the verse"—are not very helpful for these problems. Rather, as you learn to listen for these characteristics, you can better assess whether they serve the expressive needs of a given song, or are more habit-driven choices to be addressed in revision. You can also challenge yourself in new creative work to write melodies that venture beyond these limitations.

If vocal limitations are holding you back, it behooves you to work on those skills; this is slow and patient work. In the meantime, you can reduce some constricting effects on your melodic writing, and songwriting more generally, with the following supporting techniques or workarounds:

- *Lower your expectations of your vocal performance.* Focus on presenting the song; celebrate your vocal imperfections. Cultivate a fearless falsetto; unapologetically growl your lower tones. Take difficulties in singing your song as evidence that your melodic thinking is less beholden to your vocal limitations.
- *Experiment with the key of the song.* A song's key is not a fixed compositional attribute; singers transpose to suit their vocal range.

But since we play and sing as we write, a provisional choice of key can disproportionately affect the vocal melodies we compose, influencing overall melodic range, contour, etc. By experimenting with small and large shifts of key as you write, you become more aware of these effects and can make different choices. (If shifting key is instrumentally challenging, don't be proud; e.g., use a capo!)

- *Write vocal melody on your instrument.* Many songwriters sound out their vocal melodies instrumentally as they compose. This helps make your melodic ideas more distinct and definite, and separates them from your vocalist's comfort zone. This does demand a modest level of instrumental technique; but as the goal is a singable vocal melody, not an elaborate instrumental composition, simplicity is an advantage. In fact, if you are too skilled your melody may be too busy. (I suggest the technique here as an aid in writing; an instrumental melody track is also useful on work demos, as a guide for the final demo singer.)
- *Work with other vocalists.* Having other singers demo your songs, or co-writing with experienced vocalists, can offer invaluable learning opportunities. This also helps to address a risk in applying the supporting techniques mentioned so far. As you cultivate more boldness in your vocal melody writing, you can wind up with melodies that are challenging not just for you, but also for accomplished singers. Just because your melody is hard to sing doesn't guarantee it's a good melody! It may be innovative and fresh, initially hard to learn but effective; or simply awkward or contrived. Skilled vocalists do have an advantage in recognizing singable vs. problematic melodies.

Vocal strengths. Vocal prowess, in contrast—can *also* hold back your songwriting! Accomplished vocalists gain no automatic advantage in songwriting; in fact, their vocal skills may even impede their progress in songwriting—albeit for different reasons in some respects than those confronting less confident vocalists.

Strong vocalists may rely heavily on melodic aspects of their song, at the expense of aspects such as lyrics or harmony. This can also lead to tell-tale characteristics in the vocal melodies, such as overuse of:

- Range in melodic contour, where such range does not necessarily serve the song;
- Dynamics, setting the overall energy level of the song too high;
- Pronounced vocal rhythms, over-riding lyric phrasing or content; or
- Vocal effects such as stylistic riffs, melismatic runs, etc.

As vocal teachers will know, overuse of such effects can also work against the quality of the vocal performance. Here, though, our focus is on how such vocal habits can shape the actual vocal melody, the song itself, and overall songwriting skills.

One might expect that strong vocalists would at least have an edge in writing songs showcasing their own vocal style and range to best effect; yet even this is not always the case. Accomplished vocalists employ many nuances such as vocal runs and decorations in performing and interpreting songs. Writing for your own performance, nothing compels you to separate these layers of vocal interpretation from the essential song melody. Greater vocal range and ability might aid you in writing impressive vocal melodies, but not necessarily great song melodies: simple but timeless, memorable, and accessible to untrained listeners.

Performing songwriters also acquire vocal affectations, mannerisms, and habits of pronunciation and enunciation (or lack thereof). These may echo influences of current artists, or evoke genres that embed strongly marked regional dialects and styles. Artists can become habituated to and trapped in these mannerisms, fusing them consciously or unconsciously into their performer's persona. Both performance and writing can be affected by these affectations: not melodies alone, but also lyrics, themes, even the characters, points of view, and emotional stances from which they characteristically write.

In addition to contributing to compositional problems, high levels of vocal skill make it harder to hear these problems. In live performance for an audience, your job is to deliver the strongest performance you can—regardless of the state of your song. The purpose of performing a song for *critique*, on the other hand, is to obtain feedback to aid in revision. Yet many strong vocalists—or those heavily invested in their vocal skills (not always the same people!)—lean heavily on vocal performance strengths to "sell" their song, even in critique settings. In the end they may have over-sold, but not necessarily solidified, the song. The more emotive force and vocal firepower they bring to bear, the harder it becomes for writers and listeners alike to hear what is and isn't working in the song *as a song*: to distinguish a great song from a great vocal performance.

Critique practices

To counteract this interference of performance issues in song critique requires skills of both listeners and performers. Those offering critique must develop the acumen to listen past vocal stylings, to discern compositional, thematic, or structural issues in the song.

The performing songwriter can do their part with the following techniques:

- *Simplify your vocal melody*. Can you separate the essential melody of your song from your individual artist's interpretation? Could other vocalists learn the song from your rendition and add their own vocal interpretation?
- *Intentionally under-sing, under-play, under-perform*, and *under-dramatize your song*. You can also minimize the overall dynamic range of both vocals and accompaniment, especially when used for contrasting different sections of the song. That is: sing softer overall; and in sections where you feel you want to sing louder, sing less louder. Another good rule of thumb is to play the accompaniment softer than you would in a live performance setting, while strengthening the relative balance of the vocal. (Note that in demoing songs a general guideline is to set the vocal slightly hotter than might be preferable for a final artist's version.)
- *Strip away vocal affectations and effects*. As you perform, you may become aware of the performer's vocal persona you are adopting. Make a conscious effort to drop this away and let the song stand on its own: this can be disorienting at first, but is ultimately a revealing and even liberating exercise.

These deceptively simple protocols can be powerful interventions that yield keen, if uncomfortable, insights. Critique facilitators may need to coach performers in these directions. I have known such prompts to elicit indignant gasps: as if I am asking the singer to tie one hand behind his or her back. I try to approach this diplomatically: encouraging the under-singing as an experiment, strictly for purposes of obtaining feedback. More often than not, though, the listeners will judge a more understated rendition (of a good song at least) as the more moving performance as well. All these practices involve temporarily subordinating your vocalist and performer self to the song—trusting the song to do its work.

Revision practices

In critique, restraining performance aspects can help to more clearly reveal compositional issues. As we address these issues in revision, the complicating dynamics between composition and performance remain active; but their effects can be less straightforward. A guiding principle here is to trace problems, where possible, to the earliest stages in composition where they appear. Referring back to our earlier stream metaphor for the sequences of creative tasks, the idea is to "search further upstream."

Mismatches. One common source of compositional problems is a *mismatch* between song elements; an awkwardly set lyric, for example, can be considered a mismatch of lyrical vs. rhythmic elements. Mismatches arise in many ways, often lingering as artifacts of the sequence of steps by which the song was created. Depending on the elements in conflict, several alternatives for revision can usually be considered. To revise a lyric set awkwardly to a rhythm, you could change the lyric, or change the rhythm, or shift their relative placement. (While it might help to know whether lyric or rhythm came first, that doesn't determine the best revision option.) To be able to hear and test different alternatives in revision requires skills to work independently and flexibly with each element.

In this search for fixes, tensions of composition vs. performance skills can once again interfere. To address a problem in a rhythmic setting, for example, a songwriter's first instinct might be to compensate by altering performance aspects such as dynamics. Even at the compositional level, it is tempting to introduce a melodic change to fix a rhythmic issue: adding new material that only disguises the problem, leaving it unresolved and harder to revise. This is not intended to imply one normative writing process: songwriters write from different starting points, and give preference to different elements. Nevertheless, regardless of whether you start from melody, lyric, or chord progression, a remarkably consistent hierarchy of "cheats" appears to recur in song critique and revision:

- Accompaniment textures that mask repetitive chord progressions;
- Harmonic changes that support weak melody;
- Melodic contour that finesse issues in rhythmic setting of a lyric; or
- Hooky lyric rhythms that distract from problematic lyric content.

I like to share this rule of thumb with writers: "Harmony trumps dynamics; melody trumps harmony; rhythm trumps melody." Stay vigilant against revision shortcuts that shift focus away from core compositional elements where the root problems lie.

Sectional Contrast. Another common problem in revision concerns how sectional contrast is created in the song. Suppose your verse and chorus use similar chords, vocal melody and range. In performing you can try to make the chorus "bigger" by aggressively strumming chords or belting the melody; in your mind's ear you hear a full band arrangement, three-part vocal harmony, etc. But are you using lyric phrasing, harmony and harmonic rhythm, or melodic contour to create sufficient *structural* contrast between sections? You do not need to achieve contrast with these elements in every song; but to use them when the song calls for it, you must learn to listen to past performance aspects, or hold them in abeyance in revision.

Songwriting vs. Production Skills. This latter problem is especially common for songwriters with strong production skills. Such writers often pride themselves on "thinking production" from the very earliest stages in writing. But an early reliance on production often means, for example, that textural production effects become the primary elements used for sectional contrast.

The suggestions made here may appear to be in conflict with prevailing practice in some contemporary production-driven genres. New technologies and collaboration models have varied, and in some ways inverted, traditional sequencing of creative processes. Sonic/audio elements and related production artifacts may now be integral far earlier in the songwriting process. A beat, sample, or full instrumental track might precede, and directly or indirectly inspire, the writing of a topline lyric and melody. In these scenarios, where new processes are transforming aesthetics and even song form, production can't be considered a "cheat" in the sense described above. Still, even in this shifting creative landscape, I would argue that great toplines should not *depend on* the track but rather be worthy of the track. This still requires solid melodic and lyric skills. Cross-training approaches remain relevant, though they must be flexibly applied in ways appropriate to the work at hand.

Additional supporting techniques

We've looked in some depth at tensions between songwriting and performance concerns in one performance-related aspect: vocal skills. Other aspects—instrumental skills, stage performance skills, etc.—have their own dynamics and tensions, but many of the same principles apply. The following additional supporting techniques can help with many of these interactions, and in many phases: critique, revision, skill-building, and new writing.

- *Isolate and re-sequence*. Both vocal limitations and vocal strengths can affect overall choices in writing process. Here general 360° strategies can be useful: e.g., isolating steps you are accustomed to doing all at once, and altering, or reversing, habitual sequences of creative steps. You can fine-tune these into specific challenge exercises, using insights into your relative strengths in songwriting and performance skills.

  For example, some writers less comfortable with their vocal abilities might tend to focus on lyrics, giving preference to dense lyric textures in songs. Others might bury vocals beneath accompaniment, or tend to write from chord progressions, locking their vocal melodies too closely to the chords. (A tradeoff between vocal and instrumental ability is not uncommon; so less confident vocalists are often strong instrumentalists, and vice versa.) For both of these profiles of writers, the challenge of writing first from *a cappella* wordless melody would focus attention on melodic aspects, without the distractions or affordances of lyrics or chords.

- *Notation.* Notation skills are generally considered part of general musicianship; yet their role may seem tangential in some contemporary genres, where formal notations such as lead sheets are rarely used in practice.

  But notation and notation software can play a valuable role in the songwriting process itself, helping to increase independence between compositional and performance aspects. Even the limitations of conventional notation, while frustrating, can serve a purpose. To notate vocal melody, for example, you must distinguish a core, essential melody from the improvisations, variations, and rhythmic nuances of your vocal interpretation. Concretizing these decisions in the work of notating will change your way of hearing your own melodies.

  These benefits vary for different profiles of songwriters. Notation can liberate less confident vocalists to conceive and write bolder melodies, beyond their current vocal abilities. For writers more closely aligned to their own vocal skills, notation can slow down melodic thinking, enforcing a valuable if at times painfully objective view of compositional choices, quite different from a recorded performance. These dual effects of liberation and discipline apply to any notated aspect of the song.

- *Music technology.* Other music technologies—MIDI-based sequencing, digital audio workstations (DAWs), and multi-track recording, etc.—can similarly help to bridge gaps between songwriting and vocal or instrumental skills. Suppose you are writing to a chord progression that is just at the limits of your instrumental ability. Record the part; now you have a hands-free laboratory for unencumbered improvising of vocal melody and lyrics, accompanying yourself (or perhaps "co-writing with yourself") but not in real time.

Expanding the scope of your writing and performing

We have looked at principles and practices for reconciling songwriting and performance issues in critique and revision. We'll now consider two complementary sets of self-challenge exercises that you can use to expand your range in both songwriting and performance.

In the performing songwriter's dual focus—writing songs you perform, performing songs you write—several artistic choices are intertwined:

- Who do you write songs for? For yourself, or for other singers/artists as well?
- Whose songs do you sing? Your own, or also "covers" of songs by other artists?
- Do you mostly write songs alone, or with a co-writer?

In principle, these are separate and independent choices. Yet interdependencies emerge in the patterns of choices artists make. In our cross-training approach, we will tease these questions apart into separate choices and separate challenges.

Songwriter vs. performer self. Consider the interactions between the first two questions: for whom you write songs, and whose songs you sing.

To make these artistic choices more explicit, think of your creative work in terms of two separate aspects: your songwriter self and your performer self. At any given moment in your development as a performing songwriter, there is a range of songs you can write, and a range of songs you can perform. Visualize these potential repertoires as two overlapping circles. Toward the center of each circle is your "comfort zone," as a songwriter or performer respectively. Toward the periphery of each is work stretching your current capacities for that role. These respective repertoires overlap, yet are distinct. The overlapping territory or *intersection* of the circles represents the songs, and types of song, you can both write *and* perform.

We all like to do what we do well. So it is natural for us to give preference to material in this middle ground, where our strongest skills overlap. We are tugged magnetically toward this performing songwriter's sweet spot: material that feels most comfortable, natural, and authentic to us. It is easy to begin to think of your work as effectively just one circle defined and delimited by this intersection: the "songs I write."

But by confining yourself to this middle ground, you allow your respective songwriting and performance abilities to limit your range in each aspect. Significant territory, range, and repertoire, lies outside this intersection: songs you are capable of *writing* (whether or not you perform them); songs you are capable of *performing* (whether or not you wrote them). You can widen this circle, exploring your writing and performing roles independently, with the following complementary challenges.

Challenge #1: Write a song for another's voice. When you only write for your own performance, your work is defined and restricted by your perceptions of yourself as vocalist and performer. You can dramatically expand your range as a songwriter by writing songs intended for other voices, other artists.

You can try writing for a specific artist, such as a contemporary artist to whom you might actually pitch material, or for an iconic singer—a Sinatra, Nat King Cole, or Freddy Mercury. (You can write without reference to an intended singer; however, focusing on a tangible—that is, audible—alternative voice is the most powerful form of this challenge.)

Writing for another singer (or type of singer) is a different experience from writing for yourself. It reveals an internal auditory "image" of a singer's voice you hear when writing a song—a voice until now most always yours. Your first efforts may feel forced or inauthentic. Be patient: you are re-configuring intuitive connections between your writer and performer selves.

In challenge exercises, it is sometimes helpful to begin at the extremes. In this case, that means writing for a type of voice very different from your own: e.g., a singer of different gender, of marked difference in age, or in a different genre; or a singer with a very different vocal range, technical or stylistic. Writing well outside your range as a vocalist and performer requires a kind of compartmentalization, as you relinquish expectations of performing the work yourself.

This will also help you develop skills for working professionally, e.g., as a staff or team co-writer for and/or with other artists. Some highly successful writers for other artists have cultivated this ability to hear the artist's voice singing melodies they compose. Some are skilled vocalists themselves, who can imitate the artist's vocal sound and even persona in the studio.

Choosing a less intense level of challenge—i.e., writing for an "other voice" more at the immediate periphery of your current vocal range—has different benefits. The initial goal is still to expand your writing skills; but now this work has the potential to flow back to strengthen your performance. Write what you can't (yet) sing; then learn to sing it!

You can reinforce this separation of songwriter from performer self by working with a separate demo singer—in essence, a vocal "surrogate." You obviously need a demo singer for more dramatic self-challenges. But you also benefit from having other singers demo songs closer to your own vocal range—songs you *could* demo yourself. Here, there is learning value through the necessity of conveying your desired vocal phrasing to another singer.

A natural step beyond work with a demo singer—with respect to this challenge—is co-writing for, ideally with, an artist or vocalist in the style for which you are writing.

Challenge #2: Perform cover material outside your writer's comfort zone. There will be ways you simply cannot push your own vocal range with your own songs. Thus, a complementary challenge to your performer's range is to select songs outside your *writer's* comfort zone: new or familiar material, songs by other current artists, classics or standards, or even traditional folk songs.

As with the first challenge, you can approach this in diverse ways and with different learning goals. Any vocalist seeks out new repertoire to progressively challenge their vocal technique and range as a performer. You might select some songs that you can envision performing as an artist, others primarily as skill-building exercises. Some might be types of songs you have no particular interest in writing yourself: even songs you acknowledge are of high quality—but don't particularly like!

You obtain different benefits from cover repertoire that stretches you in directions difficult to explore via your own writing: songs you wish you'd written, but could not currently *write* for yourself. As you learn these songs, you also learn *from* the songs: study them from the inside, glean insights from performing them, use them as models and templates. Then at some point you loop back, challenging yourself to now write *that sort of song*—thereby stretching your songwriter self.

A natural extension of this repertoire-based challenge is to work *as* a demo singer for other writers; or to co-write *as* an artist: i.e., collaborate on songs for your own performance as an artist.

The virtuous spiral. The challenge exercises described above each have a primary focus: writing for other artists stretches your writing skills; performing cover songs stretches your performance skills. But these challenges have more far-reaching value, directly relevant to your overall creative work as a performing songwriter. This requires that you focus each respective challenge in ways that "loop back" to the complementary aspect. As you write for other voices, you learn to write in new ways *for your own voice*. As you sing songs you wish you'd written, you expand performance skills that in turn challenge your writing.

This also suggests that you tackle these exercises in an iterative, back-and-forth rhythm. As you follow one challenge with the complementary challenge, you work learning goals against each other in a benevolent antagonism, iteratively expanding both your writing and performance skills. In contrast to the proverbial vicious circle, we could call this sort of positive-feedback loop a *virtuous spiral.*

My own experience as a songwriter reflects one typical scenario. When I began writing songs, I was not a confident singer, and in any case was less focused on performing my own songs. Since I was hoping to place songs with artists, it was a natural step for me to gradually cultivate the skill of hearing distinct other voices as I wrote song melodies: both male voices with very different tonal quality or range, and female voices. As I learned to separate these imagined voices from my internal impression of my own voice, my song melodies became less constrained by my vocal limitations, more likely to appeal to stronger singers. Writing for other singers also led in a natural way to writing from other points of view: in effect, by separating my writer vs. vocalist self I was able to broaden, in turn, the narrative content and thematic range of my songwriting.

Then came a curious "boomerang" effect. Writing song melodies shaped around and for other voices encouraged me to bootstrap my own vocal abilities—to sing at least a passable rendition of the song, or to coach more accomplished demo singers. In essence: I first gave myself permission to write vocal melodies I could not sing; then forced myself to try to sing them anyway! This strengthened first my songwriting, then my own vocal abilities—a virtuous spiral in action.

Resistance, authenticity, identity

We have explored a dilemma that is also something of a paradox: the principle that performance strengths can work at cross-purposes to development of songwriting and composition skills. Yet the approaches suggested for addressing this dilemma may seem counter-intuitive in their own right. Can you really improve *as a performing songwriter* by leaving aside (even if only temporarily) attention to your own performance—or your own songwriting?

There is no small benefit in freeing your work as a songwriter from encumbrances of your performance limitations and strengths, your work as a performer from your writing skills. Thus, you can simply treat these exercises as a divide-and-conquer strategy: isolating individual skills that you eventually re-integrate into a now more seamless but expanded creative practice.

The exercises can also serve as useful preparation for broader professional skills. Even artists primarily focused on their own performing can benefit from developing skills to write for other artists; for many writers, this path has been an important steppingstone to their own artist careers. Releasing covers of strategically selected songs is an increasingly common way for new writer—artists to break out, especially via social media. Co-writing and collaboration are essential skills for contemporary writers in any genre or style—whether writing for and/or with other artists, or working with other writers for yourself as artist.

Finding your voice. But these exercises and practices offer benefits beyond risk-taking and broadening your professional skills. Through writing for another voice or artist, telling another's story, singing another's song, you also discover more about your own path as a performer of your own songs. Curiously, to fully derive these deeper insights you should expect to experience some strong feelings of resistance to these exercises—and be prepared to work through these reactions.

Venturing outside your comfort zone is, by definition, uncomfortable. Writing for another singer or type of singer will feel different from writing for your own performance. If you have shaped your performing style around your own highly personal songs, cover songs may feel awkward and posed.

But these exercises evoke discomforts that run deeper than just the unfamiliarity of new processes. They touch not only on issues of skills and scope, but on choices made and roles adopted early in your artistic path. The kinds of creative work to which you are drawn, or which you avoid, reflect strongly held values and beliefs about the nature and purpose of your artistic work. For some songwriters, the very notion of writing for another artist may feel like selling out—inauthentic almost at an ethical level. While performing songwriters might have pragmatic reasons to avoid certain cover song choices, such material can also threaten their sense of artistic integrity and identity in more subtle ways. Intervening in these choices can be profoundly unsettling, yet for this reason also transformative.

Try not worrying for a while about whether or not "this is me." At first, you cannot distinguish simple discomfort with the new and unfamiliar from what truly does not resonate with your voice and vision as an artist. The power of the experimenting comes from living with this discomfort, temporarily suspending judgment about the authenticity or integrity of results, seeing what the experience tells you.

You can support this ethos of fearless exploration with another sort of virtuous spiral. Give yourself a "sandbox": a zone for experimenting without consequences. You experiment most bravely when you can trust that your experiments will, if you so choose, vanish without a trace. At the same time, designate a later "check-in": a point in the process where you commit to invoking critical judgment and evaluating those creative results. Through this iteration—between generative and editorial phases, concerns of range and scope vs. concerns of identity and personal voice—you gradually discern the difference between habit and signature, who you can't yet be vs. who you choose to be or not to be (that is, The Question).

In my work as a teacher and mentor, I see many developing artists pulled too early and too hastily toward a safe haven, crystallizing a style and sound around their current strengths. They face intense self-expectations, reinforced by pressures of a highly competitive music industry, simultaneously luring with promises of arbitrary viral success and threatening anonymity among a clamor of other voices. This leaves these artists a precariously short window of opportunity to explore, build skills, and expand the range and scope of their work. These concerns lead me to encourage—perhaps over-emphasize—versatility and craft.

I hope working with the practices and self-challenge exercises in this chapter will help you maintain this faith: that, in songwriting, craft and inspiration, range and depth, versatility and authenticity, are not enemies but allies.

By now, our young songwriter is back at her window, guitar in hand. If she's still steaming about that annoying boyfriend, that's a dilemma we can't help with. Hopefully, though, some progress has been made with the artistic dilemmas that confront her as an aspiring performing songwriter. Perhaps her voice and guitar are weaving together in new balance; perhaps she is learning to reach past the charm of her warm contralto to a more timeless melody. There might even be a song in that.

Note

1 The author thanks the following reviewers for their insights and comments on various drafts of this chapter: Joe Bennett, Alan Blackwell (and daughter Elizabeth), Melanie Bresnan, Alyson Brill, Keppie Coutts, Ana Guigui, Søren Lyhne, Clare McLeod, Kevin Siegfried, Donnacha Toomey, and Justin Williams.

CHAPTER 3

Learning to create and creating to learn: Considering the value of popular music in higher education

Zack Moir

Introduction

Often, when I tell people that I am a music educator, specializing in higher popular music education (HPME), I am met with responses along the lines of:

> People can do degrees in popular music? Why? Paul McCartney never studied music, and look how much money he made ...

The implication of such a statement, of course, is that many (if not most) of the "stars" from the world of popular music did not *need* a degree in popular music to achieve the fame and success that they enjoy today. While this is undoubtedly true, such reasoning seems to stem from two main assumptions about HPME. First, that people who choose to study popular music all want to become "stars," and enjoy fame, commercial success, and financial reward. By extension, it is implied that such stardom *should* be a measure of success in this area. Second, that if Paul McCartney (or any of the host of other "stars" that are presented as examples of successful musicians who did not study HPME) did not *need* a degree in this subject, then neither should anyone else.

Such assumptions are problematic on a number of levels, as will be discussed in greater detail below, as they essentially imply that HPME is not a valuable pursuit in and of itself, because "success" can be achieved without studying popular music in higher education. Assumptions of this nature betray fundamental (mis)conceptions about the ethos, values, and aims of higher education (HE), while simultaneously highlighting the common-sense tensions that exist between the informal learning that popular musicians are associated with, and the inherent structures of formal education.[1] This is an issue that constantly informs and shapes my approach to course design and teaching.

This chapter will consider the "value" of popular music education, with a particular focus on the HE context. As an educator working in the U.K., I am inevitably influenced by this geographic context; however, I am confident that many of the issues raised will no doubt be recognized and relevant globally. I will argue that HPME is an important and valuable area of music education but will consider some important issues relating to curricula, pedagogy, and focus of HPME that I believe to be problematic. After providing some context on the discourses of popular music education, I will then focus specifically on the nature and value of songwriting and popular music composition in HPME courses, ultimately suggesting that this is a key area in which important skills and knowledge central to popular music practice can be developed and, consequently, that it should enjoy a more central role in HPME curricula.

Popular music in higher education

Over the last thirty years, approximately, the presence of popular music in universities, colleges, and schools has increased in many parts of the world,[2] and is a "fast-developing field of study, in terms of educational programs and activities."[3] However, despite such development and the increased presence of popular music in HE, I believe that its place within the academy remains problematic, or is at least an uncomfortable fit, in many cases. This is in part because of entrenched attitudes that result in a situation in which the study of popular music is "still treated with a certain amount of condescension."[4] Additionally, as Smith points out:

> ... since the majority of popular music education historically has existed outside of the academy, it would be perhaps rather at odds with the traditional culture of the music to reward achievement with academic accolades; it would be akin to acknowledging the achievements of fine scholars by giving them Grammy awards.[5]

Within the U.K., HPME has largely developed and flourished in those institutions that gained university status (having previously been polytechnics and colleges, for example) under the Further and Higher Education Act of 1992.[6] However, in those institutions in which popular music has been embraced, it is often treated simply as curricular content that is,[7] or can be, slotted into pre-existing institutional systems and structures that are inevitably predisposed to (or even institutionally bound by) certain values, pedagogies, and assessment practices. In such cases, HPME could be described as something of a "square pegs in round holes" situation.[8] While the history of popular music in HE is not the focus of this chapter, the fact that the increase in prevalence is such a recent phenomenon means that there is considerable continuing debate regarding what is meant when we refer to "popular music education."

It is clear that the field is characterized by variety and one obvious example of this, as reported by Cloonan and Hulstedt, is the fact that "the title of Popular Music degree programs varies across the UK,"[9] including: Popular Music, Popular Music Performance, Commercial Music, Music Business, Music (Industry) Management, and (Popular/Commercial) Music Production.[10]

One might also point to the variegated nature of the subjects included in the curricula and the various different foci of such popular music degrees.[11] This, I believe, clearly stems from the ambiguous nature of the term "popular music" and its associated practices, and such ambiguities are "problematic when trying to define the focus and parameters of popular music education."[12] Additionally, discourse differs internationally, as is reported by Mantie,[13] who conducted an interrogation of discourses of popular music pedagogy in journal articles relating to popular music education. He suggests that such differences are:

> ... reflective of both differing music education practices around the world and concomitant differing conceptions of what school music and school music teaching is or should be.[14]

Although the breadth of interest in this area is exciting for our young—but no longer nascent[15]—field, differing conceptions of the nature of popular music education, relevant content areas, and appropriate pedagogies make it difficult to develop a coherent understanding of what HPME entails. This is, of course compounded by the fact that notions of what constitutes "popular music" in the commercial context change so frequently. So, how best to consider the value of HPME if the very notion is such a fluid concept, lacking an agreed definition and focus? Should we, as academics and practitioners working in this field, strive toward an agreed definition of what HMPE is or should be? Should we abandon any such classification and just use the term "music"? Such broad and important topics are clearly beyond the remit of the current chapter; however, they do encourage us to think carefully about the purpose and, by extension, the objectives of HPME.

The purpose and objectives of HPME

Increasingly, it seems, an explicit objective of HPME is to equip students with the skills required to undertake employment in "the music industry."[16] Most institutions offering provision in popular music will make direct claims (particularly in prospectuses and advertising, etc.) that their courses "prepare" students for such employment. At a superficial level, this seems to be a sensible strategy for recruiting students, as many prospective undergraduates (and their parents) may be uncertain of the eventual employment opportunities for (popular) music graduates. However, one must question the validity, and even the ethics, of such claims and the complex issues surrounding them. Specifically, it would seem that such claims are made to pander to (a) the perceived aspirations and expectations of students, (b) the industry experience of staff involved in writing and delivering popular music courses, and (c) increased governmental pressure for HE to link more directly with employment.[17]

I would like to make it abundantly clear that I am in no way implying that industry/commercial success is the sole motivating factor for people choosing to engage in popular music, or that all popular music practices are undertaken in the hope of securing employment. As is noted by McLaughlin, "not all skills and knowledge taught and practised within educational institutions need necessarily map directly against hypothetical industrial scenarios."[18] McLaughlin's use of the word "hypothetical" in this context is especially important, particularly at a point in time in which the very notion of a singular music industry is arguably outdated,[19] and the idea that there is a stable and coherent market waiting to be provided with labor (in the form of the annual influx of music graduates) is unrealistic, at best. As Bennett suggests,[20] since the realities of work within the music industries are not well understood, institutions are "... essentially designing a curriculum for the unknown."[21] However, the view that one of the roles of music in HE is to provide "the relevant industries with the workforce of the future" is pervasive and, unquestionably, drives HPME program development and curriculum design.[22]

An inherent lack of employment (i.e., stable or regular jobs) in the music industries results in many musicians "relying on self-employment for a large proportion, if not all, of their income."[23] As such, it is common for popular music programs to include modules in music business or entrepreneurship, for example. These modules are often undertaken by students approaching the later years of their university/college education, a time at which they find themselves poised at an intersection between the relative shelter and protection of education and the real world in which (should they wish to build a career in this area) they will have to find ways to earn a living.

Obviously, such courses help to introduce students to some of the knowledge they will need to operate as self-employed musicians. However, the very notion of "entrepreneurship" and the increasing prominence it enjoys in HPME in many institutions, as both a curricular content area and an advertised reason for engaging with HPME, is flawed—not least because of the protean nature of this area of industrial/commercial activity. This uncomfortable situation is one that serves to undermine the ethos of HE and reduce the value of music, creative practice, and artistic endeavor. It also serves to reinforce and perpetuate those neoliberal ideologies that effectively frame artists and musicians as "entrepreneurs." This view of a popular music graduate (usually with a BA qualification, i.e., an arts degree) implies that their activities, behavior, and motivations are profit-driven and competitive. In my opinion this feels like an inaccurate way to describe arts graduates, and by extension an inappropriate focus for popular music programs.

Coulson uses the phrase "accidental entrepreneurs"[24] to describe those people who find themselves in such a position, since many of them did not necessarily choose to start a business. Such graduates are, arguably, only doing so in order to survive in a "product-centric" cultural and socio-political landscape created by the dominance of neoliberalism, and perpetuated by an outdated (at best) belief that the purpose of HPME is to prepare students for employment, as agents in the commercial music industries, and to provide said industries with labor. However, viewing our music graduates in this way "requires adherence to a neoliberal mindset that higher education institutions are obliged to instill."[25] Instead of designing popular music courses in ways that encourage industry-focused attitudes toward music education (based on potential employment prospects) I believe that we should be focusing on the qualities, attributes, and skills required by music graduates to function and participate in a multitude of different creative environments. By designing curricula around such abilities, and developing appropriate pedagogical approaches, we will be in a better position to design *relevant* and valuable HPME.

Clearly, there is no problem with HE institutions assisting in the development of non-musical professional skills. However, this could be more effectively achieved through non-compulsory extracurricular workshops designed to complement the musical/creative/practical aspects of the program, for example, and not occupying timetable space that could be dedicated to more relevant subjects. However, it is my belief that a curriculum that is focused on the development of skills and entrepreneurial behaviors specifically targeted toward "hypothetical industrial scenarios"[26] is wrongheaded and should not be the raison d'être, or a focus, of HPME. Additionally, many of the emerging digital tools and skills needed to engage with the commercial music industries and to monetize musical activity are already well known to, and frequently used by, young musicians before they enter HE.[27]

Designing relevant HPME curricula

I believe that the value of HPME is diminished immeasurably if popular music is treated as a mere "content area" within the prevailing systems of higher music education. Such systems have evolved and developed to support and perpetuate music which can loosely be described as Western classical. As is noted by Sarath et al.[28] in their "manifesto for progressive change" in music education:

> Contemporary tertiary-level music study—with interpretive performance and analysis of European classical repertory at its center—remains lodged in a cultural, aesthetic, and pedagogical paradigm that is notably out of step with this broader reality.[29]

Program design, curricula, and approaches to assessment serve to celebrate and enforce the values of the European classical repertory, and thus a "mutually perpetuating relationship"[30] exists between this and traditional conceptions of Western classical music education. Arguably, popular music does not have an equivalent canon, in part because it has a far shorter history than Western classical music, and also because the term popular music refers to an enormous and constantly developing range of musical forms, styles, and practices.[31] Most importantly, this is also because, in popular music, the composer/performer dichotomy is usually less pronounced as artists regularly perform their own music. Popular music practice is more associated with creativity and production, and less with learning, interpreting, and performing the works of great composers. That said, the type of approaches to popular music education alluded to in this chapter that prioritize performance and replication are in danger of replicating Western classical approaches to performance, to the detriment of other important skills and attributes.

If, HPME programs build on typical Western classical music education models (which, arguably, may also be out of touch with the world into which students will graduate) as the basis for course design, pedagogy, and assessment methods, then we are at risk of running courses that are doubly irrelevant. By this I mean that approaches to popular music program design that merely appropriate popular music into the traditional structures of a music degree can, in effect, create a situation in which the practices and skills central to the music are lost or undervalued, and that the music in the educational context bears "little resemblance to any music that exists in the world outside."[32] Thus, to adopt an approach to HPME that prioritizes and celebrates the same skills and practices as in traditional HE music courses, because of established norms and entrenched approaches, seems to be inappropriate due to the inherent differences between the two broad categories of music and their associated practices.

By way of example, consider the nature of typical approaches to instrumental performance education. Teaching occurs principally through a master–student learning model[33]—also described as an apprenticeship model.[34] In such situations, the student relies on the teaching and direction of their instructor and, while they clearly engage in an enormous amount of individual practice and (hopefully) reflection, it is fair to say that in the traditional model the teacher is arguably the "initiator, verifier and controller of a student's learning process."[35] While such an approach clearly produces results, and has been doing so for generations, it should be noted that important aspects of musical learning such as creativity and autonomy are often neglected. To my mind, this would suggest that such an approach is problematic when applied in the context of HPME.

In almost all of the popular music programs that I have had experience of, performance is assessed by means of recital-style exams, in a way that mirrors traditional Western classical music degrees to an extent.[36] While I understand that this type of assessment is designed to allow examiners to assess the technical proficiency and stylistic interpretation of the student (i.e., that which has been "passed down" and "sculpted" by the teacher), this system objectifies performance and prioritizes the values and aesthetic opinion of an assessor. Such an assessor may well be grading performances with the aid of a marking scheme but this will comprise criteria designed with the aims of this type of education in mind. This is, I believe, an entrenched practice and one that has become so closely associated with music education that it is difficult to avoid.[37] However, I would argue that this practice and the interpretive (as opposed to creative) approach to music education that it promotes does not adequately relate to or reflect the practices of popular music. It serves to promote "curation" over "creation," and should not, therefore, necessarily be a central component of a popular music program.

In order to develop *relevant* popular music curricula we must ensure that the practices of popular music are understood and respected. We must also ensure that our course design, pedagogy, and approaches to assessment (an inevitability in formal education) are well suited to enabling students to develop the skills and knowledge required to become practitioners (in the broadest sense), and empowering them to be reflective,[38] self-critical, imaginative, and confident graduates.[39]

To develop students in this way, I would argue that it is important for us to be moving away from pedagogies for employability.[40] As alluded to above, graduating from a vocational course does not lead to automatic employment (this seems to be particularly true for music graduates), and thus the emphasis for learning in HE should be less on "employ" and more on "ability."[41] The abilities that empower students to learn and develop through practice and reflection are those that should be prized and encouraged in course design and the development of learning activities.[42]

Songwriting and composition as popular music education

If our aim is to develop creative and critically reflective popular music graduates, then activities that encourage creative thinking and develop creative processes should be at the core of popular music curricula. In my first-hand experience, and through conversations with a wide range of colleagues from many institutions, this is not always the case. While there are undoubtedly elements of many popular music programs that are, in essence, "creative," the generation of new musical material is generally not the focus of the program, except in the case of a small number of "composition specialist" students. In an area of music that is so clearly linked to the production of new musical products, creative/generative musical practice should, I believe, be more prominent and more embedded within undergraduate curricula for *all* students. In my opinion, one key area of activity that facilitates such development is that which incorporates songwriting, composition, and production.

Essentially, what I am referring to is the "generation" of popular music. This is a complex and multifaceted aspect of music education that I am reluctant to refer to by the term "songwriting" alone, as this, for many, does not adequately represent the broad range of activities or products associated with those who produce popular music.[43] As such, for the remainder of this chapter, I will use the term popular music composition (PMC) to refer to those activities involved in the generation of popular music. This, while incorporating songwriting practices, is intended to refer to a broader range of "technologically informed, performance-centred skill-sets, alongside theories of traditional composition."[44]

PMC is central to popular music practice and this centrality should, I believe, be mirrored in the role and prominence it enjoys within HPME. It is my belief that a shift in focus, that would see PMC at the heart of popular music curricula, would benefit all students (not just composition specialists) as the practices involved (a) encourage the development of musical thinking, (b) consolidate musical knowledge and allow for a holistic approach to musical learning, (c) build on the prior musical knowledge and experience of students, and (d) encourage collaborative creativity.

PMC provides an important opportunity for students to develop creative musical thinking. As Hickey notes, "[A]lthough one might have tremendous talent to perform flawlessly a range of technically difficult etudes on an instrument, creative thinking in music involves *producing new ideas*."[45] That is to say that a student considered musically "talented" may not actually be particularly "creative." My fear is that in performance-driven courses that prioritize instrumental study, for example, students develop high-level technical skills but do not *necessarily* develop creative musical thinking because the production of new ideas is not a core value. Principally, such a focus prioritizes technical development and stylistic mimicry, through performances of technical studies or pre-existing pieces of music which are deemed to be of an appropriate standard by an instrumental-specialist tutor. While this has value and is an efficient way for skills and techniques to be communicated, it is not without its problems in practical and philosophical terms, and leaves little (if any) room for the development of creative practices. Embracing PMC as a *central* focus of popular music programs would be one way in which to address this issue and encourage the development of creative musical thinking.

As is noted by Kaschub and Smith, "[N]o activity within the domain of music requires a more varied palette of experiences and understandings than does composition."[46] Composing music encourages (or perhaps even requires) students to draw on all their musical knowledge and skill in order to produce new work. It encourages and develops links between the concepts and precepts of students, and thus promotes the development and consolidation of theoretical, aural, technical, improvisational, and performance abilities, in addition to stylistic knowledge and idiomatic understanding, for example. By embracing PMC as a more central element of HPME curricula, we would give more students the opportunity to consolidate and apply their musical knowledge and experiences in this holistic, interconnected way. It is, I believe, in doing so that students truly learn the value of the (arguably) otherwise disparate skills and knowledge they have acquired throughout their music education.

Due to the diverse range of knowledge and abilities employed through engagement in PMC, students actually develop many other areas of their musicianship in an interconnected way. Through PMC, students gain a deeper understanding of their creative processes, learn how to utilize their current skillset, and identify areas in which they need to develop. In this sense, PMC provides a meaningful opportunity for students to connect their theoretical and experiential learning. Direct engagement in the processes of *creating* music, through a curricular focus on PMC, would allow HPME courses to function in similar ways to the "art college model," which "condones and encourages an attitude of learning through trial and error, through day-to-day experimentation rather than through instruction."[47] This is also hugely important, as it would allow for the adoption of constructivist pedagogies within an area of music that is so often dominated by the student–master paradigm.[48] This is key when thinking about PMC as a subject area as "any generative interaction with musical materials is likely to challenge the composer to draw upon previous experiences to inform the compositional work."[49] By embracing constructivist pedagogy, educators celebrate the prior experience and knowledge of their students and allow them to pursue their own avenues of interest, while forging connections with the subject or discipline.

Simply encouraging "learning-by-doing" is not sufficient for learning to take place—it must go deeper by encouraging the learner to link their current knowledge and experience to the new subject or material "... using collaborative communities and engaging in questioning and problem-solving techniques."[50] Therefore, the emphasis is deflected from the teacher as a provider and transmitter of content or arbiter of successful performance.[51] Instead, the educator assumes the role of "facilitator," with a responsibility to provide appropriate materials, encourage collaborative enquiry and feedback, and guide students in their journey of investigation, knowledge construction, and creative enquiry. As such, learning experiences in HPME should be structured with ample opportunity for educators to offer guidance and for collaborative working among students.[52]

Unlike traditional conceptions of composition, which often view the composer as an authoritative individual who produces scores for other people to play, PMC is different in a number of key ways. Most importantly, because popular music composition often occurs as performance-centered practice,[53] it is not uncommon for this to take place in groups. This may be in the context of bands writing a song together while playing in a practice room, or professional songwriting/composition/production teams working collaboratively to produce tracks. Either way, the nature of the working practices and the performance-centered, track focused, often improvisational approach to PMC facilitates collaborative creativity at every stage. Working with other people in this creative (rather than interpretive, as when playing cover-versions in bands, for example) manner provides opportunity to gather third-party feedback (including suggestions for how to improve/develop your ideas) or different perspectives on formal, structural and stylistic elements of the composition. In this way, we might say that creativity in collaborative PMC is activated *through* working with other people and, as such, that having the opportunity to work in this way is yet another reason to advocate for PMC to take a more central role in HPME curricula.

Concluding remarks

Clearly, institutional differences exist and there are certainly many examples of wonderful practice in this area from around the world. It should be made abundantly clear that it is not my intention to undermine the work of colleagues in this area. Rather, this chapter should be viewed as a contribution to discussions on the nature and value of HPME which are vital to its continued development.[54] However, it is my strong belief—as an educator in HPME—that if the field is simply viewed as a means to provide the skills and knowledge required for employment in the music industry then we are at risk of undervaluing it. If we are merely interested in providing students with tools to gain jobs then why, indeed, should we bother to engage in three to four years of undergraduate study, at great effort and cost, if it is possible to point to a plethora of individuals ("stars" or otherwise) who have gained success and some form of "industry" employment without a degree in the subject? Likewise, if entrepreneurial skill and interpretive performance are what is prized and sought, then one could argue that this would be more efficiently achieved outside the realms of HPME curricula.

However, if HPME is (as advocated above) primarily focused on developing creative, critical, reflective practitioners who are able to draw on their wide skillset and adapt to any creative/professional situation, then I believe that it is a hugely valuable and exciting area of music education. PMC is one important area in which we have the opportunity to allow and support students to develop in this way; thus I argue that it should enjoy a more central role in HPME. In an ideal world I would suggest that we need to go even further and consider the structure and makeup of degree programs in order to facilitate an institutional structure in which learners can work in a more flexible, exploratory, and student-led way, and engage in learning experiences that reflect best practices from within *and* outside of formal education institutions.

Notes

1 In the context of the U.K., the term Higher Education (HE) primarily describes learning that takes place at universities and other institutions offering Bachelor, Master or Doctorate degrees. This is typically used in contrast with Further Education (FE) which typically refers to education that occurs in addition to that received at secondary school, usually in the form of vocational training or foundation degrees undertaken as preparation for university study. Higher education and further education are referred to as tertiary education in contrast with secondary or primary school education.

2 Gareth Dylan Smith, Zack Moir, Matt Brennan, Shara Rambarran, and Phil Kirkman, "Popular Music Education (R)evolution," in *The Routledge Research Companion to Popular Music Education*, eds. Gareth Dylan Smith, Zack Moir, Matt Brennan, Shara Rambarran, and Phil Kirkman (London: Routledge, 2016), 5–13.

3 Rupert Till, "Popular Music Education: A step into the light," in *The Routledge Research Companion to Popular Music Education*, eds. Gareth Dylan Smith, Zack Moir, Matt Brennan, Shara Rambarran, and Phil Kirkman (London: Routledge, 2016), 14. This increase is not uniform across the world, however. For example, the U.S.A. (despite being the country that spawned much of the world's popular music) is somewhat further behind other parts

of the world (see Smith, 2014) in terms of mainstream inclusion in formal education.

4 Martin Cloonan, "What is popular music studies? Some observations," *British Journal of Music Education* 22 (1) (2005): 1–17.

5 Gareth Dylan Smith, "Seeking 'success' in popular music," *Music Education Research International* 6 (2013): 36.

6 In short, this act (which radically changed the structure of post-compulsory education in the U.K.), facilitated the development of many new disciplines and areas of study due to "new universities" offering vocational courses. This also encouraged a great deal of debate on the nature and value of higher education and the role and function of university study, and it was in this environment in which popular music courses began to emerge.

7 Lucy Green, *How Popular Musicians Learn: A Way Ahead for Music Education* (Farnham: Ashgate, 2002).

8 Zack Moir and Haftor Medbøe, "Reframing popular music composition as performance-centred practice," *Journal of Music, Technology & Education* 8 (2) (2015): 148.

9 Martin Cloonan and Lauren Hulstedt, *Taking Notes: Mapping and Teaching Popular Music in Higher Education* (York: Higher Education Academy, 2012), 6.

10 Ibid.

11 See, for example, Martin Cloonan and Lauren Hulstedt, *Taking Notes: Mapping and Teaching Popular Music in Higher Education* (York: Higher Education Academy, 2012); Paul Fleet, "'I've Heard There was a Secret Chord': Do we Need to Teach Music Notation in UK Popular Music Studies?," in *The Routledge Research Companion to Popular Music Education*, eds. Gareth Dylan Smith, Zack Moir, Matt Brennan, Shara Rambarran, and Phil Kirkman (London: Routledge, 2016), 166–76; Tom Parkinson and Gareth Dylan Smith, "Towards an epistemology of authenticity in higher popular music education," *Action, Criticism, and Theory for Music Education* 14 (1) (2015): 93–127.

12 Moir and Medbøe, 148.

13 Roger Mantie, "A comparison of 'popular music pedagogy' discourses," *Journal of Research in Music Education* 61 (3) (2013): 334–52.

14 Ibid., 348.

15 Tom Parkinson, "Values of Higher Popular Music Education: Perspectives from the UK," unpublished PhD thesis, University of Reading, 2014.

16 Regretfully, this is a more wide-reaching issue and one that is true in most areas of HE. In previous decades, this was particularly true of the post-1992 institutions (which were characterized by their commitment to preparing students for employment), but this "employability agenda" is an issue that is increasingly important across the sector.

17 It is no coincidence that such focus on employment is prevalent in an environment in which graduate employability statistics are indicators of

successful education institutions. How meaningful such statistics are is a larger question and not the focus of this chapter.

18 Sean McLaughlin, "Mediations, Institutions and Post-Compulsory Popular Music Education," in *The Routledge Research Companion to Popular Music Education*, eds. Gareth Dylan Smith, Zack Moir, Matt Brennan, Shara Rambarran, and Phil Kirkman (London: Routledge, 2016), 118.

19 Michael L. Jones, *The Music Industries: From Conception to Consumption* (London: Palgrave Macmillan, 2012).

20 Dawn Bennett, "Rethinking Success: Music in Higher Education," *The International Journal of the Humanities* 5 (2012): 181–7.

21 Ibid., 182.

22 Gareth Dylan Smith, "Popular music in higher education," *Advanced Musical Performance: Investigations in Higher Education Learning*, eds. Ioulia Papageorgi and Graham Welch (Farnham: Ashgate Publishing Ltd, 2014), 36.

23 Susan Coulson, "Collaborating in a Competitive World: Musicians' Working Lives and Understandings of Entrepreneurship," *Work, Employment & Society* 26 (2) (2012): 255.

24 Ibid., 251.

25 Gareth Dylan, Smith, "Neoliberalism and symbolic violence in higher music education," in *Giving voice to democracy: Diversity and social justice in the music classroom*, ed. Lisa C. DeLorenzo (New York: Routledge, 2015), 71.

26 McLaughlin, 2016.

27 Zack Moir, "Popular Music Making and Young People: leisure, education, and industry," in *The Oxford Handbook of Music Making and Leisure*, eds. Roger Mantie and Gareth Dylan Smith, 223–40 (Oxford: Oxford University Press, 2016).

28 Ed Sarath, David Myers, John Chattah, Lee Higgins, Victoria Lindsay Levine, David Rudge, and Timothy Rice, eds., *Transforming Music Study from its Foundations: A Manifesto for Progressive Change in the Undergraduate Preparation of Music Majors* (Washington: College Music Society, 2014).

29 Ibid., 11.

30 Parkinson, 2014, 14.

31 The term "classical music" is also very broad and vague: however, when talking about popular music in the contemporary context we really are talking about a hugely fragmented, un-unified, and rapidly changing area.

32 Green, 2002, 7.

33 Don Lebler, "Student-as-master? Reflections on a learning innovation in popular music pedagogy," *International Journal of Music Education* 25 (3) (2007): 205–21.

34 Heidi Westerlund, "Garage rock bands: A future model for developing musical expertise?" *International Journal for Music Education* 24 (2) (2006): 119–25.

35 Don Lebler and Naomi Hodges, "Popular Music Pedagogy: Dual Perspectives on DIY Musicianship," in *The Routledge Research Companion to Popular Music Education*, eds. Gareth Dylan Smith, Zack Moir, Matt Brennan, Shara Rambarran, and Phil Kirkman (London: Routledge, 2016), 273.

36 While these do not always take place in the "clinical" surroundings of an auditorium (many now take place in music venues or bars, etc., to provide a sense of authenticity) they are almost exclusively assessed by an individual or panel of staff members who determine how well the music matched their expectations.

37 Incidentally, this is also true of the pop/rock and jazz exams offered by exam boards such as the ABRSM and Trinity Guildhall, etc.

38 Don Lebler, Rosie Burt-Perkins, and Gemma Carey, "What the students bring: examining the attributes of commencing conservatoire students," *International Journal of Music Education* 27 (3) (2009): 242.

39 Helena Gaunt and Ioulia Papageorgi, "Music in universities and conservatoires," in *Music Education in the 21st Century in the United Kingdom: Achievement, analysis and aspirations*, eds. Susan Hallam and Andrea Creech (London: The Institute of Education, University of London, 2010), 268.

40 Ann Pegg, Jeff Waldock, Sonia Hendy-Isaac, and Ruth Lawton, *Pedagogy for Employability* (York: Higher Education Academy, 2012).

41 Lee Harvey, "Transitions from Higher Education to Work: A briefing paper," *Centre for Research and Evaluation* (Sheffield: Sheffield Hallam University, 2003).

42 Sarath et al. (2014) suggest that, "the skills of improvisation, composition, and performance, and in some cases theorizing and pedagogy as well ..." are those "needed to navigate today's infinite array of culturally diverse treasures and to flourish professionally among them." *Transforming Music Study*, 12.

43 See, for example, Moir and Medbøe, 2015.

44 Ibid., 159.

45 Maud Hickey, *Music Outside the Lines: Ideas for Composing in K-12 Music Classrooms* (Oxford: Oxford University Press, 2012), 8–9.

46 Michele Kaschub and Janice Smith, *Minds on Music: Composition for Creative and Critical Thinking* (Lanham: Rowman and Littlefield Education, 2009), 7.

47 Simon Frith and Howard Horne, *Art into pop* (London: Methuen, 1987), 27.

48 Constructivism is based on the belief that learning should build upon existing knowledge and experience and that the process of learning occurs as learners are actively engaged and involved in meaning and knowledge construction rather than passive recipients of facts.

49 Kaschub and Smith, 2009, 7.

50 Peter Richard Webster, "Construction of Music Learning," in *MENC*

Handbook of Research on Music Learning, Vol. 1, eds. Richard Colwell and Peter Richard Webster (New York: Oxford University Press, 2011), 37.

51 Adam Gamoran, Walter G. Secada, and Cora B. Marrett, "The organizational context of teaching and learning: changing theoretical perspectives," in *Handbook of Sociology of Education*, ed. Maureen T. Hallinan (New York: Springer, 1998).

52 Jackie Wiggins, Deborah VanderLinde Blair, S. Alex Ruthmann, and Joseph L. Shively, "A heart to heart about music education practice," *The Mountain Lake Reader* (Spring) (2006): 82–91.

53 Moir and Medbøe, 2015.

54 Criticisms voiced in this chapter of certain elements of HPME are clearly not intended as criticisms of colleagues, but wider observations based on my experiences in this area.

CHAPTER 4

Professional songwriting techniques: A range of views summarized from the Sodajerker interviews

Simon Barber

Introduction

In this chapter, I distill a range of information about the songwriting process provided by internationally renowned songwriters. These conversations about the art and craft of songwriting derive from *Sodajerker On Songwriting*, an audio podcast series founded in late 2011 by the British songwriting team Sodajerker, which comprises the author, Simon Barber, and Brian O'Connor.[1] At the time of writing there are eighty episodes of the popular program in which leading songwriters discuss their approaches to writing songs, the ways in which their most recognizable hits were conceived, and what they have learned about the creative process through their practice.

The songwriters surveyed here span a broad range of professional experiences, including Brill Building and Motown songwriters prominent since the 1960s, such as Neil Sedaka, Jeff Barry, Barry Mann and Cynthia Weil, and Lamont Dozier; well-established singer-songwriters and solo artists active during the last forty years like Billy Bragg, Joan Armatrading, Todd Rundgren, Gilbert O'Sullivan, Jimmy Webb, and KT Tunstall; in-demand contemporary co-writers and collaborators such as Glen Ballard, Dan Wilson, Guy Chambers, Eg White, and Miranda Cooper, as well as leading writers from popular established bands such as Chris Difford of Squeeze, Andy Partridge of XTC, Mike Scott of The Waterboys, Neil Finn of Crowded House, and Adam Duritz of Counting Crows. In order to enable a broad variety of practitioners to share their views, I have organized this material around key themes that have emerged during these interviews, including the generation of ideas, songwriting routines, the construction of melodies and lyrics, and strategies for co-writing and collaboration.

While there are a number of books in which songwriters are interviewed about the songwriting process, such as those authored by Zollo, Egan, and Rachel, such dialogues are typically presented as discrete transcriptions and don't attempt to establish any kind of consensus among respondents.[2] A pedagogical dimension is introduced by the corpus of literature devoted to providing instruction for practitioners (Hirschhorn; Coryat and Dobson; Blume; Pattison), but this material tends to focus on practical techniques for generating new musical and lyrical ideas rather than insights into the widely adopted techniques of successful songwriters.[3] Academic literature about songwriting often does away with the above concerns altogether, tending toward either a theoretical reading of the subject (Negus; Negus and Astor); musicological approaches to analyzing song forms (Burns; Fitzgerald; Hass et al.); or reflections on the place and provenance of creativity itself (Bennett; McIntyre).[4] The aim here is to demonstrate the combined wisdom of a range of professional practitioners by juxtaposing their testimonies according to emergent themes.

Generating ideas for songs

There are a number of practical techniques that are used by professional songwriters in order to write songs. Many find that the most efficient way to produce new material is through routine work. However, some songwriters, such as Mike Scott of The Waterboys, have claimed that they can go long periods without engaging in the songwriting process, confident that when the time comes to write, their skills can be relied on and exciting ideas will quickly emerge. Among those who share Scott's confidence are singer-songwriter Joan Armatrading, who declares that one can "dust a piano and be making music," and celebrated composer Jimmy Webb, who confesses that some songs come so easily it's almost "as if a wind blew through the room and left a song on the piano." Singer-songwriter and producer Todd Rundgren relates that he achieved his optimum songwriting state around the time of writing his hit song "I Saw the Light." "At that point it was almost as if I had devised this formula for songwriting," he says, "and when it got to the point that I could finish a song in twenty minutes, I started to think 'maybe I'm not taking this seriously enough?'"

For many, the process is often much more laborious. So, what can a songwriter do to increase the odds of generating usable ideas for songs? Glen Ballard, seasoned hit-maker for artists like Michael Jackson and Alanis Morissette, believes that setting ego aside is an important first step: "I'm always willing to look foolish and to take a shot," he says; "sometimes I'll work with people who won't open their mouths, and I'm the one who is singing. If they're participating and giving you some juice, it makes all the difference." In addition to setting aside inhibitions, songwriters should also observe their surroundings for anything that might provide the spark for a song. "Look around wherever you are and be inspired by the environment," says Allen Toussaint, influential New Orleans songwriter and producer. "At a red light, don't just wait for the light to change, look around and see what's going on. Once you leave here, this is gone. It may have offered you something. You might have seen two people on the corner kiss quickly. There you are. They kissed on the corner. You don't want to miss that."

In many forms of writing, a keen observational sense can be a crucial asset. Counting Crows front man Adam Duritz wrote the hugely successful song "Mr Jones" after an evening spent in a bar observing friends and acquaintances. Chris Difford, who along with Glenn Tilbrook constitutes the songwriting partnership behind the band Squeeze, recalls that he wrote the lyrics for "Tempted," one of their most popular songs, through the simple act of writing down what he observed from a car window. "Lyrically, it came very quickly," says Difford. "I wrote it literally on a fag packet in a taxi on the way to the airport. It was a box of Senior Service. I opened it up and started writing down what I saw. By the time I got to the airport, the song was done." For others, it might be a book, film, play, or photograph that provides the seed for a song. KT Tunstall wrote "Suddenly I See" after being inspired by the front cover of the Patti Smith album, *Horses*. "The whole song is about that picture," says the Scottish singer-songwriter. "I was just listening to some music, and it was about three o'clock in the morning, and I put on *Horses* by Patti Smith. And I looked at the cover and saw it in a completely different way and just got obsessed by this photo of her." As with previous examples, Tunstall's inspired approach meant that the song was written quickly. "I probably finished that in half an hour," she says, "the most successful half hour of my life."

Many songwriters adopt a philosophical approach to their work. Some, like "Eve of Destruction" writer P. F. Sloan, view themselves as conduits for a greater spiritual source, and the act of writing as a process of transcribing music that passes through them, almost as if they had tuned to a particular frequency on some celestial radio. The concept of being inspired by spirituality, or using one's spirituality to facilitate the creative process, is so prevalent among songwriters that it has merited an entire book on the subject.[5] Indeed, the creatively consuming act of songwriting has itself been the inspiration for songs by artists from Bruce Springsteen to Barry Manilow. Some songwriters also claim to have written songs in dreams. The most well-rehearsed of such stories is Paul McCartney's account of writing "Yesterday"; however, both Dan Wilson ("Secret Smile") and Nick Lowe ("I Was Born in Bethlehem") have reported emerging from sleep with a song fully formed, needing only to transcribe it in order to realize the composition.

Writing songs successfully is possible for many artists and musicians. However, writing successful songs can be another challenge altogether. For some songwriters, the key to creating "hits" is to work according to a ratio model, producing a large volume of material in order to generate the few that connect with an audience. BBC broadcaster and singer-songwriter Tom Robinson is convinced that writing a lot of songs is the best way to stumble upon the elusive hit: "The best advice I ever heard is to be unafraid of writing rubbish," he says. "If only one song in every ten is any good, unless you write the first nine, you never get to that tenth. Write any old bit of shit! Once it exists, you can change it!" However, having the dedication to complete new song ideas can be a challenge in itself. "Most of us are tempted to give up before we get it even halfway finished as a piece of shit," says Robinson. "It's so hard to force yourself to finish that crap idea so that you can sing it all the way through."

This sort of pro-active approach is not a new concept for songwriters. Writing together during the Brill Building era of the 1960s, Barry Mann and Cynthia Weil, authors of classic songs like "You've Lost That Lovin' Feelin'," routinely completed material that they felt was unlikely to be successful in order to keep their skills sharp. "We would have what we called 'slump songs'," Weil reports. "When we were in a writing slump and we just couldn't get anything, we'd say 'let's just write something so that we don't forget that we are writers.'" At the same time, songwriters should be mindful not to simply accept the first set of songs that emerge from a writing session. "You go through all sorts of bad stuff until you get to the good stuff," says Norwegian pop star Sondre Lerche. "Sometimes the first thing that pops into your mind could be a really good thing, but what makes you a great songwriter is the filter and the quality control." Following Lerche's notion that patience is a virtue, songwriters must also then be vigilant about documenting their orphaned bridges, choruses, and lyrics so that they are not lost. "Never chuck anything out," says XTC front man Andy Partridge. "Doesn't matter how old it is. I've gone back to bits that are ten, fifteen years old thinking 'that's the piece I need! I'll change the key, speed it up, slow it down, that's going to work!'"

Undertaking daily songwriting exercises is another method used by professional writers to expedite new ideas. Dan Wilson, who wrote hits like "Secret Smile" and "Closing Time" for his band Semisonic before becoming an in-demand co-writer for artists like Adele ("Someone Like You") and the

Dixie Chicks ("Not Ready to Make Nice"), periodically attempts to produce one new song every day for thirty days: "I do a song-a-day process every three years," says Wilson. "I usually do it for thirty days and quite often it extends further. The last one I did I finished about a month and a half ago and that ended up being seven weeks." A variation on this approach is outlined in *The Frustrated Songwriter's Handbook*, in which members of a songwriting club are encouraged to attempt to write twenty songs in a single day.[6] Other songwriters prefer to work from some kind of prompt or set of limitations. Singer-songwriter Nik Kershaw describes an experimental technique in the spirit of Brian Eno's *Oblique Strategies*: "I'm always looking for ways of starting songs. I wrote with a guy a few years ago that had a deck of cards that he would shuffle and lay on the table, and whatever the cards said, that's what you would use. He called it the 'deck of *chords*'."[7]

Imposing limitations on the process is a tried and tested method for stimulating song ideas. For instance, restricting the number of chords available to use demands a greater level of melodic invention from the songwriter in order to make different sections distinctive. "That was a first for me," says Sondre Lerche, speaking about his song "Crickets," "to make something that I still felt had an arc and a dramatic structure and that I got a lot of melody out of using just four chords and this stubborn rhythm pattern. To me that felt like a breakthrough." Other methods in this category include writing with an unfamiliar instrument; a process that can encourage the songwriter to discover previously unimagined chord shapes and voicings. Similarly, experimenting with alternate tunings on string instruments like the guitar can be a helpful way to push the songwriter into uncharted territory. Sometimes an artist's idiosyncratic approach is enough to prompt ideas—for instance, Billy Bragg's so-called "chop and clang" guitar style on songs like "The Milkman of Human Kindness" has helped him to produce a catalog of distinctive sounding songs.

Limitations of time can also be a catalyst for the creation of new material. Setting a deadline or making a commitment, such as a recording date or live performance, can be powerful motivation for the completion of songs. Jeff Barry, the Brill Building songwriter behind songs like "Be My Baby" and "River Deep Mountain High," recalls having limited time to produce a B-side for a single he was working on. He and his writing partner Ellie Greenwich decamped to the corridor outside the recording studio and wrote the song "Hanky Panky" in twenty minutes before returning to record it. Beyond the prolific talents of writers like Barry and Greenwich, it is also important to note that having limitations in one's own musical, technical, or theoretical knowledge need not be a barrier to progress. Andy Partridge of XTC is a firm believer in following his instincts during the creative process: "I have no idea what the chords are. Don't ask me. That's not of interest, you know? You don't need to know the guts of music to make music."

In Western popular music, songwriters have typically used the piano and the guitar as the primary tools to develop ideas; however, songs can be just as easily facilitated through engagement with other forms of technology such as effects pedals, hardware and software sequencers, and electronic instruments. KT Tunstall's first international success was achieved with the song "Black Horse & The Cherry Tree," a song based entirely around the use of an Akai E2 Head Rush effects pedal. With this equipment, Tunstall was able to loop a number of musical parts and accompany herself as she composed and performed the song. Bassist and singer-songwriter Me'shell Ndegeocello uses a laptop as her primary writing tool. She likes to compose with the on-screen keyboard provided by her sequencing software, an act that demands less technical playing facility and greater attention to melody and arrangement. Canadian electro-pop duo, Chromeo, create music on an antiquated Pentium II PC running a music sequencing software package called Cakewalk, which dates back to 1997. Because of their familiarity with the software, and the speed with which they can operate it, the pair thrives on the limitations of the platform: "It's good to work with constructive constraints," says keyboard player Patrick Gemayel (aka P-Thugg), "that's how we do everything." Gilbert O'Sullivan, author of classic songs like "Alone Again (Naturally)," agrees that older technologies can still enable songwriters to work quickly: "all these little digital machines are brilliant, but every time I had to rewind, I had to put my glasses on to see what I was doing. So I've dumped the digital and I've gone back to cassettes. They're so easy! You stick the cassette in, press it, and move forward. Simple."

Advances in multi-track recording technology have provided other straightforward benefits for songwriters. Guy Chambers, who has co-written a string of hits with Robbie Williams, suggests that taking an existing track as inspiration, building upon it, and then removing the original track, is a helpful way to kick-start new ideas. This can be an especially useful technique for lyricists, because oftentimes your collaborator will be unaware of the inspiration for the song and will imagine a completely different melodic and rhythmic interpretation of the words. Tom Robinson provides an eloquent simile to illustrate the approach in more detail:

> It's sort of like in the old days of stone and brick bridges. They'd first of all build a wooden arch and then the bricklayers would come and lay the bricks right up the side of this wooden arch and drop the keystone in right at the top of it. When the mortar was dry, you could take the wood away and you've got a brick arch. The wood is like somebody else's song that you are writing to. It's a handy little trick.

Songwriting routines

As described previously, songwriters such as Mike Scott and Joan Armatrading regularly suspend the songwriting process, returning to it periodically in order to produce new work. While many songwriters are comfortable relying on their skills to deliver on demand in this way, it is important not to underestimate the value of routine for professional songwriters. The concept of the workaday, nine-to-five songwriter, locked away in a windowless room, bashing away at a piano in search of a popular tune, has been a construction in popular culture since the Tin Pan Alley era.[8] Though now dated and not necessarily reflective of modern practice, for some contemporary writers this image remains not too far from reality: "I'm the Brill Building kind of songwriter," says Gilbert O'Sullivan. "I sit at the piano eight hours a day, five days a week, four weeks a month if necessary. I'll sit at the piano for hours on end until I come up with a melody. That's pretty much my approach. And then I'll sit with an empty notebook for however long it takes. It's a long process." Making room for the work is essential to achieve progress. For this reason, songwriter Glen Ballard sits at his piano every day, even when he doesn't have a project at hand to work on: "There's rarely a day that goes by that I'm not going to write some phrase or something for no particular purpose," he says.

A daily routine is particularly effective in helping to sustain the success of songwriting and production teams. Speaking about his role as one third of Motown's Holland-Dozier-Holland, Lamont Dozier says, "We worked constantly. Our work ethic was spot on. We wrote all the time, from nine o'clock in the morning until two, three in the morning sometimes. It all depended on how many songs were needed for the rest of the artists at the company." Dozier reports that two successful singles he wrote came from warm-up exercises he would practice every day at the piano when he arrived at the studio. These memorable chord sequences were completed, and became "Heatwave" (Martha and the Vandellas) and "This Old Heart of Mine" (The Isley Brothers). Mike Stock, who won eight Ivor Novello awards as one third of Stock, Aitken and Waterman, maintained a daily routine of creating songs for a continuous procession of new artists who would arrive at his studio requiring material to sing: "It was a question of necessity being the mother of invention," says Stock.

Preparation is an important part of any songwriting routine. Neil Finn recommends that songwriters prepare the space in which they are going to write, ensuring that writing tools are easily accessible: "I think it's important to have a tidy room," says the Crowded House front man. "I'd also say it's important to have a shave and unclutter your mind." These kinds of activities can help ensure that it becomes as easy as possible to begin the writing process; however, creating new work remains a challenge for even the most experienced songwriter. Neil Sedaka, the author of songs like "Calendar Girl," "Happy Birthday, Sweet Sixteen," "Amarillo," and "Solitaire," adopted a regular writing routine five days per week during the Brill Building era, but despite his experience, and worldwide success, Sedaka still finds the writing process onerous: "You have to force yourself," he says. "As much as I have done it for sixty years, I'm still afraid of it." While setting goals is important, songwriters also shouldn't put too much emphasis on the daily results of a songwriting routine. "The good stuff comes when you're not expecting it," counsels singer-songwriter Josh Rouse: "I have to block out time and set aside some hours to work on song ideas, which is tough, because, for me, you can't block out time for creativity."

Although deliberate focus in a dedicated space is an essential part of the professional songwriter's routine, songs can also be written in a variety of contexts. Canadian songwriter Ron Sexsmith undertakes a daily walk, which he uses as an opportunity to consolidate his ideas. Billy Bragg relates that he can often be found playing the guitar while watching television with the sound turned down, or thinking through ideas while on the motorway driving to gigs. Talking about his song "Never Buy *The Sun*," Bragg says: "I came up with that song while I was driving on the M4. I knew what the payoff would be for the end of each verse. So when I got to the hotel room, I reverse engineered back from that line. I wrote the song that would come to that conclusion." Don Black, the lyricist behind songs like "Born Free" and "Diamonds are Forever," is similarly unpretentious about his process: "you read about these songwriters who write better on a beach or they go to Jamaica to write," he says. "I've always been very happy to do it in my kitchen, or sit in my garden and do it, or go on a bus and do it."

To work efficiently, songwriters need to be diligent about capturing song ideas, especially while on the move. Billy Bragg, Adam Duritz, and Suzanne Vega have made a habit of using "voice memos" applications on their phones for this purpose. Other writers maintain both electronic and paper archives of unused ideas. Mike Scott of The Waterboys, for instance, maintains a Word document filled with potential song titles and ideas. Prefab Sprout's Paddy McAloon has boxes full of unrecorded songs that have become the stuff of legend for fans of the band. Miranda Cooper, a founding member of the Xenomania production team, who has written hits for Girls Aloud and Sugababes among others, reports that Xenomania are diligent about cataloging and reviewing ideas for songs, be they backing tracks, melodies, or beats. Cooper has revealed that Xenomania's daily writing routine produced an archive that swelled to more than 52,000 ideas, before it was culled down to 3,000 eminently usable starts for songs.

Chords and melody

An understanding of the function of chords is a vital part of a songwriter's arsenal. As indicated previously, writing with an unfamiliar instrument can help a songwriter to avoid well-worn patterns, as can the use of alternate guitar tunings. "That's usually, for me, where a song will start – with a chord pattern," says Sondre Lerche. "And then I'm looking for a melody that deserves that chord pattern, and then I'm looking for a lyric that deserve that melody, and that can justify all of it. It all comes out of chords." Despite their central importance, many songwriters work instinctively in terms of voice leading, and don't know the names of the chords they use. Some songwriters, like Glen Ballard, who is "always exploring the chromatic possibilities of music," have a tendency to construct complicated chord sequences, primarily by adding 7th, 9th, and 11th notes to chord shapes. For others, maintaining a sense of simplicity and economy can be the key to finding interesting new motifs.

Despite the finite number of options available to songwriters, there are seemingly always new shapes to deploy in songs: "I'm always learning new chords," says Mike Scott. "I learned a new chord from working with Ian McNabb a few years ago. It's a beautiful chord and I used it on a couple of songs shortly after. There's always something new that you can pick up." Andy Partridge uses the sound of chords as a prompt to invent imagery and define the lyrical content of a song: "I found a chord and thought 'what does that sound like? It sounds like a horse trotting along. Where would a horse be? The countryside.' You're describing to yourself what you are playing and the description becomes the lyric. That's happened in ninety percent of my songs."

Another popular technique used by songwriters is to change the root of a chord, or the bass note underpinning a chord, to provide additional complexity or "color." Jimmy Webb writes extensively about alternate basses in his book, *Tunesmith: Inside the Art of Songwriting*.[9] "It's about denying expectation," says the writer of "By The Time I Get To Phoenix," "Wichita Lineman," and "MacArthur Park." "You give someone a bass note that they can't live with and there is tension and dissonance. I prefer to call my tension 'benign dissonance.' Without it, music would mean nothing to me." Approaching the same concept from a different angle, singer-songwriter KT Tunstall says that writing with a bass guitar as your primary instrument can impact the decisions you make when constructing chord sequences: "What you find is that because you're being melodic on the bass, it ends up suggesting very different chords than you would choose if you were writing on the guitar. So the chord progression comes out differently. It challenges how you put the chords together."

Attaching a melody to a chord sequence is the next logical step in a traditional songwriting process. There are numerous methods that can be used to generate melodies. Most songwriters simply improvise different melodies over a chord sequence until they find one that is striking or memorable in some way, although melodies can, of course, be written to fit the contours of pre-existing words. The "catchiness" of a melody is an important part of its appeal, and deliberately experimenting with odd leaps and unexpected intervals can aid in the construction of a memorable tune. Though melodies do not have to be simple or memorable, writing a simple, memorable tune is often the most difficult challenge of all. "Great melodies are hard," says Gilbert O'Sullivan, who insists that even the most well respected songwriters make the mistake of abandoning melody later in their careers, "but they are the thing that it's really worth pursuing."

In terms of contemporary pop song structure, the moment in which a melody arguably matters most is during the chorus. The chorus is usually the section of a song that brings together a strong melody with the title of the song and perhaps a hook or riff of some kind. This does not mean that songwriters should neglect the melodic qualities of verses, bridges, or other sections of a song; however, delivering a memorable chorus has remained a hallmark of popular songwriting since the art form first emerged. "The verse is a promise that the chorus has to keep," says Sondre Lerche. "I believe that if you have a really good verse, you need a chorus that deserves and exceeds the promise of the verse. I hate when I hear good verses and then the chorus can't deliver. It's such a breach of contract with the listener. A song with a good verse and a bad chorus is unforgivable to me." Stuart Murdoch, of the Scottish alternative pop band Belle and Sebastian, is one songwriter who frequently creates memorable verses and choruses. Murdoch accomplishes this by employing unusual intervallic leaps and elongating his melodies beyond their natural conclusions: "It's amazing how malleable melody is," he says. "You can turn pure melody into anything. That's why it's a good idea sometimes to not pin it down to chords or form too quickly, because melody can become classical, melody can become jazz; it can become any style." Murdoch keeps his options open stylistically and harmonically by inventing melodies without any kind of instrumental accompaniment: "If you start to nail down your melody with chord changes you can sometimes miss out. It's better to let your melody run as long as possible."

Maintaining an attitude of flexibility can also be important when writing melodies. At Xenomania, Miranda Cooper will generate a large number of different tunes, testing them out on different pre-recorded backing tracks. Sometimes other writers will be invited to contribute other possible melodies, which leads to surprising results: "We will have a group of all sorts of artists or songwriters writing hooks on the same track, which is incredible because sometimes I think, 'I have rinsed that, there is no other possible melody to do' and then you hear somebody else's and you're like, 'What?'" On occasion, a melody is shifted to a different section of a song to ascertain whether it works effectively in that location. This can result in a striking rhythmic and melodic combination that delivers a memorable chorus. It can also be crucial to be flexible about changing the key of a song to suit a singer's vocal range.

Approaches to lyric writing

The construction of chord sequences and melodies can be inextricably linked with particular words or phrases that have inspired them, or which are vocalized during the writing process. Sometimes this is a nonsensical phrase, an onomatopoeic sound, or a detailed lyric. Songwriters tend to accumulate interesting words and phrases, material that can act as the starting point for a new song. Some, like Mike Batt, use a dictionary to make lists of interesting words to use in songs. Others will draw on dialogue from film and television, the conversations of passing strangers, or things they hear in exchanges with friends and family. Lamont Dozier took the phrase "sugar pie, honey bunch" from his Grandfather's everyday speech, using it to great effect in the song "I Can't Help Myself" for The Four Tops. He culled the title "Stop! In the Name of Love" from a dramatic plea he made during a real life argument with a girlfriend. Songwriter, producer, and drummer, Narada Michael Walden, who has worked with Aretha Franklin and Whitney Houston among others, often talks to the women he works with about their personal lives. He obtained the song title "Who's Zooming Who?" during a casual telephone conversation with Aretha Franklin about her experiences of how men and women interact in nightclubs. Mike Stock wrote "Showin' Out (Get Fresh at the Weekend)" for pop duo Mel and Kim having heard them employing these slang phrases during conversations at the recording studio.

The goal for some songwriters is to ensure that song lyrics can stand on their own, like poetry. However, for many, the intention is to have the words function effectively in the context of a song. This kind of philosophy is evident in the work of a range of writers. For example, Paddy McAloon of Prefab Sprout acknowledges the silliness of a phrase like "hot dog, jumping frog" from his top ten hit "The King of Rock 'n' Roll," but that doesn't prevent its inclusion as a distinctive and memorable lyrical hook for the song. Richard Sherman, who as one half of The Sherman Brothers wrote songs for Disney musicals like *Mary Poppins*, believes that a nonsensical phrase like "supercalifragilisticexpialidocious" can captivate and engage listeners of all ages. Jeff Barry argues that even when writing specifically for children, there is always room to credit the listener with intelligence. Barry wrote "Sugar Sugar" for a cartoon, *The Archie Show*, and yet points out that the song contains sophisticated lines like "I just can't believe the loveliness of loving you." As Sondre Lerche puts it: "If it sounds good, it is good."

Song lyrics can act as vehicles for sharing stories, and articulating emotions. Paul Williams, recognized for writing a raft of hits for The Carpenters, Barbra Streisand, and others, believes in the importance of writing "from the center of your chest" in order to communicate heartfelt feelings. And yet, at the same time, songs don't have to be confessional. Gilbert O'Sullivan's number one hit "Alone Again (Naturally)" is a highly emotive account of loss, which O'Sullivan admits is largely fictional. In some circumstances, songs that were intended as indictments of love or politics, like 10cc's "I'm Not In Love" or Holland-Dozier-Holland's "Band of Gold," have become go-to songs for happy couples celebrating milestone events. This is not to say that songs shouldn't be straightforward in their intentions; the trilogy of politically motivated anthems written by Mann and Weil in the 1960s ("Uptown," "On Broadway," and "We Gotta Get Out Of This Place"), have all succeeded with a transparent approach to their subject matter.

There are a variety of techniques to create words for songs. Stuart Murdoch likes to store up potential song titles and use these as prompts: "'The Stars Of Track And Field' was an ancient title. That was something I wrote down in a diary in 1992 or 1993 and then just occurred to me again in '96 and then I very quickly wrote the song." Some songwriters, like Ben Folds ("Kate," "Zak and Sara," "Annie Waits") and Adam Duritz ("Mr Jones," "Anna Begins," "Goodnight Elisabeth"), frequently make use of people's names in song titles, regardless of whether these characters are real or imagined. Others will make use of some kind of wordplay or inherent contradiction in a song title. Consider, for instance, Nick Heyward's "The Day it Rained Forever," Josh Rouse's "Some Days I'm Golden All Night," or Chip Taylor's "Phoned in Dead". Humor is another important part of songwriting, from a title like Jimmy Webb's "If You See Me Getting Smaller, I'm Leaving," to the gentle satire of Nellie McKay's "I Wanna Get Married" in which the singer-songwriter essays the role of a bored housewife.

Writing to an assignment is another common function for a lyricist. Don Black and Carole Bayer Sager are often asked to craft lyrics that conform exactly to the contours of a pre-existing melody. In their collaborations with musicians like Andrew Lloyd Webber and Burt Bacharach respectively, both Black and Bayer Sager have been required to place a word on each note of a given melody, maintaining both the economy and precision of the tune without distorting the meaning of the text. When writing the song "That's What Friends Are For," Bacharach insisted that Bayer Sager add two words to the opening two notes of the melody, leading to the line "And I, never thought I'd feel this way." "We fought over everything, even an eighth note," says Bayer Sager of her writing partnership with Bacharach. Though, on reflection, she appreciates Bacharach's attention to detail on the opening of the song: "It makes it better. It's like you're coming into the middle of a conversation."

Film and television projects in particular can pose complicated challenges for songwriters responding to existing material. Mike Batt wrote the song "Bright Eyes" for the animated film *Watership Down* after he was tasked with a brief to "write a song about death". Paul Williams has written soundtracks for musical films like *Bugsy Malone*, *The Muppet Movie*, and the 1987 comedy, *Ishtar*. "Ishtar was a unique project because they were intentionally bad songs," he says. "The characters sing 'telling the truth can be dangerous business, honest and popular don't go hand in hand.' That's bright, that's good. But the next line is: 'If you admit that you can play the accordion, no one will hire you in a rock 'n' roll band.' Their self-editing hasn't evolved yet, so they put in things that don't belong in a song." "Weird Al" Yankovic is renowned for his song parodies, and his ability to take the melody from a well-known song and create new words for it. Unsurprisingly, this is a painstaking process: "I spend a lot of time and effort on it," reveals Yankovic. "Even though they are ridiculous, funny songs, that doesn't mean that they are just dashed off. I will spend weeks or months working on one song. I try to match the meter exactly, syllable for syllable, and make sure it flows correctly."

There is a variety of contexts in which the act of writing lyrics can be performed. Albert Hammond, the writer of such songs as "The Air that I Breathe" (The Hollies), recalls writing the Whitney Houston hit "One Moment in Time" with lyricist John Bettis over the phone while Bettis dictated the words. Hammond also remembers that his song "99 Miles from L.A." was written while lyricist Hal David lay on a couch beside him holding a pad of paper. The observational style, described previously in the case of Chris Difford's work on "Tempted," was also part of the writing process for Mike Scott's "The Whole of the Moon," which he wrote on a street in New York while trying to impress a girlfriend:

> We were walking down the street and I remember that it was a moonlit night and I took a piece of paper out of my pocket and looked around for some inspiration. I can't remember if it was a whole moon or a crescent moon that was in the sky, but whichever it was I got this idea for 'I saw the crescent and you saw the whole of the moon' and I wrote it down. My girlfriend was suitably impressed I'm glad to say, and I had the beginnings of a song.

Developing these sorts of skills can take a number of years, and budding lyricists should not be discouraged from experimentation. Adam Duritz, who believes in the importance of including a lot of fine detail in his lyrics, spent a great deal of time honing his inimitable style in the face of criticism that favored a more generic approach. Miranda Cooper, whose chart-topping hits for pop acts like Girls Aloud have featured words like "anesthetize" and "disinclined" in prominent positions, encourages writers to forget about the conventions of pop and just use the word that seems to work most effectively.

Collaboration and co-writing

Finding and developing an artist can be an effective route to success, as can co-writing with another songwriter, especially if they possess complementary skills. Eg White, who has written hit songs for Will Young ("Leave Right Now"), James Morrison ("You Give Me Something"), and Adele ("Chasing Pavements"), suggests that it is essential to get a sense of an artist's tastes before starting a writing session: "If we haven't met, then we'll probably talk for an hour and I'll try to figure out what they like, why they like it," he says. "Then we'll try to imagine what sort of shape the thing might take by listening to a few things they've done, and we'll talk and find a theme that we want to explore lyrically." Sacha Skarbek, who penned both "You're Beautiful" with James Blunt and co-wrote the recent Miley Cyrus hit "Wrecking Ball," agrees that a large part of co-writing is the ability to quickly develop a relationship with a stranger: "Most of it is sitting and having cups of tea and coffee and talking," he says, "but it's the talking process that gets us to where we're going to go." In addition to learning about the person you are working with, it can be useful to prepare some musical or lyrical ideas in advance, so that there is something to work with if inspiration is lacking. Ultimately, co-writers who can write great songs and respond to the emotional needs of artists will elicit the best results. "A good co-writer is one that is flexible and knows when to shut up and let the artist breathe and when to jump in and reignite it," says Skarbek. "You need to have both sides."

Giving an artist room to express themselves is critical to any collaboration. On working with Alanis Morissette during the writing of *Jagged Little Pill*, Glen Ballard recalls supporting the singer with the freedom to express whatever emotion came to the fore: "I think she asked me at one point 'can I say this?' and I said 'you just said it' and so she was fearless with it." The role of producer and co-writer affords a great deal of power, and the way in which creative matters are articulated to others can directly affect the writing process. Dan Wilson recollects that the approach taken by producer Rick Rubin is to present problems in such a way as to highlight the strengths of the writer: "The way Rick would do it is he would say 'that second verse is getting in the way of everyone in the world knowing how awesome you are. Let's find a way to make that second verse cooperate better with your greatness.'"

Meeting a stranger and sharing ideas, thoughts, and feelings can be a challenge for any creative person. Paul Williams believes that one of the best ways to learn about the art form is to work in Nashville, Tennessee, where songwriters often adopt a system of appointments to co-write with others throughout the day: "The greatest place in the world to learn about songwriting is Nashville, because in Nashville at 10 o'clock in the morning you sit across from a stranger and he says something stupid and you say something stupid back and you begin to follow the pebbles of an idea and suddenly, magically, a song has appeared." Despite the importance of in-person collaboration, many writers extoll the virtues of co-writing via Skype or email. When collaborating with Don Black, Canadian singer-songwriter Ron Sexsmith discovered that neither technological boundaries nor an age gap need be an obstacle to a successful co-writing session: "At the end of our meeting, he gave me a finished lyric and I wrote all the music in the taxi from his house back to my hotel. The first thing I did when I got to my room was to figure out the chords for what I had been singing and recorded it on GarageBand and sent it to him a few hours later via email. It was easy. We had a lot of common ground despite our age difference."

Although the Sodajerker podcast has provided insights into the writing processes of a number of writing teams, including Johnny Marr and Morrissey, They Might be Giants and Mike Stoller and Jerry Leiber, there are a number of successful writers who make it a rule never to write in the same room as their partners. Elton John and Bernie Taupin are perhaps the best-known names in this category; however, Chris Difford and Glenn Tilbrook of Squeeze also never write together: "As an experience, I didn't really enjoy it all that much," says Difford. "I found it a bit weird. If I could be so crude, it was like two guys trying to masturbate in the same room. It would have worked better if there was a red curtain in the middle." Difford considers the writing process to be very personal, and much prefers having his own space in which to explore his emotions: "When you are in the room with somebody, they bring all of their baggage, and you've got all of your baggage, and suddenly you can't move in the room because it's full of baggage." Difford is not alone in his assessment. Joan Armatrading, Me'shell Ndegeocello, Gilbert O'Sullivan, and Mike Scott are just some of the writers who have also expressed a preference for writing alone: "Why would I do it?" asks Gilbert O'Sullivan. "The satisfaction that I get out of completing a lyric, no matter how long it takes, makes the whole exercise worthwhile." Mike Scott agrees: "I'm a lone wolf when I write. I'm not one of these guys who sits in a room and exchanges chords with someone. I write on my own."

Regardless of the range of views and preferences held by professional songwriters, there is perhaps no better way to experience the thrill of the songwriting process than to be in the throes of a creative collaboration. Glen Ballard reports that, when writing with Alanis Morissette, they managed to write and record a song every day. His sessions with singer-songwriter Dave Matthews resulted in the writing of twelve songs in twelve days. Dan Wilson wrote and recorded the worldwide hit "Someone Like You" with Adele during two sessions. Albert Hammond and Graham Lyle wrote "I Don't Wanna Lose You," a top ten hit for Tina Turner, in a single session, with the bulk of the writing being completed in no more than twenty minutes. As a final illustration of how fluid this process can be, consider this anecdote from singer-songwriter Kenny Loggins, regarding his productive first meeting with Michael McDonald, which resulted in the writing of a number one hit for The Doobie Brothers:

> I went over to his house and I was unloading my guitar out of the trunk. He was in his house with the front door open, going through ideas. When I got up to the door he was singing "What a Fool Believes" but he got to the change and stopped. My imagination kept going and I heard "She had a place in his life," so I knocked on the door and I said: "Hey Mike, that thing you were just playing. I think I know how the bridge goes." So, we were collaborating before we met.

Conclusions

From the range of views expressed herein, it is clear that there is no single way to write a song. From those who write only when they are inspired, or when a project demands it, to those who adopt a daily routine, or a regular songwriting exercise of some kind, the process remains unpredictable but extremely rewarding. What we can learn from these testimonies is that there are a variety of professional songwriting techniques available to practitioners, and that experimentation and daily practice is probably the best route to finding the most productive process. These processes include: an observational approach to generating ideas and writing lyrics; staying attuned to inner thoughts, and even dreams, for potential song ideas or melodies; writing and completing a significant volume of songs, even when uninspired, and routinely capturing ideas and enforcing limitations of some kind, be it the topic you write about, the time you allot to the task, the number of chords you elect to use, or the instrument you choose.

Experimentation should be second nature for the professional songwriter, and while a lack of theoretical knowledge about music need not be an impediment to progress, engaging with technologies both old and new can be extremely productive. Despite the potential for immediate results, songwriters should not demand this of the creative process, but rather remain at play until interesting ideas emerge. Being vigilant, especially when walking, driving, or engaged in other activities, can also help a songwriter to find useful starts for songs. Songwriters should keep their standards high, ensuring that all avenues have been exhausted when crafting melodies and lyrics, particularly in terms of meter, rhythm, and structure. Altering the bass note for a chord or describing the images that a sound brings to mind can be useful ways to develop distinctive material. Trying the same melody in a different location, or in another song altogether, can produce striking and original combinations.

Making use of words and phrases heard in everyday conversation is a practice frequently adopted by songwriters. The sound of a phrase can often be more important than its literal meaning, though songwriters should not shy away from using metaphor, directly addressing political issues, or inventing fictional stories and characters. Creating memorable titles for songs, collecting unused ideas for later use, and recording ideas on a portable recorder or phone are valuable habits that help ensure creative sustainability. When collaborating with others, developing personal relationships is the fastest route to achieving productivity, and this should not be limited by distance, age difference, or any kind of censorship. Enthusiasm and perseverance are essential characteristics for success, whether alone or in collaboration with others.

Notes

1 Unless otherwise indicated, all quoted interviews are sourced from episodes of *Sodajerker On Songwriting*, an audio podcast licensed via Creative Commons, which can be found online. *Sodajerker On Songwriting*. http://www.sodajerker.com/podcast (accessed August 11, 2015).

2 Paul Zollo, *Songwriters on Songwriting* (New York: Da Capo, 2003); Sean Egan, *The Guys Who Wrote 'Em* (London: Askill Publishing, 2004); Daniel Rachel, *Isle of Noises: Conversations with Great British Songwriters* (London: Picador, 2013).

3 Joel Hirschhorn, *The Complete Idiot's Guide to Songwriting* (Indianapolis: Pearson, 2001); Karl Coryat and Nicholas Dobson, *The Frustrated Songwriter's Handbook* (San Francisco: Backbeat Books, 2006); Jason Blume, *Six Steps to Songwriting Success* (New York: Billboard, 2008); Pat Pattison, *Songwriting without Boundaries: Lyric Writing Exercises for Finding Your Voice* (Canada: Writer's Digest, 2012).

4 Keith Negus, "Narrative Time and the Popular Song," *Popular Music and Society* 35 (4) (2012): 483–500. Keith Negus and Pete Astor, "Songwriters and Song Lyrics: Architecture, Ambiguity and Repetition," *Popular Music* 34 (2) (2015): 226–44; Gary Burns, "A typology of 'hooks' in popular records," *Popular Music* 6, no. 1 (1987): 1–20; Jon Fitzgerald, "When the Brill Building met Lennon-McCartney: Continuity and Change in the Early Evolution of the Mainstream Pop Song," *Popular Music and Society* 19 (1)

(1995): 59–77; Richard W. Hass, Robert W. Weisberg, and Jimmy Choi, "Quantitative Case-studies in Musical Composition: The Development Of Creativity in Popular-songwriting Teams," *Psychology of Music* 38 (4) (2010): 463–79; Joe Bennett, "Collaborative Songwriting – the Ontology of Negotiated Creativity in Popular Music Studio Practice," *Journal on the Art of Record Production* 5 (2011): ISSN: 1754–9892. http://arpjournal.com/875/collaborative-songwriting-the-ontology-of-negotiated-creativity-in-popular-music-studio-practice (accessed August 11, 2015); Joe Bennett, "Constraint, Collaboration and Creativity in Popular Songwriting Teams," in *The Act of Musical Composition: Studies in the Creative Process*, ed. Dave Collins (Farnham: Ashgate, 2012), 139–69; Phillip McIntyre, "Creativity and Cultural Production: A Study of Contemporary Western Popular Music Songwriting," *Creativity Research Journal* 20 (1) (2008): 40–52; Phillip McIntyre, "Rethinking the creative process: The systems model of creativity applied to popular songwriting," *Journal of Music, Technology and Education* 4 (1) (2011): 77–90. I humbly identify Paul Long and Simon Barber, "Voicing passion: The emotional economy of songwriting," *European Journal of Cultural Studies* 18 (2) (2015): 142–57, as an exception to these trends.

5 Dan Kimpel, *Electrify My Soul: Songwriters and the Spiritual Source* (Boston: Thomson, 2008).

6 Karl Coryat and Nicholas Dobson, *The Frustrated Songwriter's Handbook* (San Francisco: Backbeat Books, 2006).

7 *Oblique Strategies* is a set of commercially available 7 x 9 cm cards first produced in the mid-1970s by Brian Eno and Peter Schmidt containing statements intended to provoke artists into action through lateral thinking about creative problems.

8 I have written elsewhere about the sorts of routine adopted by Brill Building-era songwriters as well as tricks and techniques employed for maintaining productivity. See, for example, Simon Barber, "The Brill Building and the Creative Labor of the Professional Songwriter," in *The Cambridge Companion to the Singer-Songwriter*, eds. Katherine Williams and Justin A. Williams (Cambridge: Cambridge University Press, 2016).

9 Jimmy Webb, *Tunesmith: Inside the Art of Songwriting* (New York: Hyperion, 1998).

FIGURE 5.1 *Lee Bob Watson (photo credit Simon Weller)*

CHAPTER 5

A river, a bible, and a broken heart

Lee Bob Watson

There are three things a songwriter needs: a river, a bible, and a broken heart. A river gives you a sense of time and place. A bible is a keeper of language and history. I will speak briefly about the river and the bible. You will find your way to a broken heart well enough on your own.

First, the river calls: "Come ... come and listen." The river has existed since before the dawn of time. The river doesn't know your name; doesn't much care who you think you are or where you think you are going. "Drop everything," the river says, "I have plans for you."

The river connects you with something timeless. An archaic language or a master drummer can be your river, showing you things which cannot be transcribed. Embed yourself in a wild patch of earth; take root in an urban corner full of colorful, uncanny characters. Sit with a river and listen. Learn the idioms, the metaphors, the rhythms, the rhymes ... Listen to how the birds talk about shifting events. Enjoy the subtleties of casual conversation and study the signs of real mayhem.

Don't fuss too much. Slow yourself down. Let the river transform the way you live, think, and breath. If you can't unplug for a day, a week, three months, three years, choose another path. If you say, "*Man, I don't have time for this*," go and do something else.

If you sit with the river long enough, part of its nature will become your nature. Part of the river's fate will become your fate. For the river, you will gladly put your life on the line. It will be impossible for you to remain neutral. From there, the songs will come.

Study the river. Write down the best lines, stories, and names you can find. There are a million ways to say, "I Love You." But, *how do you* say it? Who are the key players involved? What are their stories? What makes the love come alive for the listener?

To ground your work and make it believable, you'll want to develop some sense of perspective, some form of light and shade, some distinct sense of geography and weather: a complete worldview. This is your bible. Notebooks, napkins, an almanac, a codex—call it what you like—this is your ground zero, the genesis of all your future songs.

"The Bible" is where you keep the idioms, the motifs, the charged metaphors, and battle tested phrases. Fill your bible up with flashes of poetry, sketches, questions, quotations, and quotidian. Develop shorthand methods for charting melodies, chord progressions, and song forms. Keep a song bouncing around in your mind at all times. Observe and evaluate the lines all day, at school, through traffic jams, in casual conversations, hear the song knocking around like a pebble in the river, waiting to land on a page in your bible.

Indulge. Be wide eyed. Try different voices. Write a song for Billie Holiday or Kurt Cobain to sing. Learn a song off the radio. Make it better. Be ridiculous. Start a thousand naive little masterpieces.

If you are earnest and adventurous, in time your distinct voice as a songwriter will emerge. You will have a novel point of view. You will find slightly personal ways of pairing words and melody to get at the heart of some scenario or emotion which couldn't quite be expressed any other way. Then, one quiet morning or late, late at night: *Hallelujah!* In a frenzy, you will be scribbling down the lines of a *damn good song*. It will be completely intact. You won't have to change a thing.

The good songs come like a gift from the ether. But I don't believe they come out of nowhere. They come from the river. They come from all the time you spend listening, recording, reworking bits and pieces and filling up pages in your bible.

A great songwriter casts a spell on the initiated. They welcome the listener into a complete world of their own creation. When Tom Waits sings, "I'm going to love you until the wheels come off," it pushes a perfect little love song into a singular realm of surreal romanticism which only Waits can conjure. When Van Morrison sings, "We were born before the wind, also younger than the sun," we are instantly located within the familiar yet enigmatic center of Morrison's blues poetics. From this center, the song opens in widening circles until we are nearly lost, though gladly, in the mist. And then, with impeccable timing, "that fog horn whistle blows" to bring us back to the center.

There isn't enough space to mention all the great writers I hold in high esteem. To stay close to the theme, I think of the many who have written so eloquently of rivers: Langston Hughes, John Lee Hooker, Joni Mitchell, Leonard Cohen, and T. S. Eliot to name only a few. As high-water marks of the art, I think of Bob Dylan, who in "Blowing In The Wind" and so many other tunes has wedded the overtones of the Bible and the American Songbook with a sublime feel for the river. And finally, I think of Sam

Cooke, who put these words to a melody with such elegance and power that it forever defies explanation:

I was born by the river in a little tent.
And just like that river I've been running ever since.
It's been a long, long time coming, but I know,
a change gonna come.

PART ONE B

Songwriting in the digital era

CHAPTER 6

Composing with the digital audio workstation

Mark Marrington

Software environments for music production, or Digital Audio Workstations (DAWs), have since the early 2000s become central to the creation of commercially released music, as indispensable to the studio-based professional recording engineer as to the so-called "bedroom" producer. The proliferation of the DAW is to a certain extent the result of rapidly evolving computer power, which has revolutionized the ability to handle digital audio. However, it is also due to the unique possibilities for music creation afforded by the DAW which have, over time, effected significant transformations in popular music practice. My purpose in this chapter is to provide insights into how the singer-songwriter might benefit from using such software beyond its most typical application as a conventional recording and production engine. Part of this will involve a consideration of the DAW in general terms, identifying key aspects that are worth taking into account when using such systems to create music. I will also discuss examples of DAW-based compositional practice with reference to artists who have used the DAW to create songs. My main aim is to show that the DAW, like the piano or guitar in previous eras of songwriting, is an instrument in its own right which impacts upon the conception and organization of musical ideas. To put it another way, the DAW has its own particular creative "paradigms" to contribute to the songwriter's process, which, once understood, can be harnessed to great effect.[1]

Before dealing with the DAW itself, I wish to offer a few remarks on the DAW's relationship to the traditions of songwriting in general terms. Anyone familiar with the history of songwriting during the twentieth century will appreciate that (broadly speaking) the essential foundations of the practice were laid between the 1920s (the Tin Pan Alley period) and the 1960s (the emergence of the modern singer-songwriter)—in other words, many years prior to the wide establishment of digital technologies. Songwriting during this period evolved into a two-stage process which has since become the tradition—namely, a writing stage usually involving the piano or guitar, followed by a studio realization stage involving recording engineers, arrangers, and producers.[2] For songwriters who remain immersed in this tradition the DAW represents, at best, increased autonomy where the second stage is concerned—that is, it functions as a virtual tape recorder to capture the completed song's performance and a convenient means for the songwriter to undertake the arranging, mixing, and even mastering of the song in-house. The DAW of course has many benefits over the traditional studio in this regard, including the ability to easily recall various versions of one's project as it develops, the capacity to quickly comp[3] together multiple takes into a single convincing performance (no tape splicing required) and the ability to build up complex musical arrangements using realistic-sounding virtual instruments. However, these are essentially enhancements of an established mode of practice and, where the songwriting process itself is concerned, there is little indication, even in the most recent interview literature, that the DAW has begun to become more widely integrated into the creative thinking of instrument-based songwriters.[4] That the DAW can represent a stumbling block for the traditional songwriter is illustrated by a recent forum on the popular *Gearslutz* website, entitled "Songwriters favorite DAW and why."[5] One user states, for example, "I don't really see how a DAW can help with 'songwriting.' Song arranging and production, sure, but the writing part only requires an instrument and maybe a voice." Similarly, another commentator adds that, "most DAWs were developed for music production, but ... that's not the same thing as writing a song. Songwriting is not a linear process ... for most people."[6] This chapter is primarily aimed at this kind of singer-songwriter—one who has already spent a good deal of time developing their songwriting idiom in association with a conventional musical instrument, and considers it a reasonable question as to whether a DAW can have anything additional to contribute to the process beyond the recording and arranging stage.

The DAW: Some key concepts

A DAW is essentially a visual environment represented graphically on a computer screen, whose functionality, when reduced to its simplest terms, is to allow for the manipulation of two main forms of information—MIDI data and digital audio. The manner in which this takes place depends very much on the design of the DAW interface, which has particular consequences for creative decision-making and workflow. A range of software platforms may qualify as DAWs, each with its own metaphor for the representation of MIDI and audio, the best known of which include Apple's Logic Pro, Avid's Pro-Tools, Propellerhead's Reason, and Ableton's Live.[7] While the appearance of their interfaces may vary, many DAWs share common elements, such as the main sequencer interface (often referred to as the "arrange" page), the mixer, the "piano roll" for MIDI editing (a rather archaic interface which refers back to the era of the Player Piano), a waveform display (modeled on the oscilloscope), and the traditional score. There are also some DAWs which are more specific in their design, such as Sibelius (Avid) and Finale, whose interfaces are based predominantly on the score, and MAX MSP which is a music programming environment favored by experimental electronic musicians. Most modern DAWs offer functionality which models electronic music technology of the past, including samplers, drum machines, synthesizers, various signal processors (EQ, compressors), and effects (reverb, delay, chorus, distortion, etc.). In this sense, DAWs are essentially skeuomorphic, a property which at its most pronounced entails the precise visual emulation of these technologies, down to every last detail of the original interfaces.[8] One of the best-known examples of this is Reason (first released in 2000), which accurately represents a virtual rack of hardware (including drum machines, samplers, and effects units), even offering the capability to manually route cables at the back of its devices. Designers of third party plugins for DAWs also emphasize skeuomorphism—Arturia's "V Collection," for example, faithfully recreates iconic synthesizers and keyboards of yesteryear, while Waves's "Abbey Road" bundle models microphones, effects, and consoles associated with recordings made in the iconic London studio. Some commentators have suggested that this approach to software design is intended to play on an association with past genres of music that were created using the technologies being modeled.[9] On that basis it is possible to generalize (loosely) that Reason's rack metaphor with its drum machines and samplers is designed to appeal to hip-hop artists, Live's sample loop-trigger metaphor is meant to appeal to DJs, Pro-Tools's multi-track studio metaphor is best suited for the recording musician, Sibelius's notation metaphor is appropriate to classical musicians, and so on. The strength of these kinds of embedded musical affinities is likely to mean that a songwriter's choice of DAW will reflect their particular technical background and musical sympathies.

In addition to these broader aesthetic concerns it is also important to consider some of the specific ways in which the typical DAW interface can affect the perception of the musical material the songwriter is working with. There has been much discussion, for example, of the typical DAW "arrange" page, where a songwriter is likely to spend much of their time working. In this environment the music is represented by blocks of data (sometimes called "regions"), which encourages a certain visually oriented approach to organizing the material of a composition on-screen.[10] This is further encouraged by the typical DAW's word-processor derived editing tools—"cut," "copy" and "paste"—which can potentially turn the composition process into a graphic design exercise. Electronic musician and originator of the Folktronica genre, Kieran Hebden (aka Four Tet), has observed that, "People who make music on computers don't realize how powerful the visual element is. Whether you like it or not, your mind starts to think in terms of patterns, because it's a natural human way to do things, and you start seeing the way drums are lining up on the screen, and it becomes completely instinctive to line them up in a certain way." He adds the caution that, "It's important just to close your eyes and use your ears, and trust what's coming out of the speakers more than anything."[11]

Another aspect of the DAW which can have significant implications for a songwriter's way of working is its capacity for "linearization." This refers to the tendency of most DAWs to encourage the organization of material on a timeline, with varying degrees of flexibility for experimenting with alternative configurations. James Mooney, for example, has commented that the timeline aspect of the DAW interface suggests that the "music should be built additively by appending one item after another until the desired duration is achieved," adding that the "grid" encourages a "default state of affairs" for the creation of "rhythmical music in 4/4 time at 120 beats per minute."[12] One of my own observations, gleaned from teaching students who use the DAW for writing songs, is that a particular effect of linear sequencer interfaces is to encourage "accumulative" forms of composition, in which the constituent parts of the music are gradually introduced one layer at a time until the piece appears as a complete entity in front of the user.[13]

It may be helpful for the songwriter to consider these remarks on the DAW's structuring capacities in reference to the attributes of a more traditional songwriting instrument, such as the guitar. The grid-like patterning of the guitar fret board, for example, permits certain left hand configurations in the formation of chords, in effect informing the precise arrangement of notes within a particular harmonic structure, and thereby the characteristic chord voicings associated with that instrument. These chords will also be articulated in a certain way by the performer, dependent upon the right hand techniques they employ—strumming, rolling, plucking, "chugging," and so on—creating further pitch orderings, unique rhythmic characteristics, as well as timbral properties. In other words, the character of guitar-based music is in a certain sense the product of the user's mode of engagement with the instrument. Being aware of the ways in which a tool one uses is shaping the musical outcome is sometimes referred to as knowing the "affordance" of a particular technology. This means that you develop an appreciation of the range of actions the technology permits you to undertake and, perhaps more importantly, a sense of whether the tool might be pushed outside these boundaries.[14] Songwriters who use traditional instruments are often quite insightful where the concept of affordance is concerned.[15] Sting, for example, has stated that: "You stick something in your hand that you're unfamiliar or slightly at odds with—like the lute, which is close to a guitar but different, and complex enough to really mess you up—it will put you in that strange territory of not being in your comfort zone, and that position can be stimulating and very fruitful."[16] Jimmy Webb, in reference to piano-based songwriting, has made the interesting point that one can self-consciously ignore the instrument's traditional paradigm. His language here is interesting because he could almost be describing a DAW interface: "Sometimes I work graphically and look at the keyboard as if it had nothing to do with music and it's a mathematical grid. And going, 'What if I move that there and move that there?' And not even listen to the sound of it very much at the outset and just trying to gain another mathematical insight into how to move voices around and not be afraid to move them around."[17]

Where the DAW is concerned, two examples will serve to illustrate this notion of affordance. Imagine in the first instance that you are using the facilities of a dedicated notation-based package like Sibelius to write your song. The virtual manuscript paper design "affords" composition in accordance with the rules of staff-based notation, which you arguably need to have some familiarity with to use the software effectively. You compose onto realistic-looking pages of music (which can even be given a parchment-like texture), input score-specific performance instructions (such as tempo markings and expression) and play back the music using conventional acoustic instrument sounds. However, in reality this interface is simply acting as the front end of a MIDI sequencer which uses standard MIDI instructions to trigger audio waveforms in a sample player. Knowing what is behind the metaphor in this way is useful because the songwriter may then feel inclined to experiment with the limitations of the software to creative effect. With Sibelius, one might ask, for example, whether it is possible to notate instruments outside their standard ranges given that MIDI itself isn't limited by these kinds of conventions, assign non-typical sounds to those same tracks, or explore ways of modifying the original sounds using the onboard sample player. It may not even matter if you are unable to read music when using such a program because the interface is essentially metaphorical—that is, it is just another way of viewing MIDI data. When working with the platforms that emphasize a more studio-oriented approach, such as Cubase, Logic, and Pro-Tools, the same principles apply. In addition to the standard arrange page, MIDI, and audio editing facilities, such DAWs also provide a range of "engineering" tools (or "plugins") which are designed for use in general production tasks (compressors, EQs, effects, and other signal processing plugins). For songwriters new to the DAW, such tools can be off-putting in their complexity, requiring a certain amount of immersion in digital audio principles and mixing theory, for example, to be of use in the professional sense.[18] However, an alternative approach is to view these plugins simply as devices which can affect the character of the sound. By freely loading them onto a DAW's channel strip, choosing presets, and tweaking knobs, while carefully listening to their effect on the song's material, one may be led in surprising new directions which can themselves come to inform how you conceive songs in the future. The overarching point in both these cases is that, through exploration of the DAW's scope, the songwriter gains insight into how the software may potentially be put to creative use without necessarily being constrained by its paradigm.

Songwriting and the loop paradigm

There is, on the other hand, a sense in which it can be logical to exploit a specific characteristic of a DAW if it can help to facilitate the songwriting process. Workflow is a particular concern for the songwriter, who will often wish to spend time working out the song's content by a process of trial and error—as one *Gearslutz* user succinctly puts it, songwriting means "getting down ideas, sketches, rough arrangements, researching textures, trying alternate versions, modulations or cadences." Therefore, it makes sense to use the features of a DAW that can accommodate live experimentation as well as enable you to maintain the song's materials in a state of open-endedness. One particular aspect that is commonly exploited for this purpose is the "loop" paradigm, which can be activated in most DAWs by selecting sections of MIDI or audio material in the arrange page and using the cycle feature found on the transport bar to repeat it ad infinitum. The loop essentially acts as a stimulus for musical ideas while the songwriter jams along with an instrument, usually with the record button activated. Some DAWs make a particular point of foregrounding the loop paradigm as a real-time interactive tool. Ableton's Live (introduced in 2001), for example, offers a highly flexible "on the fly" vertical loop-trigger "Session View," which has made it particularly popular with songwriters who eschew the linear approach. Andy Barlow (one half of the electronic songwriting duo Lamb), for example, considers Live to be "by far the best tool for songwriting" because it allows the user to freely trigger the different sections of a song to try out different arrangements: "I can assign keys to different parts of the song. For example, I can press the Q key and keep cycling around the verse loop until I press the W key, which takes it to the chorus/bridge, and the E key, which then takes you to the chorus. When we're actually writing stuff that actually allows the arrangement to be completely fluid and flexible."[19] The songs of Ableton Live-based songwriter Bradford Cox (Deerhunter, and most recently his solo Atlas Sound project) are strongly characterized by the DAW's loop paradigm. Cox, who is also a guitarist, will not necessarily even begin the songwriting process with the harmonic or melodic material of the song itself—instead he may simply start with a drumbeat and gradually assemble textures over the top of this.[20] A typical example can be heard on the song "Recent Bedroom" on Atlas Sound's 2008 album, *Let the Blind Lead Those Who Can See But Cannot Feel*, which is built on looped samples of guitar, music box, and vibraphone. Creating tracks via looping has arguably become the most predominant compositional paradigm of the DAW, with Joe Bennett, a notable songwriter and educator, even suggesting that the practice has become so popular as a result of the DAW that it has now "jumped species" from computer-based genres to band-based genres.[21] It is worth adding, incidentally, that what is really being retrieved here is the aesthetic previously associated with digital loop pedals, which have long been a part of the armory of singer-songwriters. These still remain popular with artists who play live as a means of generating complex textures on the fly (notable examples include KT Tunstall's "Black Horse and the Cherry Tree" (2005) and Ed Sheeran's "You need me, I don't need you" (2011)) and the effect of the DAW has arguably been to solidify this practice as a compositional strategy for the songwriter.[22]

One further thought on this particular paradigm of the DAW relates to the fact that all these software packages also come loaded with large libraries of pre-composed loops for easy incorporation into tracks.[23] This presents an interesting creative conundrum for the artist, given that in the "auteur"-driven singer-songwriter domain at least, where originality is highly favored, it would be anathema to build one's work on such materials in the way that a hip-hop artist would do with samples. Some DAW users, it is worth adding, will even extend this to a refusal to use any of the software's given plugin presets (synthesizer patches, instrument sounds, reverb settings, etc.). This may not necessarily be the most constructive attitude to adopt, however, given that such elements can often be very helpful for both generating basic material for a song or inspiring ideas. On the originality point it is worth remembering the facetious but perceptive words of the Timelords (Bill Drummond and Jimmy Cauty) in their *Manual: How to have a Number One the easy way* (1988): "all music can only be the sum or part total of what has gone before ... There is no lost chord. No changes untried. No extra notes to the scale or hidden beats to the bar. There is no point in searching for originality."[24]

Re-imagining the song in the DAW

For the final part of my discussion, I wish to make suggestions as to how one might use the DAW as a means of experimenting with the traditional song template. Essentially this means using the DAW's various onboard editing facilities and sound processing tools to elaborate the song's basic materials, which might exist in the form of pre-recorded sketches of the song's vocal and accompaniment, or of musical ideas that have been programmed in MIDI. In practice this could, for example, entail the user engaging in detailed re-sculpting of the audio material using a DAW's sample editor, or exploring the potential of its various plugins for transforming and manipulating these sounds across an arrangement. Essentially, we are in territory more typically referred to as music production, although the implication here is that there is greater scope for exploration than simply opting for a conventional song realization. Kieran Hebden, a seasoned DAW-based artist, encapsulates this approach in the following terms: "the idea is very much that the computer's the instrument. If I wanted a guitar line or something, I'd never pick up a guitar and write a guitar melody to go on it. I might record some guitar into the computer, then start working on a track, and if I decide I need some guitar, I'd go to that recording, break it up into pieces, and then compose the melody using that sound."[25] What Hebden is emphasizing here is that the DAW is the starting point for his writing process, in which sampled sounds, comprising little more than a few short fragments, become the basis for a much more extensive compositional process carried out within the environment of the DAW itself.

Where songwriting is concerned, recent practice has typically involved conflating the traditional elements of the song with production techniques more usually associated with the electronic musician. This is illustrated, for example, by the work of James Blake, which is characterized by a fusion of songwriting with the electronica production values of Dubstep. Blake, who produces his tracks from start to finish using Logic Pro, shows a keen appreciation of the way in which the DAW's visual paradigm affects how he creates his songs: "I could record them and look at them, almost physically—graphically—and just chop up what I did like and I didn't like, it didn't have to be all in one take, it could be something I designed from the ground up, visually."[26] Aside from the incorporation of specific Dubstep traits into his style (such as the characteristic beats and sub-bass effects), fundamentally Blake's approach is to use the DAW's capacity for sound design and audio processing to create unique sonic environments that envelop his vocals and generate heightened emotional depth. This can be heard in tracks like "The Wilhelm Scream" (from c. 2:00 onwards), a remarkable tour-de-force of production in which a simple loop-based song becomes gradually immersed in and obscured by distortion and cavernous reverb (the approach here is essentially "accumulative").[27] On other tracks, the exploratory nature of Blake's production is even more apparent. The Burial-esque "I Mind," for example, with its glitch-inspired rhythmic disruptions and extreme delay effects, moves the idea of the "song" very close to its complete deconstruction. One of the most characteristic features of Blake's work is the processing that is applied in varying degrees to his vocal lines, which ranges from subtle auto-tuning to the use of a vocoder (the track "Lindisfarne" is particularly interesting in this respect). Blake's vocal parts are also frequently subject to fragmentation, an approach reminiscent of the "stutter editing" technique associated with electronic and dance music producers. This is obviously very interesting where songwriting is concerned, given that the voice is the key delivery mechanism for the song itself. As Blake comments, "When you produce your voice in certain ways, manipulating it or not, you learn to analyze it like any other sound."[28] In other words, the voice is treated as if it is another sonority in the musical arrangement, offering a unique and potentially liberating way of re-considering the function of the vocal in a songwriting context. Blake's overarching attitude to using his DAW is perhaps best summed up by his comment that "Producing just becomes part of the writing process,"[29] which is an apt way of describing the effect the DAW has had in general terms on the process of creating recorded music since its inception.

Conclusion

In this chapter I have demonstrated, at least in outline, some of the ways in which the DAW might be regarded as a creative tool for songwriters. First, it is important to be aware that all DAWs are mediating structures—that is, they each have their own properties which influence how they may be used by the songwriter and these are often bound up with particular forms of media used for music creation in the past, ranging from the score to the sampler. Theoretically, it should be possible for a songwriter to employ any DAW effectively provided they are prepared to learn to recognize these characteristics and negotiate the tool for their own purposes. I have also drawn a parallel between the DAW and traditional instruments which have been previously associated with songwriting practice, suggesting that the DAW ought to be considered an instrument in its own right, whose idiosyncrasies need to be mastered if it is to be used effectively in the heat of the moment. Ultimately, how the DAW is used in songwriting will be determined by the place it holds in the process. One might, for example, exploit a particular DAW paradigm and allow this to condition the character of the music that emerges at an early stage. This was illustrated by the loop-trigger model, a dominant characteristic of platforms such as Ableton Live, which has appealed to songwriters who use the DAW as a vehicle for on-the-fly experimentation. Alternatively, one might view the DAW as a means of elaborating "offline" musical ideas that have either been pre-recorded or pre-programmed. Here it is a question of the songwriter's imagination in employing the DAW's MIDI and audio editing facilities, signal processing tools and effects to expand upon the song's basic material. A conservative approach would be to use the DAW to arrange and produce the song in accordance with an established model, while the more adventurous songwriter might decide to experiment in the hope of discovering new possibilities for the development of their idiom.

Discography and further listening

Atlas Sound (Bradford Cox). *Let the Blind Lead Those Who Can See But Cannot Feel* (2008) and *Parallax* (2011). Use of Ableton Live for looping.

Blake, James. *James Blake* (2011) and *Overgrown* (2013). Use of Logic Pro.

Condrad, Suzy. *She of Little Faith* (2013). Use of the Boss Loopstation and vocal effects processor, with Avid's Pro-Tools as production platform; see http://www.suzycondrad.com/ (accessed August 9, 2015)

Four Tet (Kieran Hebden). *There is Love in You* (2010). Hebden was an early adopter of the Yamaha Tenori-On (essentially a hardware step-sequencer which can be used as a looper); see the track "Sing."

Lamb. *5* (2011) and *Backspace Unwind* (2014). Use of Ableton Live.

Merz. *No Compass Will Find Home* (2013). Of interest for the electronica-infused production approach using the DAW (Logic Pro); see the tracks "Eudaimonia" and "Toy," for example.

Also of interest are Radiohead's *Kid A* (2000) and *Amnesiac* (2001), electronica-influenced albums created early in the DAW era with older versions of Logic, Pro-Tools, and Cubase along with various hardware (vocoders, autotune, etc). Particularly interesting where Thom Yorke's vocal production is concerned—anticipates much of the later practice.

Notes

1 I use the word "paradigm" throughout this chapter to refer to a DAW's particular set of attributes.

2 For an involved discussion of the historical relationship between songwriters and studio practice see Albin Zak, *The Poetics of Rock* (Berkeley, CA: University of California Press, 2001).

3 Comping refers to the amalgamation of the best parts of several different takes into a single ideal performance.

4 Daniel Rachel's *Isle of Noises: Conversations with great British songwriters*. (London: Picador, 2013), for example, contains no references to the DAW (aside from a passing comment on computers by Tennant and Lowe, aka the Pet Shop Boys). Media such as the guitar and piano, on the other hand, are discussed frequently. See also Bill Flanagan, *Written in My Soul: Rock's great songwriters talk about creating their music* (Chicago: Contemporary Books, 1986); Paul Zollo, *Songwriters on Songwriting* (Cambridge, MA: Da Capo, 2003).

5 For the full thread (begun January 2012), see https://www.gearslutz.com/board/songwriting/689687-songwriters-favourite-daw-why.html (accessed 9, 2015)

6 Such views are also echoed in certain professional "how-to" guides. Stephen Citron, for example, has stated that "It is so easy to sit at a computer, toy with a MIDI input device such as a digital keyboard, play in a tune, and have the computer print it out, making a hard copy of the song or if desired, have the computer burn a CD or create an mp3 of the song. But this is, in my estimation, not songwriting." See Stephen Citron, *Songwriting: A Complete Guide to the Craft* (revised and updated edition) (New York: Limelight Editions, 2008), 284.

7 As it is neither practical nor prudent to focus extensively on any one specific DAW in a chapter of this nature, my purpose is to provide observations on common DAW characteristics that may be applicable in a number of different contexts.

8 For further discussion of skeuomorphism in the DAW, see Adam Bell, Ethan Hein, and Jarrod Ratcliffe, "Beyond Skeuomorphism: The Evolution of Music Production Software Interface Metaphors," *Journal on the Art of Record Production* 9 (2015). http://arpjournal.com/beyond-skeuomorphism-the-evolution-of-music-production-software-user-interface-metaphors-2/ (accessed August 9, 2015).

9 For an interesting analysis of the aesthetic appeal of the skeuomorphic DAW interface, see Gaute Barlindhaug, "Analog sound in the age of digital tools. The story of the failure of digital technology," in *A document (re)turn: Contributions from a research field in transition*, eds. R. Skare, N. Windfeld Lund, and Andreas Vårheim (Frankfurt am Main: Peter Lang, 2007), 73–93. http://munin.uit.no/bitstream/handle/10037/971/paper.pdf?sequence=1 (accessed August 9, 2015).

10 For a recent discussion of the visual aspects of the DAW, as well as technology and creativity in music production in general, see Simon Zagorski-Thomas, *The Musicology of Record Production* (Cambridge: Cambridge University Press, 2014).

11 See "Four Tet," *Sound on Sound*, July 2003. http://www.soundonsound.com/sos/jul03/articles/fourtet.asp (accessed August 9, 2015).

12 James Mooney, "Frameworks and affordances: Understanding the tools of music-making," *Journal of Music, Technology and Education* 3 (2/3) (2010): 147.

13 See Mark Marrington, "Experiencing musical composition in the DAW: the software interface as mediator of the musical idea," *Journal on the Art of Record Production* 5 (2011). http://arpjournal.com/experiencing-musical-composition-in-the-daw-the-software-interface-as-mediator-of-the-musical-idea-2/ (accessed August 9, 2015); for a detailed discussion of the notion of "accumulative" composition in the terms I have described here, see Mark Spicer, "(Ac)cumulative forms in Pop-Rock Music," *Twentieth Century Music* 1 (2004): 29–64.

14 Aside from Mooney, 2010, "Frameworks and Affordances," there are some useful comments on this idea in Zagorski-Thomas, *The Musicology of Record*

Production, 98–102, 145–6, where the term "affordances" becomes applied to practical problem-solving situations which themselves suggest innovative uses of technology.

15 Songwriters' awareness of the role of musical instruments in their creative approaches is well documented in the interview literature—the various commentaries compiled in Flanagan, Zollo, and Rachel, for example, contain numerous references to the use of the guitar and piano in songwriting in response to interview questions specifically designed to interrogate the effect these have on the musical outcome. Flanagan, *Written in my Soul;* Zollo, *Songwriters on Songwriting*; Rachel, *Isle of Noises.*

16 Rachel, *Isle of Noises*, 196.

17 Zollo, *Songwriters on Songwriting*, 159.

18 I do not necessarily intend to downplay the value of learning such tools "properly."

19 See "Andy Barlow," *Computer Music Special: Singer-Songwriter Production Guide* 52 (2012), 22.

20 Another track of interest is "Te Amo" on the album *Parallax* (2011). Useful commentaries on Cox's approach can be found in Mosi Reeves, "Bradford Cox: Boy Wonder," *Creative Loafing Atlanta*, February 13, 2008. http://clatl.com/atlanta/bradford-cox-boy-wonder/Content?oid=1272094 (accessed August 9, 2015); and Marc Hogan, "Interviews: Atlas Sound," *Pitchfork*, January 14, 2008. http://pitchfork.com/features/interviews/6763-atlas-sound/ (accessed August 9, 2015).

21 See Joe Bennett, "Collaborative Songwriting—the ontology of negotiated creativity in popular music studio practice," *Journal on the Art of Record Production* 5 (2011). http://arpjournal.com/collaborative-songwriting-%e2%80%93-the-ontology-of-negotiated-creativity-in-popular-music-studio-practice/ (accessed August 9, 2015). Bennett's claim requires further qualification given that 1960s blues-based rock songs, for example, were frequently based on one- or two-bar riffs (effectively loops). What is implied here perhaps is that more traditionally conceived songs have become simpler in structure as a result of the DAW's influence.

22 See also the U.K.-based artist, Suzy Condrad, who has built her style around the use of the Boss Loopstation. http://www.suzycondrad.com/ (accessed August 9, 2015).

23 It is significant that such loops have often been used in high profile released music—Rihanna's hit "Umbrella," for example, was famously built on a GarageBand drum-loop. See Adam Webb, "Is GarageBand top of the pops?," *Guardian*, October 18, 2007. http://www.theguardian.com/technology/2007/oct/18/news.apple (accessed August 9, 2015).

24 See The Timelords, *The Manual: How to have a Number One The Easy Way* (Aylesbury: KLF Publications, 1988), 28.

25 "Four Tet," *Sound on Sound.*

26 Alex Needham, "James Blake: 'I didn't make this record for Chris Moyles,

I'm in the dubstep scene,'" *Guardian*, January 22, 2011. http://www.theguardian.com/music/2011/jan/22/james-blake-dubstep-scene (accessed August 9, 2015). See also, Neil McCormick, "James Blake: pop, but not as we know it," *Telegraph*, February 16, 2011. http://www.telegraph.co.uk/culture/music/rockandpopmusic/8329194/James-Blake-pop-but-not-as-we-know-it.html (accessed August 9, 2015).

27 "The Wilhelm Scream," along with the other tracks referenced here, can be heard on Blake's debut album, *James Blake* (2011).

28 J. Poet, "James Blake," *SOMA Magazine*, September, 2011. http://www.somamagazine.com/james-blake/ (accessed August 9, 2015).

29 J. Poet, "James Blake."

CHAPTER 7

Singer-songwriter meets music production and studio technology

Richard James Burgess and Rob Toulson

Introduction

Almost every singer-songwriter who aspires to make a living from their craft will be involved in the music recording and production process at some point in their career. Recorded music allows a musician to be able to promote their material remotely, opening up the opportunity of reaching a huge global audience. Recorded music also serves the reflective songwriting process itself and allows an artist to seek professional opportunities and showcase their capabilities to labels, managers, and publishers. For professional artists, record production is a gateway to income and success that immediately adds the possibility of new revenue streams.

This chapter focuses on the music production process and a number of related aspects that a professional singer-songwriter can expect to encounter. In particular, core studio production technologies are discussed, as well as opportunities to use music production techniques as an expanded toolset for songwriting itself. The concept of working with a specialist music producer is introduced, alongside common challenges of the recording process, such as critical appraisal and a quest for sonic perfection. Finally, the avenues for using recorded music as a core revenue stream for singer-songwriters are considered, in order to provide a framework for achieving sustainable success as a songwriter and recording artist.

Essential technical skills for singer-songwriters

Music production is itself an art form. Some musicians, however, struggle to understand studio technology and music production techniques, which can leave them frustrated by the process and the final recorded result. For artists who do not self-produce, collaborating with experts and specialists can bring invaluable contributions to their career trajectory. None the less, those who do become proficient with studio technology have more opportunities for success and they open up the capability to evolve and grow artistically, especially as these technologies continue to evolve around them. The singer-songwriter is, perhaps, the type of artist who needs to directly engage with studio technology more than others. Unlike a band, whose members have complementary skills that enable them to perform the necessary musical parts, singer-songwriters often write music for multiple instruments that they cannot themselves play proficiently. For these artists, embracing studio technology can be liberating, enabling, and, indeed, essential in order to realize their personal creative vision.

In order for singer-songwriters to promote their careers and enhance their career opportunities by distributing recordings of their music, it may be economically worthwhile to learn a number of key music production skills and technologies. It is not beyond the reach of most good musicians to create high quality demonstration recordings by employing a few simple techniques. It is, however, necessary to devote some time to assimilating these basic studio recording and mixing methodologies. For example, a singer-songwriter whose main instrument is the acoustic guitar will benefit from understanding how to use microphones effectively to record both their voice and their instrument. As a simple example, the singer-songwriter may choose to record a passage of acoustic guitar into a digital audio workstation (DAW)—a personal computer with software installed specifically for recording and sequencing music (such as Avid Pro Tools, Apple Logic, or Ableton Live). To record into the DAW, a microphone is required to convert acoustic pressure disturbances (i.e., the sound) generated by the guitar into an electric signal. Once the acoustic sound is converted into an electric signal it can then be amplified by an electronic pre-amp circuit in order to raise the level of the signal sufficiently for it to be converted into digital data. An analogue-to-digital convertor unit (often referred to as an ADC or "digital audio interface") is required to convert the amplified electrical signal into the digital, or binary, data necessary for a DAW to capture, display, and play back the recording. For a non-technical person, understanding how and why this all happens can be daunting, but in practice the recording process is made simple and relatively intuitive by computer technologies specifically designed for easy accessibility. The quality of the equipment does make a difference. A good microphone that is appropriate for the specific purpose, along with a well-designed audio interface, provides the basis for a clear, professional end result. There is no secret method for recording great music though; indeed Huber and Runstein promote the "Good Rule," which quite simply states "good musician + good performance + good mic + good mic placement = good sound."[1]

There are some other basic parameters that can enhance or diminish the quality of a recording. One that is often poorly understood is gain control. Gain control is the managing of the signal level throughout the signal path. At each point in the signal chain the levels need to be optimized—not too loud and not too soft or, once the signal is electric rather than acoustic, not too high and not too low. For instance, a microphone will distort if it is placed too close to a sound source that exceeds the microphone's specifications. On the other hand, if the sound source is too quiet the microphone will pick up extraneous background noise and even its own internal noise. The same is true the entire way through the signal chain—in the mic-preamp, the ADC, within the DAW, the digital-to-analogue converter (DAC) on the way to the monitor amplifier and from the monitor amplifier to the monitor loudspeakers. If the equipment is good and each gain stage is optimized (not too high, not too low) it should be possible to make high-quality sound recordings.

There are many excellent publications with details of microphone types, audio technologies, and recording tips, and of particular interest are those by Rumsey and McCormick,[2] Crich,[3] Owsinski,[4] and Savage.[5] Additionally, these publications discuss MIDI (Musical Instrument Digital Interface) composition tools in valuable detail too, which can be of significant benefit to the singer-songwriter. It is beyond the scope of this chapter to discuss technologies and engineering terms in detail. Rather, the objective is to encourage readers to explore the more technical articles as their interest and capabilities with studio engineering and/or music production develop. It should be said that technical perfection is not synonymous with good production; there are other factors at work. Notwithstanding, most tracks we think of as "well produced" are also of a high technical recorded quality.

Returning to the example of a singer-songwriter-guitarist, a common approach to recording example songs (i.e., producing a "demo recording") is for the artist to record a vocal performance that aligns with a previously recorded guitar track. Mixing desks and DAWs are equipped to allow the performer to hear back an accompanying piece of music on headphones while recording an additional audio track, so it is possible for a single artist to record many synchronous performances and layer up multiple instruments one-by-one.

Once all the recordings (or "tracking") are complete, the audio performances need to be mixed together to achieve the highest quality sound possible and to best present the creative vision of the artist. The simplest and most powerful aspect of mixing is the "balance," which simply refers to the relative volumes of the different instruments. If a guitar and voice are recorded well then simply playing the two recordings back at suitably chosen levels will give a good quality mix.

In addition to achieving a good balance between the instruments, mixers use a number of techniques to enhance and improve the raw recordings. Some simple techniques for enhancing acoustic recordings include compression, reverb, delay, and equalization. Compression reduces the dynamic range of a vocal or instrument and makes them sound more present. Reverb and delay effects both add a sense of space and depth to the mix, whereas equalization ensures that the levels of bass, middle, and treble frequencies in the instruments and vocals are balanced and complementary within the mix. Furthermore, where multiple tracks have been recorded, panning can be used to position the various sounds to the left, right, or somewhere in-between in the stereo field, which can also add a dimension of space and width to the mix. As with recording, there are a number of excellent publications on mixdown techniques, particularly those of Case,[6] Owsinski,[7] Moylan,[8] and Savage.[9] Many advanced mixing techniques are also available to the music producer, such as sound modulation, pitch correction, and various kinds of harmonic enhancement, although these can take some time to master. The more professional singer-songwriter might therefore employ a number of audio engineers to assist with the recording, mixing, and mastering stages of a project, and some of these advanced approaches to music production will be discussed in greater detail later in the chapter.

The singer-songwriter needs to understand not only music production technologies, but also digital productivity tools that allow them to effectively manage and maximize their career potential. For example, many singer-songwriters work remotely from home studios, and, when approached to collaborate with another artist or producer, they might need to exchange audio recordings and communicate ideas via the internet. The autonomous and connected digital musician can build a sustainable career by collaborating remotely across the planet with musicians who never have to leave their home studios. Diverse creative technologies and those that support the creative industries are evolving ever more rapidly. Consequently, members of the creative community, particularly musicians and songwriters, need to embrace these advances to stay at the forefront of their industry and craft.

The studio as a tool for songwriting and composition

The recording studio has become an almost essential tool for the singer-songwriter and has come to be referred to as a "musical instrument" and songwriting tool in its own right. The equipment and software that are nowadays ubiquitous in the recording studio provide a creative palette for musicians to develop, record, and fully realize their songs. Many solo musicians are multi-instrumentalists who record each instrument one-by-one to create the finished piece. With a little technical knowledge of recording techniques and relatively inexpensive studio equipment, a solo artist can nowadays produce completed songs independently. Some people think that performing while also being responsible for the recording of the performance (commonly referred to as "engineering") can be challenging for one person to undertake. It is possible for a single person to have both artistic and engineering skills; however, the need to move regularly (mentally and physically) between creative and technical mind-sets can undermine the musical performance. For example, if a technical obstacle is encountered, the disruption can easily break down any positive creative flow. For this reason many artists work in the studio with a specialist recording engineer who is responsible for all activities involved in the setup and recording of the performances.

There have been many successful examples of a singer-songwriter or solo artist working alongside a recording engineer to produce commercially successful albums. For instance, this was the way Dave Grohl recorded his first (self-titled) *Foo Fighters* album in 1994, as recounted by Brannigan.[10] With producer/engineer Barrett Jones, Grohl perfected a process that allowed him to perform and record all of the instruments and vocals on the final productions of his songs for which he had previously produced demo recordings:

> Start with the drums, listen to playback while humming tune in head to make sure arrangement is correct, put down two or three guitar tracks, do bass track and move on to the next song, saving vocals for last.[11]

In this way, the entire album was recorded within a single week of studio time, as only Grohl and recording engineer Jones were needed for the tracking sessions. The speed with which Grohl completed the album was in large part because he had not only written his songs, finalized arrangements, melodies, and rhythmic structures, but had also produced rough demo recordings prior to entering the recording studio to make the album.

The studio as "musical instrument" generally refers to the act of entering the studio or beginning to record before any detailed songwriting or arrangements have taken place, meaning that the creative process is heavily influenced by the recording technology within the studio space. Brian Eno has particularly focused on the concept of the recording studio as a compositional tool and his 1975 album *Another Green World* was his first to be "composed almost completely in the confines of a recording studio."[12] Eno refers to the process of composing in the studio as

> working directly with sound, and there's no transmission loss between you and the sound ... It puts the composer in the identical position of the painter—he's working directly with the material, working directly onto a substance, and he always has the options to chop and change, to paint a bit out, add a piece, etc.[13]

Eno would therefore enter the recording studio with "rather a bare skeleton of the piece, or perhaps with nothing at all," meaning that all his decision-making was made during and after recordings had taken place, rather than before. The previous norm for bands and artists was that they would perfect a song in live performance or rehearsal before committing it to record. Additionally, Eno's approach embraced the ideas of experimentation and that every recorded sound, either accidental or intended, could find its place in the finished piece. Sounds that were not chosen were simply deleted and replaced. It must be noted that this approach has its pitfalls: some artists can get lost in the production details rather than focusing on the quality of the song, which can result in an elaborate production but a weak song.

Imogen Heap is an innovative singer-songwriter who has used both approaches of writing in the studio and writing prior to entering the studio.[13] Heap engineered her own Grammy Award winning album *Ellipse* and explains that, having composed her first album *Speak For Yourself* within the studio, she was pleased to return to a more traditional approach for recording *Ellipse*:

> I wanted to get the songs written, because with the last record I wrote the album and produced it in tandem, and found myself in situations where I'd have a track pretty much done, then I'd have to crowbar in this melody and lyric over the top and end up stripping it all away anyway ... [I wanted to] write the songs old-school style with the piano, and get them sounding good on their own.[14]

The process of songwriting in the studio is, therefore, a delicate one, which may suit some artists more than others. In many respects the practice of composing prior to the studio and within the studio has become somewhat merged in recent years with the development of home studio technologies, which allow any musician to "demo" their material before committing fully to the final recording. Studio recordings are nowadays almost always used in the critical appraisal process and it is not uncommon for a song to be recorded a number of times before the artist finally feels like it has been perfected in terms of composition and/or sound. One key difference between Grohl's and Eno's approaches is the time allocated for reflection and decision-making—Grohl recorded demos with his own studio equipment before tracking the final performances some weeks later. Eno on the other hand utilized a more rapid reflective process, deciding which recordings to keep or delete in a relatively short timeframe.

Given the power of modern digital recording setups, a singer-songwriter can experiment with a number of composition and production approaches in a very short space of time. With a simple MIDI interface (a MIDI keyboard or electronic drum pad, for example), it is possible to record sounds that can later be changed, enhanced, or replaced with real instruments. A songwriter can, for example, record a simple piano performance in MIDI and then adjust the notes afterwards so they appear perfectly in time and with the desired attack, sustain, and decay profiles. A novice musician can thus build apparently high quality studio performances. If a musician needs to, he or she can record musical sections separately, allowing complex musical performances to be built up in layers. Additionally, the piano can, at a later time, be changed to another sound altogether such as a harpsichord, glockenspiel or MIDI string section. This introduces new production possibilities for the singer-songwriter. Having recorded an orchestral piece using just MIDI string samples, the artist could later hire professional session players to replace the MIDI sounds with real instruments. Similarly with percussion composition: it is not uncommon for a songwriter to program a simple electronic drumbeat that will later be replaced by a session drummer. Of course, electronic drum sounds, in their own right, are extremely important in many musical genres, so it is a good idea for singer-songwriters to learn to program electronic drum sounds and patterns using the latest software and hardware tools. It is also worth noting that many studio musicians have their own recording setups, and can share audio files over the internet from remote physical locations. Professional music productions can therefore be made quickly and relatively inexpensively, considering that there is no physical travel required, and much less studio setup time.

One of the most valuable aspects of using DAWs in the process of songwriting is the flexibility in experimenting with song structures. Digital audio workstations allow a songwriter to quickly record ideas and fragments that can then be looped, copied, cut and pasted into longer sections such as intros, verses, B sections, choruses, and bridges. These sections and parts of them can easily be moved around until the writer is satisfied with the song structure. Most DAWs allow both MIDI and audio tracks to be manipulated simultaneously making the process intuitive. This allows for an iterative approach to writing and simultaneous production that can continue through the final mix and even into the mastering phase of a project. For example, it is not uncommon for artists, writers, and/or producers, at a late stage in the production process, to cut out a lengthy third verse or, perhaps, loop additional choruses at the end to give a more impactful and hooky outro. These structural decisions can be "prototyped" quickly if a song has been recorded to a consistent tempo. With some editing expertise and the flexibility of multi-track DAWs, it can be impossible for a listener to tell whether a song has been performed and recorded from start to finish or constructed piece-by-piece.

Working with music producers

The role of a music producer

A music producer's role can differ wildly from project to project, for different genres, and with different personalities. Burgess describes the many different types of music producer whose varied strengths can be characterized as creative auteur, technical enabler, direct collaborator, experienced consultant, or practical facilitator.[15] The producer's role in working with bands and ensembles often demands him or her to connect each musician's contribution together in the most complementary way to create a final track that is bigger than the sum of its parts. Producers are responsible for defining the approach to recording, meeting the brief of the record label with regard to the target market, and delivering a track that an audience will consume in vast quantities. Successful auteur producers, as described by Burgess, include Quincy Jones and Phil Spector.[16] Spector assumed responsibility for all aspects of his productions, from choosing the artists, musicians, background singers, arrangers, engineers, and studios, to participating in and overseeing the songwriting. He directed the recording process in the studio, often heavily editing the tracks post-recording and going back into the studio to overdub additional parts until he was satisfied that he had produced a hit. Spector also decided which records would be commercially released on his Philles Records label. In electronic genres, the producer may often also be the recording artist, or a creative and technical specialist who can utilize advanced production tools to design and capture the artist's desired sonic characteristics. Dr Dre, Timberland, and Dangermouse are successful electronic music producers who have worked as artists themselves and as collaborators with other artists. Successful producers take personal responsibility for the delivery and completion of the final recording, and directly or indirectly facilitate the entire recording process including arranging studio time, employing engineers, assistants, session musicians, and dealing with record labels and their artist and repertoire (A&R) representatives. A good producer shields their artists from the functional aspects of making a record to allow them to firmly focus on the creative and performance parameters.

Many successful singer-songwriters have forged long-lived collaborations with a music producer or multiple such relationships. These relationships are driven by the need for unique skills and attributes in the production process. In some cases, the singer-songwriter brings the writing and performance skills, while the producer focuses on capturing the artistic musical vision. Many producers will work with a singer-songwriter in the pre-production process, to assist with songwriting and song structures, and to help the artist fine-tune his or her vision for the recordings. Sometimes producers and singer-songwriters share responsibilities to the extent that they credit themselves as co-producers, and sometimes as co-writers. Some producers take an active role in the songwriting and/or arranging whereas others perform largely engineering functions and act as a reflective sounding board for the artist. Producer and artist may both contribute performances to the recordings, making a strong creative, technical, and performance team.

Ken Scott engineered and produced many of David Bowie's early albums. Scott suggests that he and Bowie worked well together because he didn't significantly challenge or interfere with Bowie's compositions or arrangements: "I felt the best bet was to sit back and make sure that he could do anything he wanted to do. He would create the brush strokes, and I would create the colors that he used."[17]

Phil Ramone produced and engineered many successful records with singer-songwriters such as Bob Dylan, Paul Simon, Ray Charles, and Billy Joel. Ramone produced eight studio albums with Billy Joel from 1977 to 1986, and he attributed much of their success to the smooth running of the studio sessions and the fun and humor that became part of the process. Ramone was meticulous in scheduling meal breaks, creating rules for visitors to the studio, and imposing fines for tardiness. His attention to detail allowed the sessions to run smoothly and Billy Joel and his band to operate in a relaxed and collaborative manner: "What was most satisfying about the years I spent producing Billy Joel and his band was our camaraderie and the positive effect it had on our records."[18]

Despite their unquestionable friendship, Ramone still attributed his bond with artists such as Billy Joel as being "less about dialogue and more about results."[19] Phil Ramone clearly found the balance between professionalism and friendship in his relationships with his artists and, despite his fourteen Grammy Awards, was always able to be humble in the presence of great artists and producers:

> The years I spent working with Paul Simon and Billy Joel taught me about how to work cooperatively with an artist who knows how to produce and where my own ego fits in .... taking a step back to remind

> yourself that all they want to do is make the best record possible is often helpful.[20]

Ramone's approach to collaboration epitomizes the value in being diplomatic and kind in the studio and understanding how to get the best creativity and performances out of the artist.

In many instances the music producer can be employed to bring a specific sonic signature to a project, which could be a direction or sound that the artist or label wants to achieve. The collaboration between producer Mark Ronson and singer-songwriter Amy Winehouse was underpinned by their love for very similar music from both modern and past eras. Their connection was clearly in their passion for both '60s soul music and modern electronic genres when recording Winehouse's Grammy winning album *Back To Black*.[21] Ronson and Winehouse captured a sound that was both modern and retro, fusing and utilizing Ronson's DJ and sound engineering skills with their shared passion for soul music. Ronson's clear production style is evident on the record and, while collaborating, Ronson also contributed to co-writing the title track "Back To Black."

The commercial music production process

Every music production project is different and artists, producers, and engineers work with their own preferred approaches. However, when considering only singer-songwriter recording projects, there are sufficient similarities between them that it is possible to describe some common processes that will be relevant to most projects.

A recording project usually starts with songwriting and rehearsal, often referred to as pre-production. When songwriting, which involves developing initial ideas into a finished song, is conducted within the studio, this is still considered pre-production. Pre-production may also involve demo recording, so that the artist and producer can reflect on the songs and the songwriting over a period of time.[22] The demos may just be simple live renditions with voice and piano or guitar. The producer and songwriter might then decide on a final structure for the various parts of the song, the lyrics, and the instrumentation or orchestration, to be recorded. Variously defined, pre-production is an essential part of the production process and it can often be necessary to run these sessions in a relaxed environment with a small team: often just the artist and the producer. If the songwriter intends to record songs with a full backing band, then, once the songs are written, it may be worth organizing some rehearsal sessions so that the performers are aware of the songs and arrangements. This allows the more expensive time in the recording studio to be spent focusing specifically on the feeling or vibe of the performances. Prior to about 1980 and with large orchestral sessions, pre-production might involve meeting with an arranger and discussing arrangement and orchestration ideas. Because of the expense of hiring them, top studio musicians are rarely hired to do rehearsal sessions. However, they are capable of reading an arranger/orchestrator's parts to a very high standard, and/or taking instructions from the arranger, producer, and artist, as well as listening to the other musicians, and can thus capture the perfect performance and vibe within the first few takes without prior rehearsal.

The music producer will develop a plan for taking the songs from simple demos to fully produced recordings. Generally, this involves three consecutive processes—tracking, mixing, and mastering. Tracking might involve a live ensemble performing at once, or different instruments being recorded separately. In general, larger studio spaces are only needed for live band ensembles, recording drums, or string sections and orchestras. It is not uncommon for drums to be recorded in a professional studio space and for the singer-songwriter to then revert to a project or home studio setup to overdub additional instruments and vocals. Session musicians and electronic programmers can be used to ensure a full palette of sounds and performances for the final mix stage. Some producers like to track more material than is necessary and then make the final arrangement decisions at the mixing stage. Others prefer the arrangement and a sound close to that of the final mix to emerge while tracking. During the tracking process the producer and recording engineer might manipulate the recordings to remove any unwanted noises, to "comp" vocal takes together and to experiment with audio effects and MIDI sounds. Some producers leave much of the clean-up processes for the mix engineer, which does not usually make the mix engineer happy. In any event, before going to the final mix a (variously named) "tracking, board, console, or rough mix" is usually created, which should give the producer, artist, and mixer some indication of the way the final production will or should sound.

When tracking is completed, the recordings are often forwarded to a specialist mix engineer who will manipulate and enhance the recorded audio to make it sound as clear, powerful, and relevant as possible for the intended audience. Depending on the producer and the label's desires, some mix engineers add sounds and effects to subtly enhance the finished product, whereas others add their own more dramatic, artistic interpretation to the song. Mix engineers are specialists who are familiar with the various analogue and digital tools available and how to use them to achieve the desired sonic characteristics. Mix engineer Phil Harding mastered the art of mixing to a deadline and a brief. He recounts programming and mixing Bananarama's song "*Venus*" with the same specific techniques that were used previously on Dead or Alive's records in order to find a new and exciting twist to their record: "Within 12 hours we had turned Bananarama into a female Dead or Alive and the record was huge everywhere."[23]

Mixes are usually shared with the artist and the producer who then comment and request changes until everyone is satisfied. The mix process can be delicate and mix engineers are employed for their personal approach and style. A benefit in using a specialist mix engineer is that it allows an extra set of professional ears to contribute to the project and allows the producer to maintain a broad overview of the songs, rather than getting distracted by any technicalities of the mix tasks. Mix engineers are often asked to supply the various submixes or "stems" that most labels now require and this is quite a time-consuming process. Despite George Massenburg describing mixing well-recorded songs as a "simple" task,[24] Ramone describes the mix engineer as "the star of the record-making process" and proclaims: "great records aren't recorded, they're mixed."[25] It must be said that this is a typically self-effacing comment by Ramone, whose engineering skills were of the highest standard, and it is worth noting that a poorly recorded track is one that is difficult to mix well.

Once the mixes are complete, the songs are sent to a specialist mastering engineer to be mastered. Mastering is regarded as the final creative process in the music production chain and also acts as a final quality control process before the songs are made commercially available for sale or broadcast.[26] The mastering engineer can modify, compress, and equalize the spectral balance, tighten, and refine low, middle, or high frequency sounds and manipulate the stereo width and density of tracks. These processes all allow the music to be brought to a comparable contemporary standard to that of similar current releases. During mastering, the engineer also looks at the sound qualities and levels of all the tracks on an album and ensures that the complete product is cohesive, sonically consistent, and representative of the artistic vision. The mastering engineer will also insert silence between tracks, digitally remove any undesired noise, and encode the UPC (Universal Product Code) and ISRC (International Standard Recording Code) data. The mastering engineers then prepare final masters as wave (WAV) and MP3 audio files as well as the standard DDP (disc description protocol) image, which can be used by CD manufacturing plants.[27]

In recent years there has been a tendency for mastering engineers to make songs louder and louder by adding high levels of dynamic-range compression or limiting to a track. This has become known as "the loudness war," as reported in detail by Katz among others.[28] A number of research studies have highlighted the effects of applying heavy compression at the final mastering stage, which show that unpleasant, fatiguing, and heavily distorted audio is the result—even though louder tracks might have a more immediate impact on first listen.[29] The loudness war, described in detail by Milner,[30] rages on, though in recent years broadcast technologies and listener preferences have changed somewhat in favor of celebrating more dynamic music.

Once the master files have been reviewed and all parties have "signed-off" on them, the record is ready to be manufactured onto CD and/or vinyl, and prepared for digital distribution through online digital stores and aggregators.

The quest for perfection

Knowing when a recording project is complete can be a significant challenge. There are many ways to evaluate the "quality" of a music recording, though none more than a direct reflection on whether a recording truly represents the sonic "vision" or expectation of the artist or songwriter. Some artists may have a signature sound or one of an idol that they are trying to mimic, or there may be technical aspects that have to meet a desired quality threshold—such as the frequency balance of a piano recording, or the "punchiness" of a drum set, or the personal characteristics or nuances of a singer's voice which emphasize unique or delicate features. Perhaps more importantly, singer-songwriters and music producers should consider the recorded song as a whole artifact. They should ask themselves whether it tells the intended story through its chords, melodies, lyrics, arrangement, and orchestration. They should also listen to see if they have created strong enough hooks and emotive motifs to intrigue and grab the attention of listeners.

Poor recording and production practices can under-represent a good song. There are many philosophies on how to create the ideal environment to achieve the greatest possible performance from a singer or musician. Different performers respond to different environments; many singers prefer to work later in the day when their voices have warmed up. Others like to have as few people as possible in the recording studio. For example, The Pretenders singer Chrissie Hynde was known for needing to emotionally build up to a vocal performance in the studio. As reported by recording engineer Steve Churchyard:

> When it came to her vocals, Chrissie was great so long as nobody else was in the room ... Only Chris Thomas (the producer) and myself were in the control room while Chrissie sang, and he'd have to coax a performance out of her. Chris was all about that. On a vocal day we might sit around for hours and drink tea and have lunch and chat about everything other than what we were about to do, and then at a certain point—which was part of Chris's gift as a producer—he would say "OK, how about now?"[31]

The quest for the perfect take can often overlook valuable unexpected qualities of performance anomalies. While fundamentally aiming for a perfect performance, mistakes and nuances are often accepted and embraced by highly successful singer-songwriters and producers. This may be because these imperfections enhance or highlight the personality of the artist or their performance attributes, or the fact that emotion and performance delivery is sometimes more important than perfection of pitch or timing. For example, Phil Ramone noted with reference to Billy Joel: "There was seldom any fixing or polishing on Billy's records; if there were minor flaws in the performance, they stayed in."[32]

Mixing can also be a delicate process with an often-undefined endpoint, and a process that is likely to encounter compromises. As discussed by Toulson, "All mix processes add something to enhance the audio, but often take something unnoticed away, perhaps adding small delays or noise, or reducing the clarity of the top end,"[33] indicating that, during mixing, it is possible to arrive at point of trade-off, where any further mix enhancements will inevitably involve a reduction of impact of some other aspect of the song. The person in control of the mix process therefore needs a clear understanding of the final goal for the song, and to be able to identify when the mix is finished or as good as it can possibly be.

This is a challenging and fearful time for many artists. The point of no return—as, once the mix is signed-off and sent for mastering, it is hard (if not impossible), and certainly more expensive and time-consuming, to go back and make further changes. It is not uncommon for artists at this stage to question if the sound is good enough, loud enough, or creative enough for its intended audience to value and enjoy. There is a delicate balance between perfectionism and fear of failure, which, undoubtedly, are both capable of driving a project successfully forwards or halting it in its tracks. Indeed many singer-songwriters and performers often feel dissatisfied with the studio experience, as it is never quite capable of recreating the exact experience of a live performance. Blier-Carruthers has researched extensively on the subject of perfectionism and the process of recording in classical music and has observed that performers regularly exhibit

> distrust of the technology, dislike of the process, doubts about whether you like what is captured, disillusionment with the editing process, the thought of your performance going somewhere where you are no longer in control of it, the thought of a disembodied performance existing at all.[34]

Perhaps some of the best-known singer-songwriters have been able to be so successful with their songs and music because they were able to let go of perfectionism and the fear associated with failure. In the case of the Beatles, recording engineer Ken Scott indicated that John Lennon and Paul McCartney had quite different attitudes. Describing Lennon, Scott is quoted as saying, "As a musician, he'd get bored easily. He certainly wasn't a perfectionist. He wanted it the way he wanted it, but that wasn't always sort of perfection." In relation to McCartney, Scott states: "He is a perfectionist. He will keep going on something and will belabour a point quite often, whereas John would be, 'Yea, that's good enough, let's move on.'"[35]

Developing a sustainable career through recorded music

Recorded music provides a singer-songwriter with a powerful method of interacting with their fans and a valuable potential revenue stream. There are many ways in which singer-songwriters can use their recorded music assets to both promote their personal "brand" and acquire essential income through direct sale and licensing. At an early career stage, generating a large and active audience is more important than revenues, as audience development is a pathway to large future revenue streams and a sustainable career. Particularly, given recent declines in the direct revenue from music sales, Goldstein conjectures that "the future of revenue for recorded music isn't going to come from selling music to consumers—it will come from selling music audiences to advertisers."[36]

Building an audience and gaining the participation of that audience is of great benefit to the singer-songwriter. Radio airplay is still a major asset for generating new audiences and showcasing work to people looking to discover new music. Additionally, social networks such as YouTube, Facebook, Twitter, and Instagram are currently essential communication tools for musicians and songwriters. Once a sizable audience is in place, there are a number of ways to monetize that audience. It is possible to sell music through specialist online stores; Bandcamp in particular facilitates a number of strategies for musicians to sell their recordings (for example, direct sale, "name your price," and artist subscriptions). Additionally it is possible to have short runs of CDs and vinyl records produced that can be sold by mail order through an artist's own online store and at live gigs. Royalty payments can also be received from streaming music service providers, such as Spotify and Deezer.

To sell digital downloads through Apple iTunes (and other online download stores), an artist will need to work with a digital aggregator who will deliver the music for sale. Three such aggregators who work with independent artists are Ditto Music, AWAL, and CD Baby. Additionally, if a singer-songwriter can record his or her songs, this opens up opportunities for generating income through music syncing with films, TV shows, and advertisements, as well as through writing and producing music for computer games and corporate films. In many cases, accessing the opportunities for earning sync royalties for music is best done through a publisher who will promote a songwriter's work to creative and media agencies in return for a share of earnings. For sync work, many agencies will be keen to have access to instrumental versions of original music. Therefore, at the point of final mixing, it is always worth mixing down an instrumental version in addition to the full and final mix of a song.

Essentially, a music publisher's job is to represent the songwriter (or songwriters) of a written piece of music and associated lyrics, to generate revenue from that copyright material.[37] Most commonly, in legal terms, a song is considered to be made up of the music, lyrics, and arrangement.[38] The music is defined by the melody, which is the rhythmical sequence of notes, the lyrics are the words sung within the music, and the arrangement is the chord progression, the harmonies, the rhythm, and specific sequence of parts that comprise the song. All three elements can be assigned a copyright if they constitute an original piece of work. Where there are multiple songwriters, it is always wise to define the percentage of contributions (in writing) at the time of writing or finishing the song. This is to avoid later disagreements and legal challenges over the split of royalties.

Copyright collection agencies or performing rights organizations (PROs) represent songwriters and copyright holders also. They collect royalties from performances (on radio and anywhere that plays recorded music) and "mechanical" royalties (from sales of physical goods such as CDs, and digital downloads). In the U.K., the Performing Rights Society (PRS) collects royalties for its members whenever their material is played or performed on radio or TV, used online, performed live, or otherwise played in public. Organizations that play music to the public and hold live music events are required to have a PRS license and report the music they play, so that royalties can be calculated and distributed correctly to the copyright owners. In the U.S., the performing rights organizations ASCAP, BMI, and SESAC perform a similar function.

The Mechanical Copyright Protection Service (MCPS) licenses and collects royalties for copyright songs (lyrics and music) for uses of "mechanical" forms of the copyright material in the U.K. Other countries have similar agencies, with Harry Fox being the U.S. mechanical copyright collection society. The MCPS and other similar agencies are therefore authorized to issue licenses for companies to sell mechanical copies of recorded music to the public. Record companies who wish to sell physical or digital copies of these songs must agree to pay a license fee to do so. The MCPS collects the mechanical royalties for these sales and, after subtracting a small administration fee, distributes the income to the copyright holders. Different forms of mechanical use command different royalty percentages; for example, the MCPS collects 6.5 percent of the retail price for CDs and vinyl LPs.

There are two copyrights in every sound recording which songwriters and performance artists should be aware of and recognize the separate and distinct values in each: that of the song and that of the sound recording itself. A record label makes agreements with artists to record their performances and to commercially release those sound recordings. Usually, the recording agreement with the artist assigns the rights to those specific recordings to the record company. This allows the label to use those recordings to generate income through direct and indirect music sales to the public. They also have the right to exploit the use of the recordings, and through use in other outlets, such as interactive and non-interactive digital streaming services, for radio broadcast and for licensing for use in film, TV, computer games, and for advertising purposes. Historically, record labels did not own the copyrights in any part of the songs unless they struck a separate deal for the publishing. The advent of the "360 deal" changed this in so far as record companies that use those will own contractually defined portions of all, or many, sources of revenue that accrue to the recording artist, including publishing.[39] Many labels therefore nowadays also own their own publishing companies. The terms of recording contracts are negotiable and extremely variable but most grant a royalty on sales and it is common for companies to offer an advance against those royalties, while keeping a record of all costs. Additionally, in order to enhance sales of the recordings, the label will often fund promotion and marketing of the recorded music and sometimes a live tour. There are other kinds of deals such as cash buy-outs or work-made-for-hire. These are generally to be avoided except in the case of a commissioned work (such as for a film or TV) where the buyer is specifically defining the parameters of the music and the buy-out price is sufficient to justify the lack of future royalties.

The royalties that accrue due to performances of the sound recording itself (as distinct from the song) are collected by another PRO. In the U.K. this PRO is called PPL (Phonographic Performance Limited) and in the U.S. it is SoundExchange. They claim royalties for specific pieces of recorded music that are played in public, on radio, TV, on the web, and on satellite radio. This performance royalty is completely separate from the songwriter royalties that are claimed by PRS, ASCAP, BMI, etc. PPL issues licenses to businesses that play recorded music. PPL collects fees, which are distributed to its members—i.e., the performers on and the owners of the sound recording. The money claimed by PPL is split between the recording rights holder (the record label) and the performers who contributed to the recording, usually as a 50 percent split. If there is more than one performer listed on the recording, the performer royalties are calculated from a bespoke share agreement or from PPL's Performance Allocation Policy.[40] SoundExchange collects performance royalties similarly from satellite radio, webcasts, etc., under the Digital Millennium Copyright Act (DMCA). Unfortunately, the U.S. has no similar legislation that requires a royalty to be paid by terrestrial radio nor does it have any agreement with businesses that use music. This creates an anomalous situation in the

U.S. where songwriters and publishers get paid for some uses of music but performers and producers do not. Organizations such as the American Association for Independent Music (A2IM), The Recording Academy, the RIAA, AFM, AFTRA, and musicFIRST have been lobbying for many years to get this anomaly rectified, though with no success at the time of writing in 2016.

It is worth noting at this point that producers are paid via contractual agreement. In the U.K. this agreement is with the record label and in the U.S. it is with the artist. In both instances, the money comes from the artist's share. In very general terms, the producer's contract defines where the money will come from, how much it will be, and who will pay for what. The contract encompasses what the producer's deliverables are; for example: how many sound recordings he or she will produce, when they will be completed and delivered; and there will be some requirement as to the technical (and sometimes the commercial) quality of those recordings. The agreement will define credits, how much the producer will be paid (usually as an advance) and what their royalty percentage will be from the sales and use of the recordings. In the U.S., it is necessary to have a letter of direction (LOD) from the artist instructing the record label to subtract the producer's royalty from the artist's and to pay it directly to the producer.

Accessing and understanding the experts in all aspects of the commercial music industry takes time and commitment for any artist or songwriter. In the U.K., societies including the Musicians Union (MU), the British Academy of Songwriters, Composers and Authors (BASCA), the Music Producers Guild (MPG), the Association of Independent Music (AIM), as well as the PPL and PRS, all hold valuable networking events for their members which encourage collaboration and sharing of opportunities. Likewise, in the U.S. the American Association for Independent Music (A2IM), The Recording Academy, the RIAA, AFM, AFTRA, ASCAP, BMI, SESAC, and the NMPA all offer various opportunities for networking, to better understand the industry, and ways to help improve conditions for performers, producers, and songwriters as well as record labels and publishers.

Conclusion

This chapter has aimed to explore professional approaches to music production with respect to singer-songwriters. The benefits for singer-songwriters to produce recorded music are discussed, as well as the key technologies and challenges that might be encountered through working either autonomously or with a team of professional music producers and sound engineers. The role of music production technology in the songwriting process is highlighted as a key benefit for the creative process itself. Critical appraisal of recorded music is a key to learning and development, allowing a singer-songwriter to reflect on their writing and performance in a new way. However, it is seen that in many cases this can bring challenges too, particularly with respect to perfection from both a sonic and performance viewpoint. The value of recorded music is discussed and the potential for reaching worldwide audiences is highlighted as a key benefit. With the help of the organizations who govern the royalties associated with recorded music, it is possible for a singer-songwriter to find specific channels of opportunity in the commercial music industry and develop successful and sustainable revenue streams and rewarding careers.

Notes

1 David Miles Huber and Robert E. Runstein, *Modern Recording Techniques*, 7th edn (Oxford: Focal Press, 2010), 111.

2 Francis Rumsey and Tim McCormick, *Sound and Recording: An Introduction*, 5th edn (Oxford: Focal Press, 2006).

3 Tim Crich, *Recording Tips for Engineers: For Cleaner, Brighter Tracks* (Oxford: Focal Press, 2005).

4 Bobby Oswinski, *The Recording Engineer's Handbook,* 2nd edn (Clifton Park, NY: Delmar, 2009).

5 Steve Savage, *The Art of Digital Audio Recording: A Practical Guide for Home and Studio* (New York: Oxford University Press, 2011).

6 Alex Case, *Sound FX: Unlocking the Creative Potential of Recording Studio Effects* (Oxford: Focal Press, 2007).

7 Bobby Oswinski, *The Mastering Engineer's Handbook* (Auburn Hills: MixBooks, 2000).

8 William Moylan, *Understanding and Crafting the Mix: The Art of Recording,* 3rd edn (Oxford: Focal Press, 2014).

9 Steve Savage, *Mixing and Mastering in the Box* (New York: Oxford University Press, 2014).

10 Paul Brannigan, *This is a Call: The Life and Times of Dave Grohl* (New York: Harper Collins Publishers, 2012), 235.

11 Ibid.

12 Geeta Dayal, *Brian Eno's Green World* (London: Continuum, 2010), 28.

13 Brian Eno, "Studio as Compositional Tool," in *Audio Culture: Readings in Modern Music*, eds. Christopher Cox and Daniel Warner (London: Continuum, 2007).

14 Simon Sherbourne, "Imogen Heap – Recording Ellipse, Making an Album Solo," *Sound On Sound Magazine*, December 2009, http://www.soundonsound.com/sos/dec09/articles/heap.htm (accessed May 27, 2016).

15 Richard James Burgess, *The Art of Music Production: the Theory and Practice,* 4th edn (Oxford: Oxford University Press, 2013).

16 Richard James Burgess, *The History of Music Production* (Oxford: Oxford University Press, 2013).

17 Craig Golding, Daniel Rosen, Jay Hodgson, and Russ Hepworth-Sawyer, "Interview with Ken Scott," *Journal on The Art of Record Production*, Issue 7 (2012). http://arpjournal.com/interview-with-ken-scott/ (accessed August 23, 2016).

18 Phil Ramone and Charles L. Granata, *Making Records: the Scenes Behind the Music* (New York: Hyperion Books, 2007), 183.

19 Joe Bosso, "Production legend Phil Ramone on 15 career-defining records," *musicradar*, November 15, 2012. http://www.musicradar.com/news/guitars/production-legend-phil-ramone-on-15-career-defining-records-566978 (accessed May 27, 2016).

20 Phil Ramone and Charles L. Granata, *Making Records: the Scenes Behind the Music* (New York: Hyperion Books, 2007), 80.

21 Howard Massey, *Behind The Glass: Top Record Producers Tell How They Craft The Hits,* 2nd edn (Milwaukee: Backbeat Books, 2009).

22 Russ Hepworth-Sawyer and Craig Golding, *What Is Music Production? – A producers' guide: the role, the people, the process* (Oxford: Focal Press, 2011), 141.

23 Phil Harding, *PWL from the Factory Floor* (Welwyn: WB Publishing, 2009), 64.

24 Howard Massey, *Behind The Glass: Top Record Producers Tell How They Craft The Hits* (Milwaukee: Backbeat Books, 2000), 174.

25 Phil Ramone and Charles L. Granata, *Making Records: the Scenes Behind the Music* (New York: Hyperion Books, 2007), 186.

26 Bob Katz, *Mastering Audio: the Art and the Science,* 3rd edn (Oxford: Focal Press, 2014), 1.

27 Mark Cousins and Russ Hepworth-Sawyer, *Practical Mastering: A Guide to Mastering in the Modern Studio* (Oxford: Focal Press, 2013).

28 Bob Katz, *Mastering Audio: the Art and the Science,* 3rd edn (Oxford: Focal Press, 2014), 246.

29 Thomas Lund, "Level and distortion in digital broadcasting," *EBU Technical Review,* April 2007. https://tech.ebu.ch/docs/techreview/trev_310-lund.pdf (accessed May 27, 2016); Earl Vickers, "The Loudness War: Do louder, hypercompressed recordings sell better?" *Journal of the Audio Engineering Society*, 59, No. 5 (2011): 346–51; Edward Robert Toulson, William Campbell, and Justin Paterson, "Evaluating Harmonic and Intermodulation Distortion of Mixed Signals Processed with Dynamic Range Compression," in *Innovation In Music 2013,* eds. Russ Hepworth-Sawyer, Jay Hodgson, Justin Paterson, and Edward Robert Toulson (Shoreham-by-Sea: Future Technology Press, 2014), 224–46.

30 Greg Milner, *Perfecting Sound Forever* (London: Granta Books, 2010), 237–92.

31 Richard Buskin, "The Pretenders: Back On The Chain Gang," *Sound On Sound Magazine*, September 2005. http://www.soundonsound.com/people/classic-tracks-pretenders-back-chain-gang (accessed August 23, 2016).

32 Phil Ramone and Charles L. Granata, *Making Records: the Scenes Behind the Music* (New York: Hyperion Books, 2007), 171.

33 E. Robert Toulson, "Mixing can be simple, you just have to think one step ahead," *Sound On Sound Magazine*, March 2010. http://www.soundonsound.com/people/sounding-think-one-step-ahead (accessed August 23, 2016).

34 Amy Blier-Carruthers, "The Performer's Place in the Process and Product of Recording," *Proceedings of the CMPCP Performance Studies Network Second International Conference*, University of Cambridge (April 2013), 1–17.

35 Marshall Terrill, "Beatles' recording engineer Ken Scott reveals behind the scenes details on working with The Fab Four," *Daytrippin' Beatles Magazine*, July 25, 2012. http://daytrippin.com/2012/07/25/beatles-recording-engineer-ken-scott-reveals-behind-the-scenes-details-on-working-with-the-fab-four/ (accessed May 27, 2016).

36 Paul Goldstein, "The Future of the Music Industry: Selling Audiences to Advertisers," *Recode*, April 24, 2014. http://recode.net/2014/04/24/the-future-of-the-music-industry-selling-audiences-to-advertisers/ (accessed May 27, 2016).

37 Music Publishers Association, "What is music publishing?," 2016. http://www.mpaonline.org.uk/FAQ (accessed May 27, 2016).

38 Music Publishers Association. "What is copyright?," http://www.mpaonline.org.uk/FAQ (accessed May 27, 2016).

39 Richard James Burgess, *The Art of Music Production: the Theory and Practice,* 4th edn (Oxford: Oxford University Press, 2013), 254.

40 PPL U.K. "Performer Allocation Policy," http://www.ppluk.com/Documents/Member%20Services/Performer%20Allocation%20Policy.pdf (accessed May 27, 2016).

CHAPTER 8

Collage, cut up, and pop mantras: Post-digital approaches to songwriting

Lisa Busby

Take a moment to search Google images using the word "songwriter" as your search term. The images fall into three categories: people playing acoustic guitars (and sometimes pianos), people notating 8th notes and things in pencil onto manuscript paper, and scribbled handwritten lyrics. Given the search engine's method of finding and indexing images,[1] it can give us some idea of how songwriters are perceived. The biggest challenge I face when teaching songwriting is convincing people who don't play what might be traditionally considered instruments, who may not be trained in Western tonal harmony, and who don't see themselves as poets or wordsmiths—all the things I'd suggest that are generally perceived as a necessity—that the art of songwriting is a mode of expression *accessible to everyone*, and that the limits and boundaries of song form should be determined by *the individual*, not the majority.

This chapter examines a selection of works from artists across genres that present a challenge to this image of the songwriter, and conventional songwriting forms. The focus is the role that sampling and sequencing technologies have played in the evolution of songwriting. I assert that the techniques pioneered in the formative years of hip-hop and underground dance musics (namely, looping and collage, and use of existing materials—samples or, as I'll sometimes refer to them, "audio grabs"—as the core musical content) are now ubiquitous and have had wide-reaching implications for song structures and writing styles. Tricia Rose, writing on hip-hop, explains:

> Rap music techniques, particularly the use of sampling technology, involve the repetition and reconfiguration of rhythmic elements in ways that illustrate a heightened attention to rhythmic patterns and movement between such patterns via breaks and points of musical rupture. Multiple rhythmic forces are set in motion and then suspended, selectively. Rap producers construct loops of sounds and then build in critical moments, where the established rhythm is manipulated and suspended.[2]

Simon Reynolds highlights parallel tendencies to recycle and recontextualize in dance musics:

> House music didn't just resurrect disco, it mutated the form, intensifying the very aspects of the music that most offended white rockers and black funkateers: the machinic repetition, the synthetic and electronic textures, the rootlessness, the "depraved" hypersexuality and "decadent" druggy hedonism. Stylistically, house assembled itself from disregarded and degraded pop-culture detritus ... by cut 'n' mix, segue, montage and other DJ tricks.[3]

Moreover, I assert that the compositional innovations that are derived from particular technologies, techniques, and cultural movements are not necessarily tied to them. Strategies for composition that come from a sequencing or sampling methodology have proliferated into the wider pool of popular music compositional strategies—mutated, evolved, customized. These techniques have been made available to vast numbers of people by widespread access to affordable or even free digital audio workstation software (from here on abbreviated to DAW) paired with the possibility for anyone with a smartphone to record anything at any time, and anyone with access to the internet to download anything at any time. This will be evidenced by four case studies to follow—Performing the Sample, Melodic Assemblage, Mantras, and Cut and Paste.

The purpose of the chapter is to provide points of reference and practical strategies for the contemporary songwriter working in our post-digital landscape, to empower them to work beyond the confines of a traditional musical skillset. I will not attempt to cover the histories of appropriation art, sampling, or sequencing, nor indeed the emergence and development of hip-hop or underground dance music, as these have been comprehensively covered by other authors.[4] Nor will I engage with the debates on intellectual property and the economics of appropriation arts such as sampling, or the cultural and identity politics surrounding sampling or technologized composition methodologies, as these areas too have much excellent literature already in place. However, I would like to remind songwriters that working in a post-digital context where a myriad musical materials are available does not absolve us of the responsibility to maintain an awareness of social and cultural ramifications of the use of both the materials and techniques at hand. I believe artists must use their own moral compass, self-awareness of their background and privileges, and an awareness of others when making decisions on the economic and cultural ramifications of their choices.

The Post-digital

So, first of all, what do I mean when I say post-digital? To answer this question I'll defer to the expertise of Florian Cramer, Research Professor in New Media at Hogeschool Rotterdam. In his essay "What is post-digital?"[5] Cramer reminds us that digital simply means that something is divided into discrete, countable units, and analog the converse—something instead that consists of one or more signals which vary on a continuous scale. He then asks us to consider the use of the words analog and digital in popular culture as opposed to their actual, technical meanings—specifically that analog has become synonymous with the pre-computational, and digital with the high tech and electronic. Cramer outlines various potential readings of the term 'post-digital', the three most pertinent of which for our purposes I summarize here:

- Post-digital is the state of media, arts, and design after their digitization or at least the digitization of crucial aspects of the channels through which they are communicated.
- Post-digital is a landscape in which the disruption brought on by digital information technology has already occurred. The prefix "post" does not suggest a world beyond the digital, but rather one in which the digital is ubiquitous. Post-digital is not the end of digital, rather its mutation.
- Post-digital is the hybrid of old and new media. Artists in a post-digital environment choose media for their own particular material aesthetic qualities regardless of whether these are a result of analog material properties or of digital processing.

As Kim Cascone puts it, "The tendrils of digital technology have in some way touched everyone."[6] So when I use the word post-digital in reference to popular music I am referring to a world where the main method of musical distribution (legal and illegal) is the internet; a world where anyone with a computer can have access to a DAW capable of recording and making music to industry broadcast and release quality, for free.

It is not only the tools and technologies that have become ubiquitous, but approaches and methodologies for creation. Nicolas Bourriaud in

Postproduction notes that, "since the early nineties, an ever increasing number of artworks have been created on the basis of pre-existing works; more and more artists re-interpret, re-produce, re-exhibit, or use works made by others or available cultural products,"[7] and that "today artists' intuitive relationship with art history is now going beyond what we call 'the art of appropriation' which naturally infers an ideology of ownership and moving toward a culture of the use of forms, a culture of constant activity of signs based on a collective ideal: sharing."[8]

Ideas of collective creation are not new to popular musicians, as Jason Toynbee rightly notes—all authors in popular music are "social authors,"[9] nodes in creative networks inhabiting their own particular "radius of creativity"[10] but whose mutual relations are a necessary element of any possible creative innovation. So we know that the cartography of pop is a messy and complex one indeed. Sometimes we can trace straight lines from one point to another, and make clear observations as to development of ideas and techniques across time—but very often traditional and newer strategies work in parallel, not least because of the diverse interests and skills of the artists.

The four sections that follow will trace specific post-digital compositional ideas not by genre but by technique, and will each provide a set of practical reflections for songwriters to explore these techniques themselves.

Preparations

I'd advise that all songwriters who'd like to engage with the practical strategies in this chapter keep an audio sketchbook as part of their ongoing practice. You may already have a paper notebook where you jot down ideas for songs, scraps of lyrics, chord sequences, and more. I'm suggesting that this practice should be directly translated to keeping a library of recordings and audio materials. This can be anything—recordings you've made yourself of melodic motifs or chord structures, or even just interesting standalone sounds; field recordings you've made in your daily travels: found material from the internet or other samples and audio grabs.

It perhaps, then, goes without saying that the practical strategies for songwriting explored in this chapter are most likely to be employed within the DAW or perhaps within audio apps on a smartphone; or you might even be using hardware samplers or sequencers. However you choose to work you will need to be able to record and manipulate audio.

Finally, I urge everyone to remember that even in an exploded post-digital context artists have to negotiate frameworks of copyright and intellectual property law intended to curtail sampling of existing musical materials. What are the various ways artists navigate this? Some use material already in the public domain, i.e., works that are no longer in copyright, works that are available via Creative Commons licenses,[11] or library music.[12] Others who want to use samples of copyrighted material ask the owner's permission and negotiate a deal for the samples' use. Some artists have more complex and uncertain relationships to the legal frameworks, for example using samples of a very short duration, samples they recontextualize or heavily process to the point that they become unrecognizable. Furthest from any secure legal center are those who sample freely, trusting that if a sample owner wishes to enforce their rights they'll do so down the line.

Performing the sample

One interesting way in which sampling as a compositional idea or sonic fingerprint has proliferated is by artists composing and recording in ways that do not involve actually sampling but sound like they do—works that have the structural, musical, or sonic qualities we associate with sampling, or sample-based genres. Joseph G. Schloss has written in critical detail about the discourse in the hip-hop community around the perceived authenticity of "breaks" ("any short captured sound whatsoever")[13] as opposed to live instrumentation. His chapter "It just doesn't sound authentic" in the book *Making Beats: The Art of Sample-based Hip-hop*[14] is an excellent starting point for any scholar interested in the complex relationship between the live and the sampled. Schloss concludes that the act of sampling is less central to practitioners in this field than the sound of sampling,[15] and the examples I will present here offer an interesting inversion of usual perspectives, and seem to confirm this position.

We see complex interactions between the found and the played throughout the history of U.S. hip-hop and across the "Black Atlantic."[16] For example, in his lecture for the Red Bull Music Academy,[17] Ahmir "Questlove" Thompson discusses the intricacies of J. Dilla's approach to the performance of microsamples of Roy Ayers's "Ain't Got Time"[18] in his role as producer for Black Star's "Little Brother."[19] On this track Dilla seamlessly merges in performance short fractured samples using an MPC to create the impression of a continuous sampled loop, when actually it was impossible to directly sample as Ayers talks throughout the original track. Questlove himself is a key musician in The Roots, a hip-hop outfit where live playing is at the heart of the compositions and recordings, and was part of the larger Soulquarians collective working in Electric Ladyland Studios between 1996 and 2002. This collective included D'Angelo, Common, Erykah Badu, James Poyser, J. Dilla, Bilal, Q-Tip, Mos Def, and Talib Kweli—a vibrant atmosphere informed by the input of singers, MCs, instrumentalists as well as technologists and producers like Dilla—and produced a number of critically acclaimed albums.[20]

Charting the trajectory of compositional development in a band like Portishead also highlights the complex and changing relationship between the live and the sampled. While they have always incorporated instruments (acoustic and electronic) into their methodology, their debut album *Dummy*[21] made significant use of samples, for example the track "Glory Box"[22] in which extensive sections were used from "Ike's Rap II"[23] by Isaac Hayes to form the basis of the song. On their second self-titled album significantly fewer samples are credited, and moreover they had begun exploring in a live context the use of large ensembles, emulating live the orchestral soundtracks and library music they had sampled.[24] On *Third*,[25] while there is audibly more traditional live band instrumentation, there are clues across the album that the compositional processes formed and defined by the particular technological environment of sampling are still present. "The Rip"[26] is a good example—its central fingerpicked guitar line is no doubt "played" (it has various live characteristics such as fret buzzes and dead notes) but its repetitive, block-like structure is reminiscent of their older work and created by digital assemblage, one chord at a time.[27] Later in the same track, we hear a subtle example of a looped vocal between 2:09 and 2:58 where a single vocal "oh" appears to be held for an impossibly long time. This blurring of the obviously live with the obviously manipulated or looped is evident on other tracks such as "Threads."[28] It demonstrates that Portishead have diversified their modes of sampling (i.e., to incorporate their own original "samples") but that it is still very much a core compositional strategy.[29]

This practice of "sampling without sampling" is important to us here because it provides a particularly clear illustration of a phenomenon observed in the introduction to this chapter—it clearly separates the aesthetic or compositional device from the technology that was responsible for its proliferation. The rhythmic, textural, and compositional characteristics of sampling and sequencing are increasingly forming an important part of the vocabulary of all contemporary songwriters, and need to be understood not simply as consequences of a particular technology or way of working, but as conscious choices, tools available to the songwriter/composer even where the hardware sampler or DAW is not.

Performing the sample—practical exercises

How might you perform the sample? Inspired by Portishead, or similar recording techniques on Joy Division's "She's Lost Control,"[30] why not record vocal instrumental parts in individual segments, even individual notes, and sequence or layer them afterwards? What sonic interest might this bring? What flexibility does it give you to experiment with note placement, timbral juxtapositions, repetition, and rhythmic phrasing?

Why not try out some transformation and interpretation experiments? For example, translating an existing polyphonic sample to a monophonic instrument. What about a non-musical sample to a pitched instrument? What about an instrument you've never played before?

Or try some performed versions of digital effects; for example take an existing short phrase and perform it over a much longer duration—a form of manual time-stretching. What other digital FX could be emulated physically/acoustically, and when performed generate interesting compositional results—pitchshift, delay?

Melodic assemblages

One area of particular interest to the songwriter is how samples can be used to construct or craft melodies.

"Be good to them always"[31] by The Books, from their 2005 album *Lost and Safe*,[32] has one such unique approach to melodic writing. From the outset, we can hear that clear cut "audio grabs" are a key part of the sonic tapestry of this work. In the opening section (0:00 and 1:30) we hear a series of short, sharply edited speech samples slotted between interjecting synth lines. The sung melody enters at 1:35—note the unusual delivery and structure of the melody, the lines are delivered curtly, they have a strange sense of all being different lengths and shapes, not repeating or forming any recognizable pattern rhythmically. From about 2:00 onward the listener starts to realize why—the meter and structure of the lyric delivery is entirely based on the speech samples layered underneath and slowly emerging in the mix. It has a wonderfully serendipitous effect, what is an obviously a fractured narrative (they are audibly samples from a number of different sources) becoming connected, creating an abstract story of sorts. The interpretation and articulation of pitch by the vocalist in part helps this sense of unity—he is to some extent choosing where to insert melodic intervals (and the size of those intervals) based on the speech shapes in the original sampled voices—but of course the overall tonality of the melody is being led too by the instrumental harmonic setting composed by the band.

The approach of London artist Burial demonstrates an inverse of this approach—rather than samples singing through the musician, the musician is singing through his manipulation of the samples. In an interview with Mark Fisher in *The Wire*, Burial discusses the importance of vocals to U.K. dance music forms:

> I was brought up on old jungle tunes and garage tunes that had lots of vocals in but me and my brothers loved intense, darker tunes too, I found something I could believe in ... but sometimes I used to listen to the ones with vocals on my own and it was almost a secret thing. I'd love these vocals that would come in, not proper singing but cut-up and repeating, and executed coldly. It was like a forbidden siren. I was into the cut-up singing as much as the dark basslines. Something happens when I hear the subs, the rolling drums and vocals together. To me it's like a pure UK style of music, and I wanted to make tunes based on what UK underground hardcore tunes mean to me, and I want a dose of real life in there too, something people can relate to. So when I started doing tunes, I didn't have the kit and I didn't understand how to do it properly, so I can't make the drums and bass sound massive, no loud sounds taking up the whole tune. But as long as it had a bit of singing in it, it forgave the rest of the tune. It was the thing that made me excited about doing it. Then I couldn't believe that I'd done a tune that gave me that feeling that proper real records used to, and the vocal was the one thing that seemed to take the tune to that place.[33]

In "Archangel"[34] from the 2007 album *Untrue*,[35] the artist has sampled minute sections of Ray J's "One Wish"[36] and changed the length and pitches of notes to create a completely new melody for his own composition. The original vocalist is still present, his phrases intact as statements—but their shape, pitch, and articulation are the expression of Burial's voice, perhaps what Joseph Auner might categorize as the posthuman voice.[37] While it is not unusual for obscure parts or single lines from an existing track to be sampled, looped, and used as the basis for a new composition, the extent to which the individual words and syllables here have been altered and manipulated to reshape them into a new melodic line is more unusual. To my mind, it follows on from the sorts of manipulations and "revoicing" found in the work of Aphex Twin in the 1990s, in particular the melodic vocal manipulations found on the wordless earworm "Windowlicker."[38] And what's critical is the minutiae of detail here, this is still "audio grabbing," yes, but it is more akin to the rhythmic microsampling approach of Björk, Matmos, or Matthew Herbert. Modern DAW technology has made possible the application of micro manipulation and programming to all aspects of songwriting—anyone, vocalist or not, can now sing, the pitches you choose for the lengths you choose, the words you wish in the voice you wish, and regardless of whether you choose to use your own voice or not.

By adopting existing musical material as a building block for composition, we are stepping away from a reliance on instrumental virtuosity or theoretical knowledge. This is of course fundamentally the same as the use of music technology in the creation of dance and hip-hop, which certainly had a democratizing influence (without wishing to undermine the extraordinary performance virtuosity developed by practitioners on new instruments such as the turntable and the hardware sampler). However, as the Burial quote above indicates, as availability of technology in those instances freed the music from a dependence on instrumental technique, it sometimes replaced that constraint with a similarly limiting set of stylistic/technical parameters (needing the drums and bass to sound massive for it to be a proper tune). By interpreting the potential afforded by musical technology as a songwriting tool, as valuable to us in the initial creation of work as it can be in its eventual recorded realization, we return to technology as a possibility space, where we work with raw materials to an undefined end, and generic expectations may be set aside.

Melodic assemblages—practical exercises

Like The Books you could try and apply or extract melody from a found sound source—birdsong, a news report, or anything with ongoing rhythm or pitch. Or like Burial try microsampling and extreme manipulation (by pitchshift, timestretch, etc.) of existing vocal articulations to construct a new melody. Perhaps song fragments from your audio sketchbook could be woven into a new and complete tapestry?

As a lyric and melody generating exercise play with back-masking and phonetic reversal. For example, reverse a recording of a sung lyric—your own or an existing work—and listen for new lyrics and interesting melodic motifs. Or use chance to stitch together a melody for you—pick a selection of songs at random (perhaps the last ten you listened to that day), from each pick one word, tone or motif, then literally collage them together. Like The Books, any spoken or textual source could be used here, not just existing songs.

If you have a melody you want to change or develop, again chance forms of organization could provide some interesting compositional results. Rearrange the lyrics alphabetically, or by shortest to longest word—how does it affect the melody, how does is affect the narrative meaning?

After employing these and other chance procedures outlined in this chapter you don't have to stop there—you can always fill in the gaps, edit, and adjust as you see fit to reshape and restore the sense of a narrative or emotionally communicative song. But they will have taken your writing to some interesting places along the way and thrown up ideas that you might not have come to otherwise.

Mantras

> Repetition is evidently a major part of popular song and is a prerequisite for all popular songs.[39]

Pete Astor and Keith Negus, in their examination of songwriting and song lyric as analogous with architecture, observe three pertinent categories (often blurred or used flexibly) in the use of lyrical repetition in pop songs. First, to emphasize a point, the meaning of the repeated phrase; second, as a compositional tool similar to the way other forms (sonic art, visual art) might use motifs or repetition; and third, for the pleasure of repeating the sounding word or phrase.[40] However, the type of repetition that might be more applicable to the case studies in this section is what Luis-Manuel Garcia called "process repetition."[41] This is the pleasure of repetition itself, not necessarily the pleasure of repetition derived from the character of the sound object. The sound object itself may be quite blank—the value is derived from the repetition of it, not its inherent qualities in the first instance. Garcia relates this specifically to electronic dance music but suggests that his reading of "repetition and repetitive processes may also help to explicate the manifold pleasures of listening to other musical traditions that rely heavily on repetition"[42]—what I intend to do in this section.

First, to contextualize my observations it is useful to identify the different uses of vocals in early underground dance musics in Detroit and Chicago in the 1980s. Simon Reynolds identifies two vocal structures that developed—the soulful and song-like, and the more mechanized sound of the "jack track" with its "functional" catchphrase-like hooks and electronic stutter effects.[43] I'd suggest that in both categories, as well as in pioneering crossover works such as Moroder/Summer "I Feel Love,"[44] the emphasis on a single-line or mantra is key.

In a post-digital landscape we hear repeating mantras and the use of other classic dance music tropes extensively in the work of Animal Collective. In "Guys Eyes"[45] short loops of insistent rhythm and the drench of reverb that epitomizes the production speak to a psychedelic tradition that had manifested in the trance-like qualities of early acid house.[46] The track is made up of a number of single-line phrases repeated and layered extensively. We also hear single words at the end of lines isolated and repeated (for example "need you" at 1:26), evoking the digital stuttering Simon Reynolds identifies as a key signifier of the jack track. In FKA twigs's work repetition is a common feature—the long form repetition of "Water Me,"[47] or the more small scale repetition and development of phrases and vocal articulations that are deftly woven into a powerful and climactic structure in "Papi Pacify."[48] Possibly most interesting for our analysis here is "Preface,"[49] where the single mantra "I love another and thus I hate myself" is repeated, layered, fractured across this miniature track, until finally we are left with simply "I hate myself" ringing resoundingly. Much of the setting is obsessively focused on sensual texture—the vocals are processed and manipulated, displaced and swirling across the rhythm, and single digitally twisted syllables pop out of the mix like fireworks—and implies a "blissed out" transcendental "E experience." However there is a self-conscious duality here—the subject of the track is quite nihilistic in contrast to the setting, and reflects her own interpretation of the track as both like a hymn and punk.[50]

The repeating mantras here *could* be perceived as the first of Pete Astor and Keith Negus's categories outlined earlier—repetition for emphasis of meaning. However, Butler suggests that cyclical repetition, and thus repeated listening, allows for the perceptual separation of electronic dance music's complex timbral and rhythmic layers[51] and these mantras do feel somewhere between pure sound objects and meaningful text. Could Butler's methodology apply to the fractured and complex layers of lyrics and melodies we have observed here? The work of German producer AGF (Antye Greie) is in part concerned with chopped, layered, and processed vocals, recalling the lineage of sound poetry.[52] Greie seems to have moved toward the idea of abstractions from text as a way to *preserve* the complexities of meaning that are flattened when lyrical expression becomes too explicit and direct. In Greie's music, through technology and the processing of the text the message is deconstructed, fractured, processed, and thereby interrogated. Ambiguity is introduced. I'd suggest that both the Negus/Astor and the Butler models are in in evidence in the Animal Collective and FKA twigs examples previously discussed. These artists use repetition both to reinforce meaning and to obfuscate it.

One more thing we can observe from these examples is that what might have been considered esoteric or more accurately a niche underground practice in process repetition in the past, is increasingly looking like a mainstream direction today. When Thom Yorke and Radiohead introduced similar jack track techniques to their mournful indie pop writing style circa *Kid A*[53] it was met with a mixture of trepidation from some fans and acclaim by others. Fifteen years on ...? Minimalist and extreme repetition in rock is as old as the form itself, and indeed was made a central focus of the music by Glenn Branca.[54] Michael Gira's Swans is a group who from the start have traded in punishing, unapologetic cyclical repetition, but in their most recent formation (2010 onwards) have attained a mass popularity that would have been unthinkable when they recorded *Cop* in 1984.[55] The musical world has changed around these established repetition-based practices. The DAW, sequencing and sampling have brought repetition as creative practice to the very heart of contemporary popular music, and today's artists are exploring it in new contexts and with diverse and interesting consequences.

Mantras—practical exercises

Do you have unfinished, incomplete, or orphaned lines or vocal hooks in your audio sketchbook? Perhaps they've been so difficult to finish because they already say everything they need to. Try thinking of them as a mantra instead. How might a selection of different and unconnected mantras function together in a single work?

How might you arrange around a mantra that you've chosen? Take a single line and repeat it; for every repeat cut and paste in a completely new sound texture or instrumental setting—played or found—so that your mantra is the only constant in your composition. Your collaged materials might be in different keys at different tempi; try to find ways to make the sequence work anyway.

Cut and paste

The KLF were by no means wrong when they suggested in their [only partially] tongue-in-cheek *The Manual* that a song form that goes something like this, "an intro, a verse, a chorus, second verse, a second chorus, a breakdown section, back into a double length chorus and outro," was a guaranteed way to "have a number one hit the easy way."[56] This wisdom notwithstanding, of interest to me in this section are songs not in a verse/chorus/bridge form, or a 12-bar blues form, or in fact in any of the familiar forms we recognize in pop's rich history, but rather songs that bring together independent sectional ideas to form their own unique structures dependent on the ability to stick various sections together in the studio. Is this a post-digital phenomenon? Certainly not—some of the most commercially successful, beloved songs (The Beach Boys, "Good Vibrations"[57]), and critically revered albums (Miles Davis, *In a Silent Way*[58]) were created using this very methodology. What I do want to examine in the post-digital landscape is the emergence of the following three phenomena in so-called "modular songwriting":[59]

- the centrality of quick and easy overdubbing to a compositional process;
- the tendency to work in easily replicable and manipulable building blocks;
- the prevalence of a compositional approach where every part of the song is a hook.

The creative process of Sufjan Stevens provides a useful opening case study. In a panel discussion on creative processes at The Guggenheim in 2012, Stevens explained the value of listening and overdubbing to his compositional process:

> I kinda work with my hands and my ears, and I'm a craftsperson so I just do a lot of recording and overdubbing and responding to what I hear. Maybe later I'll bring in other musicians, but I do a lot of overdubbing myself and playing different instruments myself. And so it's not abstract, it's not on the score at all. You just kinda feel if something's going in the right direction.[60]

Furthermore, the impact that this methodology has on the eventual outcomes in terms of shape and scale of the compositions:

> I don't think I set out to make epic projects. I think the projects themselves become unmanageable in the process and I end up producing so much for a single project that they end up taking over and becoming much bigger and grander than I'd anticipated. I really work on a very microscopic level. I really think in terms of the song or folk song, and I work within a very conservative frame of melody, accompaniment, and narrative. So really basic, simple forms, and they just end up becoming hybrids or amended or expanded to form greater, epic, set pieces.[61]

Let's examine these methodologies with reference to the track "Come on! Feel The Illinoise!"[62] The track comprises two parts in distinct time signatures but each is similar in its construction. Part 1 has three melodic modules (the modules that begin "Oh ...," and "Cannot conversations ... /Ancient Hieroglyphics ...," and lastly "Chicago ..."), while Part 2 has two ("I cried ... /We laughed ..." and "Even with ..."). Underneath this, the arrangement largely comprises an extensive pool of interlocking instrumental parts. Listening closely to what initially might seem like a very repetitive piece of writing, we actually hear that in arrangement the song is constantly changing, determined by the introduction or removal of instruments and voices in an astoundingly dense sonic landscape.

This is reminiscent of Talking Heads' process when working on *Remain in Light* in 1980:

> The basic tracks Talking Heads laid down were rhythmical, pulsing and minimal – they were all in one chord. Each part was recorded as a long loop of song. Compositions were created by switching loops on and off. Or merging them together. David explained it like this, "Any part you play is going to fit with any other part. So you can close your eyes and switch a bunch of them in and out and you'll get this dramatic

change of texture, but everything will still at least melodically work together."[63]

What's different with Stevens is the sheer scale on which he is able to work, made possible by the digital environment. Talking Heads were working on tape, a self-regulating system, given the time and financial investment involved. In a DAW environment Stevens has none of these constraints, and as a result often ends up with densely arranged and, in his own words, "epic projects," or furthermore "hybrids" where disparate blocks (and what might even be considered by other songwriters as different songs) get glued together because in a digital environment it's so easy to just keep producing, to keep making.

A useful comparison at this point might be Animal Collective's track "My Girls."[64] It employs similar strategies of extensive repetition of three individual modules all built around a singular arpeggiating synth pattern. It's not as densely arranged and features a predominantly electronic sound-world as opposed to the lush orchestral setting of Stevens's work, but none the less on a basic level they are employing similar musical strategies. What's not the same is the approach to lyric. While Stevens's modules often repeat melodically, they very rarely repeat lyrically. The long form repetition is used as a tool to allow the setting of detailed narratives for the listener—not surprising when the topic concerned is the history of an entire American State. The Animal Collective does quite the opposite, with every modular repeat of the three sections we hear the same words: repetition is used to emphasize the heartfelt simplicity and universality of the statement. In this respect the Sufjan Stevens track might be thought of as a song without a chorus, while Animal Collective's is a song made up entirely of chorus(es). This distinction of the modules' purpose, when considered alongside the aesthetic distinctions, perhaps serves to highlight the ways in which the post-digital environment is shaping both folk and club music traditions.

My last case study seeks to show how these techniques are being used in mainstream pop writing, not simply the experimental fringes or indie scenes. Girls Aloud's "Biology"[65] is similarly modular with five distinct melodic sections (the first "Why don't you ..." at 0:00, second "I got one ..." at 0:33, third "Closer ..." at 0:59, fourth "You give it up ..." at 1:32, and finally "You can't escape ..." at 1:57). Rather than make a virtue of melodic repetition as we've seen in the previous examples, this song takes quite the opposite approach—throwing as much development as it can cram into its short radio edit timeframe.

Aside from the distinct melodic content in each module, there are other interesting things to note. Let's consider the evolving harmonic structure—in section 1 a single chord repeating, in sections 2 and 3 a two-chord pattern, and in sections 4 and 5 a four-chord pattern. Similarly the rhythmic structure—in section 1 we hear first of all the kit and the right hand of the piano simply bashing out the four beats of the bar before the drummer introduces a backbeat, in section 2 the backbeat continues but moves from a shuffle feel to a straight 8th feel, and in section 3 onwards steps up into a 16th note disco feel. These layers of structural change alongside the gradually developing arrangement and production choices make for a sense of accumulation and growth across the track. Their overlaps allow the sections to flow on from one another smoothly, despite the fact that melodically they all have quite a distinct character and could arguably belong to different songs. You start to hear this evolution everywhere once you know it's happening—listen for example to the mobile synth bass line starting in section 3 that becomes more insistent and present as the sweeping filter gives a changing sense of pitch emphasis and textural edge; or indeed the slow build of the vocals from solo voices in sections 1 and 2, a duet in section 3, the ensemble in unison in section 4, to finally the ensemble segmented and being led in a call and response while the backing vocals that had started to creep in at the halfway point in section 4 finally play out their role fully.

Alex Petridis in his review of *Chemistry*[66] for the *Guardian* was astute to observe that it is "a record that dispenses with the tiresome business of verses and instead opts for songs apparently constructed by stitching eight different choruses together."[67] "Biology" is an excellent example of the phenomenon observed earlier in "My Girls"—the five distinct melodic sections do feel "stitched" together but the threads that bind them are the more subtle overlapping and intersecting arrangement and production choices. In the end the song structure wittily reveals its own inner working—after all five sections have cycled through we jump back to the beginning but then straight into section 5 again ... and crucially it works, it doesn't feel like an unnatural juxtaposition.

The music video[68] might even be argued as the perfect visual allegory of the DAW. It sees the five girls perform within three small, contrasting sets that they move between via digital emulation of a revolving stage. The color palette and dressing of the three rooms change in sync with the three harmonic changes (i.e., sections 1, 3, and 5), as do their costumes. Not only does this highlight the independence of the sections: more importantly, these crude revolving cardboard sets and "before your eyes" outfit cross fades reflect the ability to simply lift sections and lay them over each other or next to each other in the DAW, to change the feel or character of a voice or instrument with different production choices. The video demonstrates visually the ease with which the contemporary songwriter may access limitless sonic possibilities, and furthermore, as The KLF note, that the process of songwriting is one of construction and "you will have to find the Frankenstein in you to make it work."[69]

So Spicer's notion of "accumulative form,"[70] the practice of looping specifically resulting in what Garcia suggests is "an ever changing same,"[71] and the importance of the studio as instrument (and the Frankenstein-like opportunities it can afford) continue to be powerful tools for musicians, just as they have been for years. I suggest in post-digital music making songwriters are taking these ideas, removing them from established contexts, pushing them to logical extremes, and creating innovative new structures.

Cut and paste—practical exercises

Write your song vertically instead of horizontally, start with a single idea, and arrange it completely before moving on. Ideas in your extended arrangement might become as important to the song as the initial melody or lyric.

Treat your sketches like samples—export a complete arrangement as audio, reimport into a new project, cut and paste, and process it as if it were a sample to form the basis of a new composition. Try challenging yourself to use all of the bounced material in some way and still arrive at something new and different.

When working with MIDI, consider that any part written could be voiced on any instrument. Extreme examples of revoicings like translating the MIDI information from a drum part to a pitched instrument or vice versa can produce unexpected and exciting results.

Take the successful sections from a handful of unsuccessful or incomplete songs and make a Frankenstein's monster from them. Consider moving the sections into the same key and meter, or allowing them to retain their original parameters.

Conclusion

To return to where I began, the purpose of this article was to empower the songwriter working in ways that do not conform to perceptions of the musician as instrumentalist and performer. The value of the expansions and interrogations of a song's shapes and materials that the artists herein explore is in the space that it makes in the songwriting landscape for those marginalized by traditional music making—either from a lack of access to it, or an alienation by it.

Discography

Animal Collective, "My Girls." *Merriweather Post Pavilion*, Domino WIGLP216, 2009, CD.
Aphex Twin, "Windowlicker." Warp Records WAP105CD, 1999, CD [Single].
Roy Ayers, "Ain't got time." *He's Coming*, Polydor PD 5022, 2391 027, 1972, LP.
The Beach Boys, "Good Vibrations." Capitol Records 5676, 1966, 7" [Single].
Björk, *Vespertine*, One Little Indian TPLP101CD, 2001, CD.
The Books, "Be good to them always." *Lost and Safe*, Tomlab 50, 2005, CD.
The Books, *Lost and Safe*, Tomlab 50, 2005, CD.
Black Star, "Little Brother." *The Hurricane (Music From And Inspired By The Motion Picture)*, MCA 170 116–2, 1999, CD.
Glenn Branca, *Lessons No 1*, 99 Records 99–01, 1980, 12".
Burial, "Archangel." *Untrue*, Hyperdub HDBCD002, 2007, CD.
Burial, *Untrue*, Hyperdub HDBCD002, 2007, CD.
Miles Davis, *In a Silent Way*, Columbia CS 9875, 1969, LP.
Girls Aloud, "Biology." *Chemistry*, Polydor 9875390, 2005, CD.
Girls Aloud, *Chemistry*, Polydor 9875390, 2005, CD.
FKA twigs, "Papi Pacify." *EP2*, Young Turks YT098, 2013, 12".
FKA twigs, "Preface." *LP1*, Young Turks YTCD118, 2014, 12".
FKA twigs, "Water Me." *EP2*, Young Turks YT098, 2013, 12".
Isaac Hayes, "Ike's Rap II." *Black Moses*, Stax 2628–004, 1972, LP.
Matthew Herbert, *Plat Du Jour*, Accidental AC19CD, 2005, CD.
Joy Division, "She's Lost Control." *Unknown Pleasures*, Factory FACT 10, 1979, LP.
Matmos, *A chance to cut is a chance to cure*, Matador OLE 489–2, 2001, CD.
Portishead, "Glory Box." *Dummy*, Go Beat 828 553–2, 1994, CD.
Portishead, *Dummy*, Go Beat 828 553–2, 1994, CD.
Portishead, *Roseland NYC Live*, Go Beat 559 424–2, 1998, CD.
Portishead, "The Rip." *Third*, Island 1764013, 2008, CD.
Portishead, "Threads." *Third*, Island 1764013, 2008, CD.
Portishead, *Third*, Island 1764013, 2008, CD.
Radiohead, *Kid A*, Parlophone CDKIDA 4, 2000, CD.
Ray J, "One Wish." Sanctuary Records SANXD424, 2005, CD [Single].
Sufjan Stevens, "Come On! Feel The Illinoise! Part I: The World's Columbian Exposition Part II: Carl Sandburg Visits Me In A Dream." *Sufjan Stevens Invites You To: Come On Feel The Illinoise*, Ashmatic Kitty Records AKR014, 2005, CD.
Donna Summer, "I Feel Love." Casablanca Records NBD 20104, 1977, 12" [Single].
Swans, *Cop*, K.422 KCC1, 1984, LP.

Videography

"New York City Ballet—Justin Peck & Sufjan Stevens" YouTube video, 1:04:21. Posted by "Works and Process at The Guggenheim" October 2, 2012. https://www.youtube.com/watch?v=pqfJiL5o_5A (accessed October 9, 2015).

"Questlove (2013)." *Red Bull Academy Lecture* video, 2:00:29, 2013, http://www.redbullmusicacademy.com/lectures/questlove-new-york-2013 (accessed August 9, 2015).

"Girls Aloud—Biology." YouTube video, 3:42, Posted by "GirlsAloudVEVO", June 29, 2009. https://www.youtube.com/watch?v=bBPtP4t2J1k (accessed August 9, 2015).

Notes

1 Google "Google Image Publishing Guidelines," https://support.google.com/webmasters/answer/114016 (accessed October 18, 2015).

2 Tricia Rose, *Black Noise: Rap Music and Black Culture in Contemporary America* (Hanover: Wesleyan University Press, 1994), 67.

3 Simon Reynolds, *Energy Flash* (London: Faber and Faber, 2013), 19–20.

4 The aforementioned books *Energy Flash* by Reynolds and *Black Noise* by Rose would be excellent studies from which to begin to explore the histories of electronic dance music and hip-hop respectively. The culture and politics of dance music is explored by Jeremy Gilbert and Ewan Pearson in their book *Discographies* (London: Routledge, 1999). While Mark Katz and Joseph G. Schloss have written specifically on the DJ culture and use of samples within hip-hop in, respectively, *Groove Music* (Oxford: Oxford University Press, 2012) and *Making Beats* (Middletown: Wesleyan University Press, 2004); Dick Hebdige and Julian Henriques have explored Caribbean musics and sound system culture, important precursors to hip-hop, respectively in *Cut 'n' Mix* (London: Comedia, 1987) and *Sonic Bodies* (London: Continuum, 2011).

Nicholas Bourriaud's succinct study *Postproduction* (New York: Lukas & Sternberg, 2010) gives an excellent overview to appropriation as practice in the arts broadly, and Paul D. Miller's edited collection *Sound Unbound* (London: MIT Press, 2008) provides a variety of viewpoints on sampling culture within a musical landscape. Katz's book *Capturing Sound* (Berkeley: University of California Press, 2010) provides a historical overview to the many ways in which recording technology and playback media have impacted on music making, as well as its dissemination.

5 Florian Cramer, "What is Post-digital?" *APRJA* 3 (1)1 (2014), http://www.aprja.net/?page_id=1291 (accessed October 9, 2015).

6 Kim Cascone, "The Aesthetics of Failure: 'Post-Digital' Tendencies in Contemporary Computer Music," *Computer Music Journal* 24 (4) (2000): 12.

7 Bourriaud, *Postproduction*, 13.

8 Ibid., 9.

9 Jason Toynbee, *Making Popular Music: Musicians, Creativity and Institutions* (London: Arnold, 2000), 46.

10 Ibid., 40–1.

11 Creative Commons, "What we do," https://creativecommons.org/about/ (accessed June 25, 2016).

12 Nate Patrin has compiled an interesting overview of library music's use in popular music in his article "The Strange World of Library Music," *Pitchfork*, May 20, 2014, http://pitchfork.com/features/starter/9410-library-music/ (accessed June 25, 2016).

13 Kodwo Eshun, *More Brilliant than the Sun: Adventures in Sonic Fiction* (London: Quartet Books, 1999), 14.

14 Joseph G. Schloss, *Making Beats: The Art of Sample-based Hip-hop* (Middletown: Wesleyan University Press, 2004).

15 Ibid., 78.

16 Paul Gilroy, *The Black Atlantic: Modernity and Double Consciousness* (London: Verso, 1993).

17 "Questlove (2013)," *Red Bull Academy Lecture* video, 2:00:29, 2013, http://www.redbullmusicacademy.com/lectures/questlove-new-york-2013

18 Roy Ayers, "Ain't got time," *He's Coming*, Polydor PD 5022, 2391 027, 1972, LP.

19 Black Star, "Little Brother," *The Hurricane (Music From And Inspired By The Motion Picture)*, MCA 170 116–2, 1999, CD.

20 Chris Williams, "The Soulquarians at Electric Lady: An Oral History." *Red Bull Music Academy Daily*, June 1, 2015, http://daily.redbullmusicacademy.com/2015/06/the-soulquarians-at-electric-lady (accessed October 4, 2015).

21 Portishead, *Dummy*, Go Beat 828 553–2, 1994, CD.

22 Portishead, "Glory Box." *Dummy*, Go Beat 828 553–2, 1994, CD.

23 Isaac Hayes, 'Ike's Rap II,' *Black Moses*, Stax 2628–004, 1972, LP.

24 Portishead, *Roseland NYC Live*, Go Beat 559 424–2, 1998, CD.

25 Portishead, *Third*, Island 1764013, 2008, CD.

26 Portishead, "The Rip." *Third*, Island 1764013, 2008, CD.

27 Peter Forrest, "Adrian Utley: Recording Third." *Sound on Sound*, November 2008, http://www.soundonsound.com/sos/nov08/articles/portishead.htm (accessed October 4, 2015).

28 Portishead, "Threads." *Third*, Island 1764013, 2008, CD.

29 Forrest, "Adrian Utley."

30 Joy Division, "She's Lost Control." *Unknown Pleasures*, Factory FACT 10, 1979, LP.

31 The Books, "Be good to them always." *Lost and Safe*, Tomlab 50, 2005, CD.

32 Ibid.

33 Mark Fisher, "Burial: Unedited Transcript." *The Wire*, December 2012, http://www.thewire.co.uk/in-writing/interviews/burial_unedited-transcript (accessed September 30, 2015).

34 Burial, "Archangel." *Untrue*, Hyperdub HDBCD002, 2007, CD.

35 Burial, *Untrue*, Hyperdub HDBCD002, 2007, CD.

36 Ray J, "One Wish." Sanctuary Records SANXD424, 2005, CD [Single].

37 Joseph Auner, "Sing It for Me: Posthuman Ventriloquism in Recent Popular Music," *Journal of the Royal Musical Association* 128 (1) (2003), 98–122.

38 Aphex Twin, "Windowlicker." Warp Records WAP105CD, 1999, CD [Single].

39 Keith Negus and Pete Astor, "Songwriters and song lyrics: architecture, ambiguity and repetition," *Popular Music*, 34 (2) (May 2015): 236.

40 Ibid., 238–9.

41 Luis-Manuel Garcia, "On and On: Repetition as Process and Pleasure in Electronic Dance Music," *Music Theory Online* 11 (4) (October 2005): http://www.mtosmt.org/issues/mto.05.11.4/mto.05.11.4.garcia.html (accessed October 19, 2015).

42 Ibid.

43 Reynolds, *Energy Flash*, 23–4.

44 Donna Summer, "I Feel Love." Casablanca Records NBD 20104, 1977, 12" [Single].

45 Animal Collective, "Guys Eyes." *Merriweather Post Pavilion*, Domino WIGLP216, 2009, CD.

46 Hillegonda C. Rietveld, *This is our House: House Music, Cultural Spaces and Technologies* (Farnham: Ashgate, 1998), 52.

47 FKA twigs, "Water Me." *EP2*, Young Turks YT098, 2013, 12".

48 FKA twigs, "Papi Pacify." *EP2*, Young Turks YT098, 2013, 12".

49 FKA twigs, "Preface." *LP1*, Young Turks YTCD118, 2014, 12".

50 Ben Beaumont-Thomas, "Weird things can be sexy," *Guardian*, August 9, 2014, http://www.theguardian.com/music/2014/aug/09/fka-twigs-two-weeks-lp1 (accessed September 30, 2015).

51 Mark J. Butler, *Unlocking the Groove: Rhythm, Meter, and Musical Design in Electronic Dance Music* (Indiana University Press, 2006), 166–75.

52 Keith Moliné, "Tongue Twister," *The Wire* 267, May 2006, 45.

53 Radiohead, *Kid A*, Parlophone CDKIDA 4, 2000, CD.

54 Glenn Branca, *Lessons No 1*, 99 Records 99–01, 1980, 12".

55 Swans, *Cop*, K.422 KCC1, 1984, LP.

56 Jimmy Cauty and Bill Drummond, *The Manual: How to Have a Number One Hit the Easy Way* (KLF Publications, 1988), http://freshonthenet.co.uk/the-manual-by-the-klf/ (accessed September 28, 2015).

57 The Beach Boys, "Good Vibrations" Capitol Records 5676, 1966, 7" [Single].

58 Miles Davis, *In a Silent Way*, Columbia CS 9875, 1969, LP.

59 Marshall Heiser, "SMiLE: Brian Wilson's Musical Mosaic," *Journal on the Art of Record Production* 7 (2012), http://arpjournal.com/smile-brian-wilson's-musical-mosaic/ (accessed September 28, 2015).

60 "New York City Ballet – Justin Peck & Sufjan Stevens," YouTube video, 1:04:21. Posted by "Works and Process at The Guggenheim," October 2,

2012, https://www.youtube.com/watch?v=pqfJiL5o_5A (accessed August 9, 2015)

61 Vish Khanna, "Interview with Sufjan Stevens: An excerpt," *Kreative Kontrol*, October 12, 2009, http://vishkhanna.com/2009/10/12/sufjan-stevens-interview-an-excerpt/ (accessed September 27, 2015).

62 Sufjan Stevens, "Come On! Feel The Illinoise! Part I: The World's Columbian Exposition; Part II: Carl Sandburg Visits Me In A Dream," *Sufjan Stevens Invites You To: Come On Feel The Illinoise*, Ashmatic Kitty Records AKR014, 2005, CD.

63 David Bowman, *fa fa fa fa fa fa: The Adventures of Talking Heads in the 20th Century* (London: Bloomsbury, 2002), 168–9.

64 Animal Collective, "My Girls." *Merriweather Post Pavilion*, Domino WIGLP216, 2009, CD.

65 Girls Aloud, "Biology." *Chemistry*, Polydor 9875390, 2005, CD.

66 Girls Aloud, *Chemistry*, Polydor 9875390, 2005, CD.

67 Alexis Petridis, "Girls Aloud, Chemistry," *Guardian*, December 2, 2005, http://www.theguardian.com/music/2005/dec/02/popandrock.shopping5 (accessed September 27, 2015).

68 "Girls Aloud-Biology," YouTube video, 3:42. Posted by "GirlsAloudVEVO," June 29, 2009. https://www.youtube.com/watch?v=bBPtP4t2J1k (accessed October 19, 2015).

69 Cauty and Drummond, *The Manual: How to Have a Number One Hit the Easy Way*.

70 Mark Spicer, "(Ac)cumulative Form in Pop-Rock Music," *twentieth-century music* 1 (1) March 2004, 29–64.

71 Luis-Manuel Garcia, "On and On: Repetition as Process and Pleasure in Electronic Dance Music," *Music Theory Online* 11 (4) (October 2005): http://www.mtosmt.org/issues/mto.05.11.4/mto.05.11.4.garcia.html (accessed October 19, 2015).

PART TWO

Performance

CHAPTER 9

From "me" to "we": Audience-focused practical tools for interpretation and performance

Dane Chalfin

Introduction

Writing and performing your own songs is a wonderfully personal experience. To bring your unique perspective on the human condition and the world around you to an audience in an emotionally charged medium like music, with an emotionally charged instrument like your voice, can be a life-affirming process for both the singer and the spectator. One problem singer-songwriters sometimes face in a live performance situation is that the very personal nature of the performing experience can lead to an introverted and sometimes even self-indulgent performance that can alienate the audience without the singer even realizing it. When working with singer-songwriters, one phrase I often hear is, "It's all about the music, not putting on a show." Singer-songwriters sometimes feel that if they are too outwardly emotive or "showy" they are somehow selling out or diminishing their authenticity. The flipside to this idea is that if we just wanted to hear the music we could easily put on the record without leaving the comfort of our home. There is something about a successful live performance that transcends the recorded medium. As a species, we have used song as a way of passing down our history and building community as well as the background for dancing, partying and relaxing. I believe that the magic live performance offers versus recorded music comes from an open and unashamed sharing of our views and feelings with a receptive audience.

In other words, the audience is 50 percent of the experience. That is why it is crucial that as singer-songwriters we move away from an idea of "me, the artist" toward a notion of "we, the artist and audience," the two halves sharing a single experience.

Very little practical work on stagecraft for singer-songwriters has been written about and this is why I am presenting this piece as an original, usable, pedagogy-based resource rather than a literature review. The following perspectives, exercises, and guidance are based on my work with singers over the last decade as both a lecturer in performance and a private commercial performance coach. We will begin by looking at a model for interpreting lyrics with you, the artist, as the main focus. By examining your own experience and understanding of what you are saying we can then move on to a model for physicalizing your emotional experience in a way that will focus on the audience and what they receive from your performance.

Interpretation

We will begin by breaking down the interpretation process into an exploration of your identity, the person or people you are addressing, how you feel about what you are saying and, most importantly, how you want them to feel when they hear your words. The first step toward being able to clearly convey our worldview to an audience is a clear understanding of what we have written in the song. You might think that having written the song you know exactly what every word is about, and song interpretation is best left for approaching covers. My experience of working with singer-songwriters is that they often have a clear idea of the overall point of the songs, but lack specificity when trying to describe what each verse, chorus, or line is trying to achieve and how those ideas develop as the song progresses. I usually encourage my clients to work backward from the general to the very specific using the following process of asking questions:

1. What is the one emotional word that describes the general essence of what the song is about? Try to move beyond general words like "love, happiness, sadness" to juicier more specific words like "elation, lust, loss," etc.
2. Now do the same things for each section of the song and look at how the emotions develop. Make sure that you constantly refer to the actual lyrics rather than just your idea of each section to make sure that your interpretation makes sense. For example, a song might take an emotional journey like:
   - a Verse 1: melancholy
   - b Verse 2: anger

c Chorus 1: loss
d Bridge: reflection
e Verse 3: hope
f Chorus 2: joy

3 Now take each section line-by-line or thought-by-thought and specify the important emotional words and nuances in each.

Most singer-songwriters find that by dissecting their emotional interpretation in this way they discover there was more going on in the song than they originally noticed. This alone can bring out new layers in the performance of the song.

Getting more specific

Once an artist realizes the benefit of interpretation I will introduce a more specific model for interpretation that looks like this:

1. Identity—Who are you in the world of the song?
2. Level of Address—Who are you addressing in the world of the song?
3. Underlying Emotion—How are you feeling in the world of the song?
4. Objective—What are you trying to achieve in the world of the song?
5. Primal Sound—How does that voice sound in real life?

You'll notice that I refer to "the world of the song" specifically. This is because, apart from a few rare song types like "war protest" or "mob song," the object of your attention in the song is rarely the audience itself, but the person or people you were writing the song to or about at the time. This imaginary world of the song is an important thing to identify to good song interpretation and ultimately give communicative performance.

Identity

Identifying your role in the world of the song is usually very easy. Typical roles include:

- The Happy Lover
- The Betrayed Lover

- The Unrequited Lover
- The Encouraging Friend
- The Chastising Friend
- The Voice of Reason

Obviously, these are not the only identities we write from and please feel free to assign your own that fit with your interpretation.

Level of address

The level of address identifies who you are talking to at each point in the song and will also help you assume appropriate eye-lines and postures onstage in performance. The levels of address I use are:

1. Self—talking to yourself, your internal monologue sung out loud;
2. Someone in the Room—a person you are addressing face to face;
3. Someone in Your Imagination—a person who has left or is not present for some other reason;
4. The Mob—only used in "war protest" or "mob song" type scenarios, very rare in typical pop/rock these days;
5. Gods/Universe—the great outpouring of emotion to the gods, the sky, the universe, etc.

It is not uncommon for the level of address to change throughout the development of the song. For example, a song might begin addressing The Self in the first verses and move to The Gods/Universe in the final chorus.

Underlying emotion

The underlying emotion might be quite obvious if the lyric is direct and in vernacular language. Sometimes it is trickier to identify if the language is more poetic. It is also possible that the lyric presents one emotion on the surface while hiding an underlying emotion beneath that can color the performance in a different way. I ask singers to work section-by section-initially, then line-by-line or thought-by-thought afterward to really get specific with the emotional content of the song. Try to use really juicy, descriptive emotional words rather than general ones like "happy, sad, mad" wherever possible. Some evocative emotional words include:

Delighted
Overjoyed
Thankful
Ecstatic
Satisfied
Elated
Courageous
Liberated
Provocative
Frisky
Peaceful
Encouraged
Tender
Devoted
Passionate
Loved

Eager
Anxious
Inspired
Determined
Brave
Daring
Hopeful
Rebellious
Irritated
Enraged
Hostile
Hateful
Resentful
Bitter
Provoked
Fuming

Indignant
Ashamed
Powerless
Despairing
Lonely
Vulnerable
Pathetic
Weary
Lifeless
Terrified
Shaky
Crushed
Injured
Aching
Humiliated
Alienated

Objective

Like the underlying emotion, I will ask singers to identify the objective of each section, line, or thought in keeping with who they are, whom they are addressing and what related emotions are. Objectives are verbs, and like emotional words, objective words should be very descriptive and specific. Some common objectives include:

Comfort
Berate
Chastise
Convince
Seduce
Tease
Adore
Alarm
Attract
Care (for)

Cajole
Encourage
Exhilarate
Gee Up
Hurt
Guilt-trip
Insult
Beg
Plead
Shock

Sympathize
Empathize
Wound
Confide
Provoke
Empower
Enthuse
Reassure
Soothe
Win

Primal sound

Once the previous questions have been answered I will then ask the singer to identify a primal sound or "everyday noise" associated with the real life version of that scenario. Primal sounds include things like:

Sigh	Cry	Yell
Whisper	Whine	Shout
Whimper	Groan	Cheer
Coo	Moan	Scream

By identifying the primal sound that fits the scenario we can troubleshoot the voice quality the singer is using. Often a singer will present with too light or too heavy a sound for the emotions and objectives before they are interpreted well. For example, a jilted lover comforting themself over their grief is more likely to be sighing or whimpering rather than yelling or screaming. By making sure that the emotive sound we are singing with is true to the intention of the section of the song, we are more likely to engage an audience and win their trust. We have all heard singers who show off on the high notes where the words do not dictate such acrobatics. It is easy to "switch off" to a singer who is more interested in their own vocal vanity than the honest, communicative purpose of the song and its intended effect on the audience. Singers will often limit themselves in terms of their technique by approaching singing like an unnatural act—a technique of its own with rules and regulations. All of the sounds we make when singing, and the related muscles, have reflexive, emotive connections in our brain and body. We use the same muscles that we need to laugh, cry, and call out when we sing. Singing could easily be viewed as making sustained emotive noise on pitch. I often find that simply asking a singer to "whine" the line in the chorus with their perceived problematic high note, or "call out" that tricky belt section, makes the problems vanish. But this is always in line with the interpretation. I believe that your body knows when you are "BS-ing" it and responds accordingly, usually with vocal constriction or instability.

Physicalizing the interpretation

Once you have a deeply meaningful understanding of the context of the lyric and emotional energy you are trying to project, we can move on to how your eyes, face, and body engage with those emotions and sounds so that your performance technique and stagecraft support the interpretive work you have done. The next stage of developing the performance is taking the information gained from lyric and musical interpretation and making it translate visually to the audience. Posture, eye line, gesture, and movement need to be appropriately aligned with the song in order to give the audience a holistic experience. As society has become increasingly visually stimulated through the easy and constant access to video via smartphones and tablets, it is my feeling that we cannot rely on the old cliché that "It's all about the music, man ..." Modern audiences have come to expect their music to be a visual as well as auditory experience.

Posture

Posture has been a hot topic of discussion in singing pedagogy for hundreds of years as a technical issue. I would like to divorce posture from technical purity and look more at how it interacts with interpretation and performance.

We have all seen a singer-songwriter sitting down behind a piano or with a guitar, hunching over and effectively playing to themselves. There may be moments of a song where this extreme introversion is emotionally appropriate, but maintaining this posture can be alienating to an audience as it sends the message, "I do not want you included in this." Sadly, many performers mistake this posture for credibility. An audience wants to be able to engage in your whole spectrum of emotion and experience without feeling cut off or uncomfortable about watching. In my experience, performance posture can impact positively or negatively on the audience's perception of you, so being in control of it is essential.

Going back to our interpretation questions, the first thing I ask a performer regarding posture is, "How would you be standing in real life if the emotional experience of the song/section/line was happening?" For example, if the song dictated that you were the jilted lover, soothing yourself over your feelings of loss, would you be staring at the heavens or down at yourself? If you were the joyous celebrator, praising the gods for your fortune, would you be singing at the sky or at the front row of the audience? The answers are obvious based on the emotional circumstances of that part of the song. As the emotional journey of the song develops, so do the postures, and this creates a good foundation of movement in the song and set. Even if you are stuck behind a guitar or piano there is still plenty of scope for movement when singing and in between phrases. Jeff Buckley and Tori Amos never let an instrument get in the way of physicalizing their performances.

Eye line

It is very easy for singer-songwriters to get lost in the imaginary world of the song and stare either at their instrument or off into space indiscriminately. I find that tying eye line to Level of Address (LoA) quite useful for audience communication.

1. Self—eyes down or closed
2. Someone in the Room—eyes directly over the audience
3. Someone in Your Imagination—eyes further above the audience and sometimes to one side
4. The Mob—eyes at the audience
5. Gods/Universe—eyes to the sky

With the exception of LoA4, it is not advisable to look directly into the eyes of the audience, as being sung at in this way can create anxiety or a desire to look away. I advise performers to give the audience direct eye contact when speaking to them in between songs, but keep the eye line less direct when singing so the audience can watch the emotional journey of the song as "invisible voyeurs" without any sense of self-consciousness.

Gesture and movement

Performers often take for granted that gesture is purely a function of the arms and hands. Gestures happen with the legs, pelvis, torso, shoulders, neck, head, and instruments/microphone/mic-stands. As many singer-songwriters will be self-accompanying on guitar or piano, and increasingly with pedals, laptops, and other gear simultaneously, it is important to note which parts of the body are free to gesture when playing/singing and which ones are available in the musical/vocal breaks. The gestures in the breaks are easy to overlook, but we know that watching a performer become inanimate when waiting for their next cue can be awkward to watch.

As before, when addressing gesture the first question to answer is, "What would you be doing physically in real life if you were saying those lyrics?" If there are no ergonomic blocks to those kinds of physicalizations, then you can keep the movements in their purest form during performance. If there are instruments or other gear that prevent the full movement, you can synthesize an adapted version that helps put across the appropriate message. It cannot be overstated that the underlying emotional content should always inform the style of movement. The way we move in sadness or mourning has a different aesthetic quality than how we dance with joy or celebration. When moving around the stage or dancing in instrumental breaks it is important to remember the overall mood of the song and keep that represented in any physicality.

Keeping gesture specific to the LoA is also a useful tool. If you are singing out to the gods, gestures that do not fully extend through the limbs can look uncommitted or self-conscious. Conversely, if the lyric is intimate and self-focused, larger movements may look showy and inauthentic.

Finally

The overriding thought to take away from this work is simple:

> "How would the imaginary world of the song feel, look and communicate in real life?"

Applying that question to every area of the performance from the interpretation of the lyric to the way you use your body will tackle most problems that singer-songwriters face when trying to communicate with audiences. This question fosters an attitude of inclusion of the audience in the performer's mind and opens a channel of communication synergy that separates live performance from recordings. In my experience, audiences that feel included openly into the world of the performer's psyche and physicality are more receptive to the performance and more forgiving of any stumbles that may happen. Alienating audiences through lack of consideration of their needs is, in my view, the cardinal sin committed by artists that I work with. It could be said that without a captive audience our artistic work lacks meaning and a reason for existing. I have never met a singer-songwriter who was truly content with being the only member of their audience. By changing the thinking from "me" to "we," I hope that artists and audiences can share in more meaningful and life-affirming artistic exchanges and develop more lasting relationships through music and live performance.

CHAPTER 10

The Mariposa Folk Festival and the Canadian singer-songwriter tradition

Sija Tsai and Andrew Hillhouse

The following article examines an under-discussed aspect of the music industry: festivals. Across the world, these events provide opportunities for singer-songwriters of many genres to gain exposure in the music industry. In North America, the folk/roots genre[1] offers an illustrative example of how music festivals can serve as important vehicles for the career development of singer-songwriters. Although the current festival circuit in which North American singer-songwriters work reflects a variety of genres one might expect in this digital, globalized age (folk, hip-hop, electronic, country, rock, etc.), folk/roots festivals have a special historical significance to North American singer-songwriters. The early large-scale folk festivals of mid-twentieth-century North America came into existence before rock festivals,[2] co-existing only with classical and jazz festivals.[3] As such, folk festivals were arguably the first to actively engage performers who wrote and sang their own material.

In the first section of this article, Andrew Hillhouse (a musician, artistic director, and ethnomusicologist) offers his observations on the application and programming processes of these events within Canada and the U.S. These current processes, however, follow a long evolution that has occurred since the 1960s and 1970s, when the application system was more ad hoc and programming was more curatorial. During that time, the folk festival was particularly significant to the nascent music scene in English-speaking Canada. One event in particular, the Mariposa Folk Festival, was especially important for its contributions to the professional landscape of singer-songwriters. Founded in 1961, the MFF was the first event of its kind in Canada, with its closest North American precedent (programming-wise) being the Newport Folk Festival (founded in 1959).[4] In the second section of this article, music historian Sija Tsai discusses how the Mariposa[5] Folk Festival, in its founding decades, helped to shape the Canadian singer-songwriter tradition.

The current festival circuit (Andrew Hillhouse)

Folk festivals are prized gigs—by which I mean professional performance opportunities—for emerging singer-songwriters. A festival[6] booking offers potential for audience growth, network expansion, and product sales unmatched by smaller gigs such as house concerts, coffee houses, clubs, or theaters. Even an appearance at a minor festival can have a significant impact on a singer-songwriter's career. If a performance is well received, it can be a stepping-stone to developing a regional touring circuit. Larger and better-known festival appearances offer additional prestige and promotional power. As a touring folk musician through the 1990s who has performed at a number of festivals in the U.S. and Canada, including so-called major folk festivals such as the Winnipeg, Vancouver, and Philadelphia Folk Festivals,[7] I have experienced the career benefits of festivals and the challenges of getting booked into them. Now, as the Artistic Director of a mid-sized festival in western Canada, I have noticed some trends in the application and programming of festivals that point to practical considerations for singer-songwriters attempting to establish a career.

Applying for festivals

Since the mid-1990s, the increasing consolidation of a professional folk/roots music infrastructure has had a significant impact on the way singer-songwriters obtain gigs at festivals. While the mainstream popularity of singer-songwriters has ebbed and flowed over the years, a relatively grass-roots yet increasingly business-savvy industry centered on notions of folk and roots music has steadily evolved since the 1990s. In this field, large networking events, considered by many as essential to the development of singer-songwriters' careers, are meeting places for this interconnected web of presenters, labels, agents, managers, and of course artists.

Conferences such as the North American Folk Alliance Conference, The Americana Music Conference in Nashville, and South by Southwest in Austin, Texas, have become important events in festival directors' yearly calendars. While these conferences may vary greatly in structure and mission,[8] they all present the opportunity to showcase, to perform one's best material with the intention of building networks. Directors travel to such events as a type of one-stop shopping and to maximize their travel dollars, where they can see showcase performances of both established and lesser-known artists. These events may ultimately save presenters the expense of traveling in the field to curate their festivals; however, showcasing is an expensive proposition for musicians. Independent artists wishing to make the most of their trip must pay for registration fees, hotel rooms, and, if they choose, a booth in the contact room. Further, opportunities for higher profile so-called "official" showcases are limited, leaving most performers to organize their own so-called guerilla, or independent, showcases, which take place in hotel rooms and suites late at night. It is not uncommon for singer-songwriters to spend well beyond their means in order to travel to a conference, only to have other musicians attend their hotel room showcase.

The basic application process for festivals has changed little since I started touring in the mid-1990s; performers send unsolicited materials to festivals from roughly six months to a year before the festival begins. However, the technological formats through which directors first encounter artists has shifted, with video now playing a greater role in promotion. In the 1990s, the promotional package I sent to festivals contained a small folder with a CD, a "one sheet," which was a single document that included a bio and reviews, and a picture of my band. Now, as a festival director, I receive very few CDs from performers (to the degree that it actually draws my attention to receive one). Today, artists email Electronic Press Kits (EPKs) to directors, including sound files, links to online hosting sites such as SoundCloud, videos, and biographical information. The expectations of high production quality in promotional packages have risen, and artistic directors often rely on video representations to give a sense of live performance. With this in mind, a growing concern among artists is their control over their presence on social media and formats such as YouTube, where a poorly recorded video performance, whether posted by the performer or an audience member, can have a damaging impact on their reputation.

Programming/selection

Since becoming a festival director I have become aware of a sensitive topic among artistic directors: the fear that their curatorial autonomy is being compromised by the growing power of larger agencies. Large agencies offer diverse rosters covering a variety of genres, with so-called headliners as well as emerging artists. They maintain high profiles at industry events, presenting their own showcases in larger rooms. Emerging singer-songwriters are affected by this dominance, as they may feel that signing onto such an agency is essential to success. There are however numerous small agencies that are arguably more effective than the larger ones in representing their artists, who they handpick with passion and commitment. As a festival director, I enjoy working with such small agencies, or indeed directly with artists, a sentiment expressed by several of my colleagues.

Another trend in booking is the growth in presenter's networks, such as Canada's Western Roots Artistic Directors (WRAD). Technology and mobility facilitate communication among directors, who share performers, enabling block booking of tours.

Finally, there is another, fairly recent trend affecting the landscape of folk festivals that will likely have an impact on bookings and applications. The seeming explosion of large, corporate rock festivals poses opportunities and challenges for singer-songwriters and the folk festivals that have traditionally been their terrain. It is still a question as to whether such corporate festivals will have a negative impact on audiences for smaller and mid-sized festivals. Perhaps folk festivals, with their underlying ethos of community development and participation, will attract new audiences with the sense of alternative they offer, and will continue to exist as spaces for creative and professional growth for singer-songwriters.

The Mariposa Folk Festival and the Canadian singer-songwriter tradition (Sija Tsai)

As my colleague Andrew Hillhouse points out, the current festival circuit almost necessitates that singer-songwriters be business-savvy and tech-savvy. This milieu functions like an industry, with its own kind of "middlemen" (and women) and trade shows.

Although many Canadian folk/roots festivals are long-running events, their current procedures reflect a gradual transformation that has occurred since the 1970s and 1980s. In their nascent forms these events were, ironically, pioneering an industry through community values and close interaction between directors and performers—an environment where artistic directors were curators, agents were often unnecessary, and opportunities for creative exchange between performers were built into the structure of the event.

An important prototype for these events was the Mariposa Folk Festival. This still-running event had its heyday in the 1960s/70s helped to shape the singer-songwriter tradition in English-speaking Canada. This section examines aspects of the MFF that were conducive to creative interaction between performers, inter-artist networking, and inter-genre exchange. These include its daytime workshops, egalitarian perspective, and diversity in programming.

FIGURE 10.1 *Joan Baez performing in the "heyday" of the Mariposa Folk Festival (Toronto Islands, 1969) (Photo by Bettmann/Getty Images): http://media.gettyimages.com/photos/7271969toronto-canada-thousands-of-folk-music-fans-flocked-onto-in-picture-id515448596*

FIGURE 10.2 *Mariposa Folk Festival 2008. Tudhope Park (Orillia, Ontario, Canada).*

Brief history

Founded in 1961, the MFF was the brainchild of Ruth Jones.[9] Early programming was inspired by the Newport Folk Festival, with its mixture of traditional performers and newer singers of folk songs with commercial appeal. Throughout the 1960s it relocated a few times while finding its financial footing. It was held in various locations in the province of Ontario, most notably Orillia (1961–3), Toronto (Maple Leaf Ball Club, 1964), and Innis Lake (1965–7). The MFF's first long-term home became the Toronto Islands, where it stayed from 1968 to 1979 and found its first period of financial stability. After leaving Islands, it faced financial difficulties and a more competitive music scene, spending the next two decades moving between various locales (which included Barrie's Molson Park, Toronto's Exhibition Place, and various rural Ontario settings). This long period of itinerancy only came to a close in 2000, when administrators managed to secure a long-term location in Orillia—the town of the festival's inception—where it is still staged today.

While the festival is now over fifty years old, it is still best-remembered for the 1960s and 1970s, when it implemented key features that nurtured the careers of singer-songwriters and set the stage for future festivals. A key figure who oversaw these developments was Estelle Klein.

Estelle Klein and the development of the festival format

Born in 1930, Estelle Klein was active in the Toronto folk scene by the early 1960s. Around this time, she founded the Toronto Guild of Canadian Folk Artists, which began publishing *Hoot* magazine in 1963. Although not yet a director of the Mariposa Folk Festival, she was nevertheless sitting on its advisory board.

In 1963, Klein attended the Newport Folk Festival for the first time. The review she wrote for *Hoot* magazine shows her particular fondness for its daytime workshops:[10]

> Those which I managed to attend were The Ballad, The Blues (part), Old Time Banjo Styles (part), and Whither Folk Music. I felt all of these to be so worthwhile that at one point, attending a concert seemed unnecessary.[11]

Klein ended her review with the statement: "Festivals of the caliber of the Newport Folk Festival should happen in Canada."[12]

In 1964, when MFF organizers Randy Ferris and Joe Lewis were attempting to save the floundering event, they solicited Klein's help with the artistic programming. After requesting full control of this aspect, Klein began to incorporate more daytime workshops into the program. By the late 1960s, the MFF's format consisted of daytime workshops and evening concerts.

Klein would lead the artistic vision of the MFF throughout the 1970s, which remains the best-known decade of the event's history. Under her direction, some key aspects of the festival operations and format were shaped by: 1) her views on stardom, 2) her belief in an interactive atmosphere.

During Klein's tenure, any partiality toward famous or mainstream performers was tempered by the equal pay scale and the events following the 1970 gate crashing. The equal pay scale was adopted at MFF in the late 1960s.[13] Essentially, all musicians performing at Mariposa received union-scale rates, whether they were lesser-known or well-known performers.[14] The fact that artists chose to come in spite of this is a testament to their love of the festival. As explained by Owen McBride (an Irish ballad singer):

> In most other festivals, there were big bucks. If you were very famous, you got big bucks, if you were not so famous, you didn't get paid as well, so at the other festivals there were always negotiations between performers and their managers, trying to get more money. With Mariposa ... you'd see trucks and cars and vans from California where people had *driven up* to be a part of Mariposa Folk Festival. It made the careers of *so many* people.[15]

Aside from the career-building capacity of the festival, it was also viewed as a positive peer experience. As Marna Snitman (a former administrator) put it: "Performers wanted to come because not only would they get to see their old buddies, but they'd meet new people that were every bit as good musicians as they were, or better, that no one had ever heard of."[16]

Having no expectations of lavish remuneration, performers thus participated for the opportunity to interact with their peers in the folk scene. The egalitarian approach to performance fees adopted by Klein thus had strong experiential implications for MFF artists.

In addition to the equal pay scale, the 1970 gate crashing was also a key factor in mitigating stardom at the festival. That year, Joni Mitchell and James Taylor were scheduled for the Sunday evening concert. According to most accounts, a group of people tried to dodge ticket prices by swimming across the channel to Olympic Island.[17] Klein later described her reaction to this incident in a letter to the iconic American folksinger/activist Pete Seeger:

> ... big concerts have a certain drama but that a kind of excitement is kindled that sometimes creates these problems—esp. if you have a

> situation in which a "star" type appears only once all weekend ... Finally, the one thing I feel to be most important is that "name" artists must appear daily[18] in some kind of program in order to avoid the build-up of excitement I mentioned earlier that happens with only one appearance.[19]

True to her word, Klein dispersed the more mainstream performers by eliminating evening concerts. In 1971, additional stages were set up around the island to facilitate concurrent performances throughout the day, and well-known artists were now mixed in with lesser-known performers. The concept of multiple daytime stages was later adopted by many festivals across Canada (such as those in Winnipeg and Vancouver) and reportedly by some in the U.S.[20]

Another factor shaping the festival format was Klein's belief in fostering an interactive atmosphere. Many Mariposa performers have spoken of the countless hours she spent organizing workshops with engaging topics and selecting performers who had chemistry with each other. Although the concept of topical workshops would later become common at Canadian folk festivals, some people have noted that Klein was at the forefront of this concept, having transformed the instrumental or genre themes (e.g., "Banjos," "Gospel music") into conceptual ones. An example of workshop themes from the 1972 program includes "Songs and Tales of the Supernatural," "The Woman's Image in Song," and "Scotland to Cape Breton in Song and Story."[21] Ken Whiteley (a Toronto musician who later aided Klein with programming),[22] recalls that, for all of March and April, they spent hours on the phone with performers to solicit ideas for workshop themes, and the names of people they wanted to work with. As he put it: "Sometimes it would be 'pair up a younger musician with an older musician,' and have that younger person interview the older performer to elicit an oral history."[23] Ever the curator, Klein also had a gift for recognizing the potential compatibility of artists who had never worked with each other. As recalled by singer-folklorist Sheldon Posen:

> She would put together the most unlikely people that you would think of, and she would see that there were going to be connections between them ... that they would strike sparks off each other ... And ... make that workshop more than the sum of their parts.[24]

Occasionally the workshop stages saw performer pairings that did lack chemistry; but these still generated insightful moments to those involved. Chris Rawlings, a singer-songwriter, provides a vivid recollection of one such incident from a 1970s workshop:

> I was plunked down in a workshop with a number of people, including David Amram. And David—he's a pretty accomplished musician. You

> know, orchestral, and folk, and many things in between. But we got into this workshop that was for songwriting. And the basic tenet that came from the workshop is that "if you're a songwriter, you should be able to—well, what rappers now call 'freestyle.'" In other words, you should be able to improvise a song. And I totally, totally disagreed with that. And I was on the wrong end. Even my partner, Gilles Losier, was following in step. I just said, you know, "David, beyond this workshop, nothing, nothing will last of what you just improvised." And when I write a song, whether or not it's remembered down the line, I sure want it to be. And so I work the hell out of it. I put as much effort as I can into it, I draw from all of the folk styles, and writers that I've learned, that I've sung the songs of, and I want it to be damn good. And what I was hearing in *that* particular workshop was that it didn't matter. It was basically a jazz workshop. In the context of a songwriting workshop. So, I mean, that was a little bit of a "stand up for your craft/your art" [scenario], and I've never forgotten that.[25]

The MFF workshop format thus provided this singer-songwriter with a valuable opportunity to reflect on his creative process. Such interactions between performers were not limited to the festival stage, however. For many musicians, a much-anticipated feature of each festival was its hotel parties. Regardless of their status, all performers were housed in the Executive Motor Hotel (located at 621 King St.). Many participants remember this hotel as a central spot for networking and the true pinnacle of musical interaction at Mariposa. As Owen McBride recounts:

> ... that was another big thing about Mariposa, regardless of who was playing. Back at the hotel, afterwards—after the concert was over, everyone would go back and there would be yahooing and good fellowship. There would be jam sessions in every room, and the party would go on all night. It was just wonderful.[26]

Many reports attest that, while on-site festival music was good, "the best music was made back at the hotel."[27]

The format of 1970s Mariposa was shaped by organizers' vision of an interactive environment for performers that favored egalitarianism over stardom. This approach helped foster a dialogue between singer-songwriters, traditional singers, and artists with a more improvisatory approach—many of whom had different views on the use of pre-existing material and improvised elements.

This atmosphere pervaded Mariposa for the duration of its tenure on the Toronto Islands. Klein's format would influence future Canadian folk festivals through the work of Mitch Podolak, who founded the Winnipeg Folk Festival. Podolak attended Mariposa in the mid-1970s, and recalls his enthrallment with the workshops. He attributes the on-stage energy to Klein's acute curatorial sensibilities:

> She'd take a person like Steve Goodman ... she'd put him together with a composer like David Amram. Why would you put those people together in a "make it up as you go along workshop"? ... You'd do that because you think the energy's gonna match. You have to have a relatively instinctive understanding of human energy, of how people are gonna do that ... I've never seen a workshop better ... ever. [laughs] Those two guys making up a song [*recording unclear*]. "What should we sing about?" And some of the audience yells, "Moby Dick!" And they wrote a 25-minute song which was a whole Herman Melville story. The audience went *nuts*.[28]

Inspired by what he saw at Mariposa, Podolak founded the Winnipeg Folk Festival in 1974; and many aspects of this event were modeled after Mariposa. As he describes:

> I got about twelve years of Mariposa programs. Including a whole bunch of Estelle's stuff. And then I would sit down, workshop by workshop, and listen to the music and try to figure out why she put those people together. ... Estelle was somebody to study. I don't think anybody's close, actually. ... She was my teacher. [But] she didn't know it.[29]

Later in his career, Podolak would help to set up other festivals, in Vancouver, Edmonton, Calgary, and Canso. Many ideas germinated at Mariposa—such as daytime stages, topical sessions, and the children's area—were carried across Canada, providing new performance and networking opportunities for singer-songwriters. Podolak also elaborated on the model in many ways; and one of his biggest contributions was the integration of volunteers and performers. His chief vehicle for this was the hotel parties:

> ... the first thing I did when I got back to Winnipeg is I realized, "Wait a second. The fun is the parties, if you want to keep volunteers." So now if you go to Edmonton, or Calgary, or Vancouver, or Winnipeg, what you find is these huge roaring parties at the hotels, where in some rooms are big dance bands, right? And others are acoustic picking rooms. And the whole spectrum of things happening. Edmonton and Calgary are spectacularly famous for their parties, and for taking care of performers and volunteers. Now, every one of the Western festivals, the volunteers eat with the performers, the volunteers work with the performers, the volunteers party with the performers.[30]

Interactivity therefore remains a significant aspect of these events. Although many present-day Canadian folk festivals have deviated from the original workshop format (in favor of afternoon concerts), the hotel parties serve as important sites for connection between performers and volunteers. It should also be added that many festival volunteers[31] are aspiring singer-songwriters themselves.

Other programming

Children's music

Canada has held a long association with children's music, with some of North America's best-known children's artists—notably Sharon, Lois, Bram, Fred Penner, and Raffi—being Canadian. A lesser-known history is the strong ties between children's music and the Mariposa Folk Festival. The event contributed to the development of children's music in two ways: 1) its year-round Mariposa In The Schools program, and 2) its on-site children's area at the festival.

Before these two initiatives were developed, several Mariposa affiliates had been involved with children's music on an individual basis. Among others, Alan Mills, Ed McCurdy, and Sharon Hampson had released children's records by the early 1960s, and singer Lois Lilienstein was performing children's music in nursery schools and public libraries.

By the end of the decade, the interests of the folk community merged with those of other stakeholders in Toronto—notably the Toronto Separate School Board. Musician Klaas van Graft—both a Mariposa performer and member of the Toronto Musicians' Association—helped to arrange a joint funding system with the school board to sponsor in-school concerts. The MFF ultimately acted as liaison between the school board and the Musicians' Performance Trust Fund by organizing the funding from these entities toward employing folk musicians in their roster.

By 1972, the initiative had become more formalized, with the MFF supplying performers to both the public and private school boards. By 1973, the program had officially been named Mariposa In The Schools. It was the first initiative of the MFF to receive government funding, and was so successful that, in 1983, it would incorporate as a separate organization.

Aside from bringing folk music into schools, the MFF continued to nurture children's music on site at the summer festival. Since its founding year (1961) the festival had often featured a small representation of children's music; but in 1976, Lois Lilienstein and Sharon Hampson (both established children's performers at that time) began a dedicated children's area on the festival grounds. According to the 1976 program notes, "the workshops are carefully scheduled to take into account the ups and downs, highs and lows of children's activity and interest levels."[32] The programming that year featured a mixture of children's music specialists, singer-songwriters, and traditional performers.

The Mariposa Folk Festival's children's initiatives—namely the MITS program and the children's area—had far-reaching influence, both in Canada and abroad. The MITS program (now a separate organization) has continued operating into the present day, serving schools across the province of Ontario. The on-site children's area remained a mainstay of MFF programming, and its format was later adopted by other festivals. Authors Sheldon Posen[33] and Anna Hoefnagels[34] point to additional ways in which Mariposa influenced the development of children's music. According to Posen, the development of MITS and the children's area coincided with an increasing taste for children's music in broader society; particularly among young parents who had come of age during the folk boom of the late 1960s and early 1970s. Also, many MITS performers continued their involvement with children's music through recordings and/or large-scale touring. The most famous example began with Lois Lilienstein and Sharon Hampson. While producing a record for MITS, the two artists decided to make their own children's recording. They teamed up with Bram Morrison (also a MITS performer) for the collaboration, and later went on to release dozens of albums and have their own Canadian Broadcasting Corporation (CBC) television show, *The Elephant Show*, in the 1980s.[35] Their example demonstrates how networking in the festival milieu could lead to further commercial opportunities.

Cultural diversity

In the broader context of arts events in Canada (which included ballet, symphonies, and theatrical production), the MFF was at the forefront of diversifying its cultural representation. As Canadian society was itself seeing an increased amount of dialogue on multiculturalism and First Nations activism, the MFF opened its gates widely to artists from First Nations communities and ethno-cultural groups.

First Nations performers had participated at MFF at various points in the 1960s; but it wasn't until 1970 that the MFF created a dedicated program for aboriginal artists. This owed to the efforts of Alanis Obomsawin, an Abenaki singer and storyteller[36] who used her contacts in various communities to bring a larger number of indigenous artists to the festival. Over the next eight years, the program would feature a mixture of musicians, dancers, storytellers, and artisans. However, aboriginal singer-songwriters were also numerous, with some key participants being Tom Jackson, Shingoose, and Willy Dunn.[37]

Since many of the First Nations artists came from remote regions, the MFF was their first opportunity to network with artists outside of their home communities. As Obomsawin has explained:

> For a lot of them it was their first time. And to be next to so many incredible performers—it was very exciting ... Some of them were starting, they were getting known in their area, and then coming to Mariposa really gave them another view of themselves.[38]

For many audience members, the MFF provided them with their first exposure to both traditional and contemporary aboriginal art forms. As indicated by audience surveys from the mid-1970s, the Native People's Area was a common highlight for many festival goers.

In addition to a designated First Nations program, the representation of ethno-cultural musics similarly gained more emphasis in the 1970s. At first, the recruitment of such performers began informally. Klein mobilized MFF volunteers—particularly Leigh Cline, a Toronto musician and sound engineer—to recruit their contacts from Toronto's many cultural enclaves. The process became more formalized in 1972, when the MFF created its first "Ethnic Committee" to conduct outreach in ethno-cultural communities. Over the next few years, the festival would continue to broaden its range, featuring both music and dance groups from Macedonian, Portuguese, Chinese, Filipino, and Turkish immigrant communities, to name a few.

The reception of the ethnic and dance area was largely positive, but it was not without tension. Leigh Cline recalls a performance with a group of Greek musicians:[39]

> It was sort of like the first time Bukka White and Son House and those kind of guys were playing for a white audience. It was the same kind of mentality ... We go and we play on stage; we played it exactly the way we did it for Greeks. Which was electric bouzouki, electric clarinet, electric organ and electric guitar. And a drummer. And we were playing folk music—we were playing folk *dance* music, actually. Because they don't separate the music and the dance. And the audience actually *hated* it. We got comments like, "Well when are you going to play the real thing?" It's like, "This *is* the real thing, guys ... This is the way they do it in Greece." But—no. They were used to Caravan.[40] And the other line we got is "Where are the costumes?"[41]

While such performances may not have appealed to some audience members, they challenged dominant perceptions of certain cultural groups. And regardless of audience perceptions, the MFF's efforts in cultural diversification soon became utilized by the broader arts community, as MFF organizers were often approached to work on multicultural projects on television and radio.

In its efforts to diversify throughout the 1970s, the MFF expanded its offerings of First Nations and ethno-cultural musics. This programming frequently displayed cultural traditions in a state of flux and/or in a process of interchange with other traditions; and also introduced many musical traditions to new audiences. This atmosphere anticipated the environment of the later twentieth and early twenty-first centuries, which, of course, were marked by an unprecedented level of global exchange. Many contemporary festivals feature globe-trotting musicians who perform material outside of its original context;[42] and the story of 1970s Mariposa may offer a lesson to singer-songwriters who draw from their cultural heritage.

Legacy

From 1969 and into the early 1970s, the MFF was considered to be one of the top folk festivals in North America, and garnered glowing reviews in the U.S.-based *Sing Out* magazine.[43] The festival was popular among not only critics and laypeople, but also well-known musicians, who would stop in to jam. The most famous example occurred in 1972, when Bob Dylan, Neil Young, Gordon Lightfoot, and Joni Mitchell dropped by on the same weekend in hopes of participating.[44]

The 1960s and 1970s were ultimately considered to be the MFF's heyday. In the 1980s, the MFF entered a decade of experimentation, with frequent adjustments to programming, locale, and marketing strategies.[45] From 1989 to 1991, organizers even changed the name of the event to "Mariposa: A festival of roots music" to reflect the larger proportion of mainstream programming and to attract younger audiences. At the same time, however, other folk festivals began to spring up and flourish across the country—and over the next thirty-plus years the phenomenon would crystallize into the industry we see today.[46]

Festivals remain an important career-building opportunity for today's singer-songwriters. Networking at these events is essential as it was in the 1970s;[47] but as we see from Hillhouse's opening section, the process of application and programming has changed significantly. What was once a more curatorial process, involving a lot of direct contact between directors and performers, has become an interconnected web of industry events and multiple stakeholders.

Despite these changes, however, contemporary Canadian roots festivals share the same historical continuum as their 1970s prototype. The "mother" festival that helped to shape the Canadian singer-songwriter tradition is still running today; and its "offspring" are providing an updated context to continue re-shaping what is now a well-established musical genre.

Notes

1 A note on our use of the terms "folk," "roots," and "singer-songwriter": In English-speaking Canada, the term "folk" is sometimes used interchangeably with "roots," as well as with "singer-songwriter." In this chapter, the term "folk" is largely applied to two things: 1) performers of the 1960s/1970s who were influenced by the mid-twentieth-century North American folk revival (see Gillian Mitchell—citation below), 2) performers from later decades who modelled themselves after the group above. While artists from either group may have performed some traditional repertoire and embodied the values of traditional performers (on the latter, see Chris McDonald—citation below), their inclusion of original material led others to call them "singer-songwriters." The use of the term "roots" in this chapter generally refers to the more contemporary musicians or singer-songwriters (from roughly the late 1980s onward) who are influenced by the same vernacular music (to borrow Benjamin Filene's use of the term—see citation below) that inspired the original 1960s/1970s folk revivalists (though perhaps with a wider scope, including blues and bluegrass) but who operate on a more commercial level. For a historical analysis of the North American folk revival, see Gillian Mitchell, *The North American folk music revival: Nation and identity in the United States and Canada, 1945–1980* (Aldershot: Ashgate Publishing Ltd, 2007). For a discussion about the rise of singer-songwriters in a Canadian context, see Chris McDonald, "'From both sides now?': Ethnomusicology, folklore and the rise of the Canadian singer-songwriter," *Folk Music, Traditional Music, Ethnomusicology: Canadian Perspectives, Past and Present,* eds. Anna Hoefnagels and Gordon E. Smith (Toronto: Cambridge Scholars Publishing, 2007), 50–60. For a more general discussion of the historical juncture between folk ideology and popular/rock singer-songwriters, see also Simon Frith, "'The magic that can set you free': The Ideology of the Folk and the Myth of the Rock Community," *Popular Music* 1 (1981): 159–68. And for a more in-depth discussion of American roots music in a historical context, see Benjamin Filene, *Romancing the folk: Public memory and American roots music* (Chapel Hill and London: The University of North Carolina Press, 2000).

2 To date, the earliest large-scale rock festivals in North America are understood to be the Fantasy Fair and Magic Mountain Music Festival and the Monterey International Pop Festival (both staged in the summer of 1967).

3 Examples are the Tanglewood Music Festival (which began in 1934), and the Newport Jazz Festival (inaugurated in 1954).

4 Neither Newport nor Mariposa were the first events in their respective countries to bear the title of "Folk Festival," however. In the U.S., events such as the White Top Folk Festival and the National Folk Festival were running in the 1930s, and various smaller-scale folk festivals existed before Newport's founding. In Canada, Mariposa was preceded by the Miramichi Folk Festival (founded in 1958). The difference between these earlier events and Newport/Mariposa was that the former tended to present regional musical traditions,

or music associated with particular ethnic groups. Newport and Mariposa (both widely promoted) straddled the boundaries between traditional performers and those with commercial appeal (this, in turn, made these events more conducive to programming singer-songwriters). For a more in-depth historical discussion of earlier American folk festivals, see Ronald Cohen, *A history of folk music festivals in the United States: Feasts of musical celebration* (Lanham, Toronto, and Plymouth: The Scarecrow Press Inc., 2008).

5 The first edition of the Mariposa Folk Festival was staged in the town of Orillia in the Canadian province of Ontario. The name "Mariposa" (the Spanish word for "butterfly") came to be associated with Orillia through author Stephen Leacock's 1912 work *Sunshine Sketches of a Little Town.* The town featured in this collection of stories was modelled after Orillia, but given the fictitious name of Mariposa.

6 In this chapter we use the word "festival" as it is commonly understood in popular music, that is "An organized series of concerts, plays, or films, typically one held annually in the same place". http://www.oxforddictionaries.com/definition/english/festival (accessed February 15, 2015).

7 These festivals are commonly referred to among musicians as major festivals due to their audience sizes, as well as their prestigious reputations. Now into their fourth and fifth decades of existence, they have a quasi-institutional, established quality to them. At the Philadelphia Folk Festival (founded 1962), The Winnipeg Folk Festival (founded 1974), and the Vancouver Folk Festival (founded 1978), along with several other Western Canadian festivals such as the Edmonton Folk Festival (founded 1980), audience numbers can range from 15,000 to 40,000 attendees for the weekend.

8 Two conferences that demonstrate such a contrast are The North American Folk Alliance Conference and South by Southwest. To highlight one major difference, the former takes place in a single conference hotel, and all events are directed to conference attendees, with little or no ticketed, public concerts. South by Southwest, by contrast, consists of a series of performances in venues around the city, including several featuring marquee performers.

9 Now known as Ruth Jones-McVeigh, she was a resident of Orillia, Ontario, and a prominent supporter of the folk scene at the time. For a more detailed discussion of key organizers, advisors, and general administration of the inaugural Mariposa Folk Festival, see Sija Tsai, "Surface sketches of a wandering festival," *Canadian Folk Music/Musique Folklorique Canadienne* 45 (1) (2011): 8–14, and Sija Tsai, "Public Policy and the Mariposa Folk Festival: Shared Ideals in the 1960s and 1970s," *Musicultures* 38 (2011): 147–58.

10 These were differentiated from concerts. While the latter referred to standard onstage musical performances (often in the evening), the daytime workshops had a stronger didactic content, and were more likely to include discussions and demonstrations of a particular instrument, tradition, or musical style.

11 Estelle Klein, "Newport Folk Festival: A review," *Hoot* 2 (1963): 31–3.

12 Ibid., 33.

13 The equal pay scale may have been another aspect borrowed from Newport Folk Festival, which was reportedly using this system in the 1960s.

14 Many MFF performers and administrators enjoy mentioning that Joan Baez—already internationally famous by the late 1960s/early 1970s—performed at Mariposa for union-scale rates in 1969.

15 Owen McBride, interview by author, Toronto, ON, February 11, 2013.

16 Marna Snitman, interview by author, Toronto, ON, October 12, 2011.

17 The number of people involved, however, is said to have been greatly exaggerated in the media. For example, one of my research participants recalls seeing only about two dozen freeloaders.

18 Klein's underlining.

19 Estelle Klein, letter to Pete Seeger, February 8, 1971, Clara Thomas Archives and Special Collections, York University, Toronto.

20 Specific examples of U.S. festivals influenced by Mariposa's stage format were not provided by research participants. Further inquiry is needed in this area.

21 *Mariposa Folk Festival program book*, 1972, n.p.

22 In addition to his involvement as a performer, Whiteley was mentored by Klein in various aspects of festival programming and administration. He later programmed the workshops as festival coordinator in 1976, and served as Artistic Director in 1978 and 1980.

23 Ken Whiteley, interview by author, telephone, ca. September, 2011.

24 Sheldon Posen, interview by author, telephone, November 29, 2011.

25 Chris Rawlings, interview by author, telephone, April 6, 2011.

26 Owen McBride, interview by author, telephone, February 11, 2013.

27 Sheldon Posen, interview by author, telephone, November 29, 2011.

28 Mitch Podolak, interview by author, telephone, September 15, 2011.

29 Ibid.

30 Ibid. See also Michael Macdonald, "The best laid plans of Marx and men: Mitch Podolak, revolution, and the Winnipeg Folk Festival," *Ethnologies* 30 (2) (2008): 73–91.

31 Volunteers at contemporary Canadian folk festivals can work in a wide range of departments, of which there can be upwards of fifty for the larger festivals. Examples of volunteer departments include technical crew, campground, backstage traffic, environment crew, family area, artisan village, tavern, first aid, raffle, etc.

32 Sharon Hampson and Lois Lilienstein, "Children's Area," *Mariposa Folk Festival Program Book* (1976): 17.

33 See Sheldon Posen, "The beginnings of the children's (folk) music industry in Canada: An Overview," *Canadian Folk Music Journal/Revue de musique folklorique canadienne* 21 (1993): 19–30.

34 See Anna Hoefnagels, "Children's folk music in Canada: Histories, Performers, Canons," *Musicultures* 37 (2010): 14–31.

35 This show was later rebroadcast on the U.S. network Nickelodeon through the mid-1990s.

36 Obomsawin later went on to become a prolific documentary filmmaker with the National Film Board of Canada, and has won several awards for her work.

37 Jackson is also widely known for his work as an actor, and as organizer of Huron Carole, an annual series of Christmas concerts.

38 Alanis Obomsawin, interview by author, telephone, January 8, 2013.

39 The performers were Yannis Antos (keyboard), Nikos Kaltsas (clarinet), Tassos Marinos (bouzouki), Takis Koroneos (drums). Cline, while not from Greece, performed with this group for several years as a guitar player.

40 Caravan was a multicultural festival that ran in Toronto from 1969 to 2004. The event featured various "pavilions" around the city which allowed ethno-cultural communities to showcase their cuisine and traditional performance arts.

41 Leigh Cline, interview by author, telephone, November 6, 2011.

42 For an in-depth discussion of transnationalistm at contemporary festivals, see Andrew Hillhouse, "Touring as social practice: Transnational festivals, personalized networks, and new folk music sensibilities," PhD dissertation, 2013, University of Toronto, Toronto.

43 See, for example, Adele Gradz, "Summer Festivals, 1971," *Sing Out!* 20 (6) (1971): 8–9, 25.

44 For a detailed account of this incident, see Dave Bidini, *Writing Gordon Lightfoot: The man, the music, and the world in 1972* (Toronto: McClelland & Stewart Ltd, 2011).

45 For more details, see Sija Tsai, "Mariposa Folk Festival: The sounds, sights and costs of a 50-year road trip," PhD dissertation, 2013, York University, Toronto.

46 See Sija Tsai, "Surface sketches of a wandering festival," *Canadian Folk Music/Musique Folklorique Canadienne* 45 (1) (2011): 8–14.

47 For a detailed discussion on networking in a global festival context, see Andrew Hillhouse, "Touring as social practice: Transnational festivals, personalized networks, and new folk music sensibilities," PhD dissertation, 2013, University of Toronto, Toronto.

CHAPTER 11

Seth Lakeman testimonial: Stories from my life, and tips for getting ahead

Seth Lakeman (b. 1977, Devon, U.K.) is an English folk singer, songwriter, and multi-instrumentalist. He describes his style as indie-folk, drawing on rock and electric styles. Lakeman's second album Kitty Jay *was shortlisted for the Mercury Music Prize in 2005. In this interview with Katherine Williams, he talks about his early musical experiences and development, crucial turning points in his career, and tips for up-and-coming singer-songwriters.*

KW: Good evening Seth. Thanks for talking to me—I am sure our readers will benefit from hearing your experiences and advice.

First question: How would you describe your style?

SL: "I would say it's indie-folk. It's contemporary folk songs, so it's looking at people, and the environment and place that you live in—which I would describe as folk music—and taking it, and using it with contemporary sounds. It's important to give quite a nod to, and keep your roots in, the tradition as well. It's a careful balance, but it's important to have your own independence as well ... I've always played and kept to acoustic traditional instruments as in the fiddle, viola, mandolins, and bouzoukis. I've kept the instrumentation quite rigid to tradition, but I think the ways it's approached have come from other idioms ... My music crosses between various styles and genres."

KW: It seems that the most successful music—and your music comes into this category—is music that has a continuation with the past, and yet has something new to attract audiences.

"The idea is to give depth. It could be historical, it could be a window into someone's life ... It's a certain amount of depth, which folk song has. That's what I'm trying to achieve, or find, when I'm writing."

KW: How did your interest in music start?

"It was all very much family based. I learnt most of it from my parents, who ran a folk club locally in the South-West Dartmoor area. [I] used to listen to performers as they came to the club throughout all the 80s ... So that was the platform really, and the education into music. I didn't go to university, didn't study in that sense. [I was] mostly self-taught, but very much motivated by family ... We all [Seth Lakeman, and brothers Sean (b. 1974) and Sam (b. 1975)] helped and spurred each other on. It was that intrigue, and that age group when you are looking to experiment, and you're looking to find different sounds. It was a crucial part of what [I'm] doing now."

KW: How old were you when you started playing with your brothers? And was that jamming in the house, or playing publicly?

"About fifteen. [We played] publicly, busking all over the place, and then we started playing festivals. Things like Sidmouth and Fylde. Big folk festivals all over the U.K., and a few overseas venues as well. Then [we] met a couple of singers, and experimented within songwriting. So I started thinking about songs [at] about seventeen or eighteen years old. But mostly before that I was writing instrumental music."

KW: Sure. So when you get to songwriting, do you write the lyrics as well as the musical content?

"Yeah. Generally—90 percent of the time, I do. I write a lot of tunes for the fiddle. A lot of melodies. I'm usually looking at melody and rhythm. The lyrics are something you focus on for each project. It's a big part of getting your head into a concept record. I'm always writing, but generally I get my head into it for a whole record. A good three to six-month period. The lyrics come after the melody, usually."

KW: When you first started songwriting, was that with your brothers, or was that when you started to do your own thing?

"I was working with a band called Equation, who signed to an American label [Time Warner] in 1995.[1] I spent three years over there, I guess from the age of eighteen/nineteen to twenty-two. We toured all over America, and were signed to the World Music Label [branch of Time Warner: Blanco y Negro, then independent label Putamayo]. We sang traditional songs, in the folk-rock, Fairport-Convention style. I came back here, and I worked with my sister-in-law Cara Dillon. I worked with her on the single 'Black is the Colour.'[2] I toured with her for about two years, around the globe, and then came back and started to work on my own thing ...

I was mostly writing songs when I was doing my own thing. That was with *The Punch Bowl* [2002, iScream], where I experimented with songwriting, and then into *Kitty Jay* [2004, iScream]. It wasn't until my early to mid-twenties that I was really songwriting."

KW: Over your time performing publicly since you were young, where have you preferred playing?

"There's so many different ways I would perform. From [sitting] there in the pub, playing sessions, to performing at the Minack Theatre or something like that, something really quite magical and poignant to the songs you're singing.[3] [Venues range from] festivals, which are raucous, where people are drinking, upbeat, enjoying themselves, to a [sitting down] theatre like Regent's Park or Shepherd's Bush. You get different rewards out of each kind of venue."

KW: Does a particular gig in your career stand out to you, either for the status of the venue, or for marking a career turning point?

"The Minack Theatre [in 2009] is a big one for me. It was a big moment in my career. There was a DVD made.[4] The poignancy of 'Solomon Browne', which is quite a big song that I wrote, [in that] stunning setting."

KW: These days, do you have a regular practice routine?

"I'm always playing, always practicing. Every morning I get up, and I will play to the kids for a good half hour, and then depending on what is going on work-wise—whether I've got a solo gig, or a band gig, I might work and practice things with that in mind. [I might practice] the lyrics, particular songs. But generally I'm trying to come up with new ideas as well. I just generally play tunes, and improvise. When I play, I generally just improvise. People say you don't need to practice, but I think you do. You've got to keep fit. Gig fit."

KW: Do you have any tips on songwriting you would like to pass on?

"I've always thought trying to find a story is always a great way to weave together four or five minutes constructively. It can be about yourself of course, or it can be about someone else, but I think that is interesting for a listener. You take them on a journey. So as well as the music taking people on a journey, it's lyrically taking them on a journey."

KW: And how about tips on performing live? Is there anything that you find particularly effective?

"These days, people want immediacy. They need something that's going to hit them fast. I just think people's patience has run down. So I think gimmicks are important. I think ways of trying to grab people's attention as quickly as possible is that way that it works in a live show. If you're a new act, I think that is vital."

KW: And my final question: do you have any tips on marketing yourself?

"I think marketing is all about getting out there, and being in people's consciousness. As soon as you can become word of mouth, or get something up online that [audiences/fans] can share—that's the key. If you've got something on YouTube, if you've got something there, it's important to get it out there to people. If you're trying to market yourself, you need to stand out from the crowd. Standing out from the crowd is—playing at service stations, busking in streets. All sorts of crazy ideas. You stand out."

KW: It sounds like you're saying, "Be visible. Be in peoples' consciousness."

"Yeah. Music is almost suffocating a bit as an industry. People don't want to pay money to consume it. You need to stand up and be counted. Make sure people want to invest in what you're doing."

FIGURES 11.1 AND 11.2 *Lakeman performing at the Minack Theatre, Cornwall May 2009*

Seth Lakeman Discography

With the Lakeman Brothers

Three Piece Suite (1994)

With Equation

Hazy Days (Putamayo, 1998)
The Lucky Few (Putamayo, 1999)
Dark Ages E.P. (2000)
First Name Terms (iScream Records 2002)

Return to Me (recorded Blanco y Negro 1996, released Rough Trade 2003)

Seth Lakeman

The Punch Bowl (2002, iScream)
Kitty Jay (2004, iScream)
Freedom Fields (2006, iScream)
Poor Man's Heaven (2008, Relentless)
Hearts & Minds (2010, Virgin Records)
Tales from the Barrel House (2011, Honour Oak Records)
Word of Mouth (2014, Honour Oak Records, Cooking Vinyl)

Notes

1 Equation consisted of singers Kathryn Smith, Kate Rusby, and the three Lakeman Brothers. Rusby was replaced by Cara Dillon in 1995. Dillon and Sam Lakeman left the group due to musical differences in the late nineties, and began performing together under the name Polar Star. In summer 2000, Dillon and Lakeman signed to the indie record label Rough Trade Records, with manager Geoff Travis. The couple married in 2002.

2 "Black is the Colour," the opening track of the singer's eponymous album, *Cara Dillon* (Rough Trade Records, 2001).

3 The Minack is set on a cliff edge in Cornwall, U.K., and is a famous outdoor venue for theater. Lakeman's performance was the first solely music show.

4 *Seth Lakeman Live at The Minack*, 2009.

PART THREE

The music industry

CHAPTER 12

Audience engagement and alternative revenue streams

Samuel Nicholls

Introduction

Singer-songwriters have traditionally gained direct income from a few defined sources—revenue generated through their performance and composition of work, primarily through recordings and public performances. While these income streams remain at the heart of an artist's income, the accountability and reliability of how money reaches an artist has become more variable, which includes a number of new intermediaries. Where once, recorded music would be sold through a record shop, and performance royalties distributed from live event and media broadcasts, there are now many ways audiences consume music. These include digital record shops, such as iTunes, streaming services licensed in numerous permutations, and directly from an artist. Offering their music through a wider range of platforms allows many artists direct access to these new income streams and circumvent the traditional intermediaries involved in income collection. Artists can therefore tailor their music and related products direct to an audience with more immediate feedback and financial gratification.

As the ability to derive primary income from recorded music has fallen,[1] major labels have looked to tie up additional rights to justify their investment in artists. Where traditional activity such as touring was seen as a supplementary activity to promote the core purpose of increasing record sales, now the inverse is true and in order for an album's full economic potential to be realized, major labels now deem it necessary to invest in a whole "360 degree" package, and take royalties from other relevant streams, including ticket sales, merchandise, publishing, and more.

Live music revenue has become such a dominant income source that major companies such as Live Nation have also started acquiring additional rights, such as recordings, in order to maximize their income from touring artists such as Madonna.[2] These high-value deals replicate the realities independents face, with an increase in services such as Bandcamp, Kickstarter, and Patreon, allowing them the flexibility to offer their music in alternative desirable forms, attuned to reap the most effective financial reward from their fans, with direct remuneration from the relevant platform in a process defined in corporate business as Direct To Consumer (D2C), but often referred to as Direct-To-Fan (D2F) within the music industries.

The success for any artist in taking advantage of any of these recent innovations in consumer exploitation is made possible and profitable by an artist's ability to directly communicate with their fan base, most commonly through social media and direct marketing. Kevin Kelly's "1000 True Fans" article introduces the theory that by creating a strong connection with an achievable number of fans ("you can count to 1000"), who "will purchase anything and everything you produce," a creative producer can be financially sustained, as well as providing a platform for nurturing "Lesser Fans."[3] How you build that connection, add value to your work, and maximize monetization is discussed in this chapter, drawing upon current literature, industry statistics, case studies, and publications and interviews with independent artists from an individual empirical study.

Background

For any artist, the key to maximizing their income and taking advantage of alternative revenue streams is audience engagement, or fan interaction. Serviant, in his blog for Midem,[4] details three steps to increased revenue for new artists—"[First,] engage the fans. Second, use that fan engagement to push the message virally. Lastly, leverage that viral engagement to drive purchases of music and music-related products like concert tickets, fan gear and the like."[5] Driving engaged fans to music purchases is obviously a key factor, but when an artist is able to attain a significant level of direct engagement, it is vital to retain this. There are now various means to selling music direct to fans, and capturing and using the data from these sales can aid the process of developing strategies to upsell and offer customized products.[6] Kelly argues that the key challenge is to have direct contact with your fans, with fewer organizations eligible to take a percentage off the artist's revenue (the most common example being the traditional record label). By offering a direct solution for fans to finance an artist, it is possible to both retain a high percentage of income and collect the relative personal data from fans in order to continue a high level of engagement with them.

Studies in the virility of an artist's content, and the level to which viral marketing engages audiences have been in some depth.[7] Following the successes of "Gangnam Style" and "Harlem Shake," "Viral" marketing can be seen as an online equivalent of word of mouth marketing, effective when representing something interesting, memorable, succinct, shareable and crucially, popular. Converting this ability to elicit a reaction into a social connection, and then an increased commercial gain has become a key strategy in the recording music industry. For example, a Nielsen report claims that creating a platform for fans to better connect with an artist will generate at least $450 million in additional revenue across the industry.[8] The report further argues that this commercial gain isn't restricted to the most profitable artists, rather the ability to build community and relationships that fans can invest in emotionally and financially can happen at any level. The notion that an artist requires a large number of fans before their music can be monetized appears to permeate the creative class. This however, has been dismissed as "just that, a myth."[9]

Direct-To-Fan

One of the most common ways independent artists are self-distributing their own music is through Direct-To-Fan (D2F) or Direct-To-Consumer (D2C) platforms. Direct-To-Fan typically describes the means by which artists sell their products by their own means, usually online through third-party providers such as Bandcamp,[10] Topspin,[11] and Music Glue.[12] These platforms are often used in conjunction with an artist's own website, or they provide varying degrees of association with an artist's existing web presence, through widgets or "apps" on platforms such as Facebook. This allows artists to post their own music, merchandise, concert tickets, and other physical and digital goods online, allowing the fan to directly purchase these goods from the artist. Producing these goods and managing and dispatching these orders to the fan are, at a basic level, the responsibility of the artist, unless specifically agreed otherwise. Artists are generally able to dictate their own price for their products, with remuneration to the artist usually facilitated by the third-party platform. Payment goes through an intermediary such as PayPal, or is invoiced regularly and paid directly—all less the platform's commission rate (typically 10 to 15 percent). In addition to providing the artist with the means to collect valuable engagement data, this model also provides the artist with a higher revenue share of sales and freedom of licensing.

Direct-To-Fan platforms are not solely utilized by independent artists and labels. As well as a higher revenue share, the availability of fan data and relative analytics is viewed as increasingly valuable marketing information.

Therefore, major labels also use a combination of existing independent platforms and commission bespoke services for specific artists, to take advantage of this. Streaming services, such as Spotify and Apple Music, also provide similar value to artists and rights holders by making the equivalent information available in order to establish a stronger connection between artists and fans on their platforms, with services such as Spotify Artist Services, Apple Connect, and Pandora's acquisition and integration of Next Big Sound.[13] These new services are an important development within streaming platforms, as they give the artist, or a specific representative of the artist, a direct method of communication with their fans. It has been noted, specifically by Rogers and Braun, that direct communication builds a much stronger artist–fan relationship emotionally and economically, and that an abundance of artist-relevant information from third parties, mutually promoting other, potentially irrelevant products to the fan, can be a large turn off.[14]

The ability to tailor and to offer a discounted rate of a collection of products[15] is also a notable advantage of utilizing Direct-To-Fan platforms. As U.K. chart regulations have changed to accommodate streaming, instant gratification incentives, and a variety of merchandise and ticket bundles,[16] artists and management are able to find new ways to attract sales, especially within the first week of a record's release. For example, acting independently of major record labels, Noel Gallagher's High Flying Birds and Stereophonics have been able to promote new album releases to their fans, primarily through live appearances, by creating a combination of products, and specifically tying new live events to the album releases where they saw demand—resulting in number 1 selling albums in the U.K.[17]

American Hip hop artists Run The Jewels use the Direct-To-Fan model as an effective platform to increase their fanbase and maximize revenue, despite making their albums available for free download through their website. Their albums are not given away for free, given that in order to be sent a download for any of their albums (and they have used this strategy for each of their three album releases to date), their fans are required to sign up to their mailing list in order to receive it. This activity around their second album, *Run The Jewels 2*, resulted in a 66 percent growth in the band's mailing list, and as their co-manager Amaechi Uzoigwe says, this list is one of their most effective marketing tools.[18] This certainly holds true for the band's Direct-To-Fan offering, which includes a wide variety of products within a range of prices. Items are available at an initial tier of $10 to $100, additional limited edition bundles at $250 and $5,000, and a humorous tier of "Bonu$ Packages" including "The Show And Tell Package" at $25,000 (Run The Jewels will accompany your child to their school show and tell), the "We Are Gordon Ramsey Package" at $150,000 (Run The Jewels will self-produce their own episode of Kitchen Nightmares) and the "Meow The Jewels" package.[19] The "Meow The Jewels" package—that Run The Jewels would recreate the album using "nothing but cat sounds for music"—resonated so strongly that one fan created a crowd-funding campaign to finance the creation of this album. With the band's blessing, $65,783 was raised from 2,828 fans, with the profits donated to the families of Eric Garner and Michael Brown, Jr.[20] The album brought about collaborations with Prince Paul, Dan The Automator, and members of Portishead and Massive Attack.[21]

Variable pricing models (Pay What You Want)

Direct-To-Fan platforms offer the artist or rights holder the ability to control the flow, distribution, and marketing of their products and, by controlling additional aspects of the selling process, they are also able to adapt their offering to reap the largest financial reward. Pay What You Want (PWYW) pricing came to public prominence when the band Radiohead released their seventh studio album *In Rainbows* in 2007, with the option for fans to pay any desired price for the album's digital download. Traditionally, PWYW had been hard to implement, as the production and distribution costs of physical records made the pricing structure too variable and prohibitive to implement effectively and confidently. With the advent of digital downloads however, Radiohead were able to release their album with a structure for fans to choose the price they paid to obtain the music.

The Pay What You Want model is something that many Direct-To-Fan platforms have taken advantage of, most prominently Bandcamp, who offer the ability to "name your price." Many artists recognize the ability to offer fans a choice of payment option as a vital component in effectively building a strong fan–artist relationship. The ease of access for music ownership is seen as the most important factor in this model, building the connection with fans, but financial reward is also influenced greatly. Artist Steve Lawson states that often "people who've downloaded one album for free come back to pay for others,"[22] while Hope & Social describe giving the option of payment to the fans as an issue of trust and respect.[23]

Lawson, a solo bass player, benefits from the removal of financial barriers to artist discovery and the risk of experimenting on new music/artforms. The Stockton-On-Tees ARC theater experimented with a "Pay What You Decide" pricing strategy in early 2015, where theatergoers could book tickets with no obligation to pay, in the hope of exposing a wider audience to new productions.[24] The results of ARC's audience engagement strategy[25] showed that not only did audience numbers improve by 58 percent, crucially its income increased by 82 percent.[26]

These figures are much more accurate than those available for music projects, but certainly correlate with evidence from *In Rainbows* and

Steve Lawson's experience. *In Rainbows* was at the time an incomparable success for Radiohead, even in the context of their existing popularity,[27] totaling sales of more than three million copies in the year immediately after release. This figure includes all purchased formats of the album, and crucially includes around 1.75 million Pay What You Want downloads, sold Direct-To-Fan through Radiohead's website alongside 100,000 high value box sets. The album outsold the band's previous three album releases by a wide margin, and created such a marketing statement that when the album was released through traditional channels almost three months after initial release, it went to number 1 in the U.K. and U.S. charts.[28] Lawson's figures may not be as extravagant, but demonstrate equally interesting sales patterns. With a full back catalog available on a Pay What You Want basis, he has estimated he receives an average of approximately £6.49 for each download he receives payment for—notably close to the average album download price on services such as iTunes (£7.99)—and even more impressively, Lawson's data includes sales income for single tracks alongside album purchases.[29] PWYW is clearly a valuable tool in both facilitating an improved artist–fan relationship, and increasing gross revenue.

Crowd funding

Crowd funding, fan funding or micro-patronage is often defined as the funding of a project through contributions from a number of engaged members of the public, usually prior to the product's or project's creation, where the contributor is without any claim to ownership of the product. There is a crucial differentiation between this funding and traditional investment, where an artist could give fans or non-traditional wealthy benefactors ownership over creative works in return for financial contributions. One of the main contributing factors in artists turning to crowd funding, is the ability to own their own creative work.

The band Marillion were one of the first bands to achieve notable success from crowd funding, first financing a North American tour in 1997, before utilizing the concept to offer pre-orders of their as yet to be created twelfth album *Araknophobia* upon later being out of contract in 2000.[30] By current standards, this was a crude version of crowd funding, but the band received close to 13,000 orders at £15 each for their embryonic album project.[31] With the functionality of specific crowd-funding platforms and intermediaries available in the current markets, crowd-funding campaigns have become easier to initiate and more accessible for fans. Services like Pledge Music offer in-house advice and support from industry professionals, and are now driven by the ability to offer a variety of different goods and services at a range of prices. This allows the artist a much higher rate of return when a fan is willing to spend above an album's RRP. Nielson's 2013 study states that it is this better set of "products and experiences to fans" that will yield higher revenue for artists and stakeholders, cultivating True Fans.[32]

With the difference between the "lesser" fan and the "true" fan being that the latter is more likely to "buy the super-deluxe re-issued hi-res box set,"[33] it has never before been easier to offer not just one tier of added-value product for the fan, but an increasing scale of reward linked to a high investment, seemingly tailored to any fan's budget. With entry-level rewards like downloads, through to extra artwork, living room concerts, or studio visits, many of these not only provide an opportunity for a fan to reward an artist with significant recompense, they mostly bond the artist and fan together, completing the 'true fan' conversion.

It is notable that the figures from Kickstarter show $25 as the most popular reward, but $100 as the most successful in total gross income for a project,[34] while Pledge Music claim the average spend per transaction on their site is $61.[35] All these figures are above the standard album download price point of £7.99, and are impacted on by a much smaller commission rate from the host service—15 percent from Pledge Music, approximately 8 percent from Kickstarter, against approximately 30 percent from a traditional music download service (e.g., iTunes, Amazon, 7Digital).

Kickstarter is currently the most popular crowd-funding platform, founded in 2009, operating across a range of creative projects including film, games, comics, technology, and music. As of September 2015, music has the highest number of successful projects, against any other category, with over 42,000 projects launched over the last six years, raising over $140 million in investment.[36]

One significant contribution to this figure is that of Amanda Palmer, ex-Dresden Doll lead singer, now solo artist, songwriter, and crowd-funding 'pioneer'. Palmer has a long history of fan interaction based around direct communication from before her utilization of crowd-funding platforms, managing to generate income through webcasts and Twitter conversations. In 2009, in the middle of the lengthy dissolution of her recording contract with Warner Music Group offshoot Roadrunner Records, she boasted of making $19,000 in one night, firstly through a t-shirt, collaboratively designed with her Twitter audience/online fanbase, followed by a webcast auction.[37]

Even within her major label deal, she was able to create a high level of fan engagement with her album *Who Killed Amanda Palmer*. Referencing the plot of Twin Peaks and the death/disappearance of Laura Palmer in the TV program, Palmer and her then label created promotional artifacts for fans to buy into this fictional plot, including a fake radio station (WKAP-FM) and an alternate reality game, which was in turn inspired by the overarching story arch and associated multimedia the band Nine Inch

Nails created around their Year Zero album.[38] As well as promotional material, Palmer was also able to create higher value, desirable goods around the project, such as the photo book *Who Killed Amanda Palmer: A Collection of Photographic Evidence*—all of which established a precedent and relationship with her audience that she was able to take advantage of through a formal crowd-funding campaign.[39] When Palmer was eventually released from her WMG/Roadrunner contract in 2012, she used Kickstarter to raise funds for her second album *Theatre Is Evil* in order to bring the project to life with ideal collaborators, in both its music and its art and design. Backers could pledge from $1 for a digital download, to $300 bundles to include vinyl, signed items, and "surprise arts 'n' crafts." Those wishing to make a large contribution to the project were able to do so with specialist, unique rewards for a small number of backers, offering up to $10,000.[40] The campaign was an unprecedented success and remains the highest grossing music project on the platform, raising $1,192,739 from 24,883 backers.[41]

As well as becoming Palmer's most successful album, it also established her credentials as an artist who explicitly understands the relationship an artist has with their fans, and the need and ability to derive revenue from this in order to survive. Shortly after the culmination of her successful Kickstarter campaign, she expanded on her ethos in the TED talk *The Art Of Asking*,[42] where she discussed the skill and need to ask for help "or How I Learned To Stop Worrying And Let People Help."[43]

Palmer's campaign didn't occur without criticism however, and it should be noted that for all the success crowd funding can bring, almost half the music projects launched on Kickstarter fail to reach their target on the site, earning no revenue for the creatives involved.[44] "Successful" projects that do reach their target, still face a myriad problems, noted by writer and music maker Chris Thorpe-Tracey in his article *The Case Against Crowd Funding*.[45] Thorpe-Tracey critiques the need for the formal structures of the current crowd-funding platforms, as well as what he feels are the restrictions a crowd-funding campaign place on artists' creativity, with distractions such as the need to issue order fulfillment. This was certainly an issue that frustrated Palmer after her campaign, when she berated problems such as the unpredictability of shipping costs and the general administrative burden of a massive one-off project in particular.[46]

With Palmer, this manifested itself in a larger problem, as transparency over the usage of the money raised was questioned in responce to her request for additional musicians—unpaid members of her fan base, to perform in her shows. This was met with immense criticism,[47] as was the list and figures of planned expenses she published,[48] raising the question what responsibility of liability do artists have for the usage of money acquired through crowd funding once they have fulfilled all their rewards, and what accountability the public demands of them. Palmer maintains her project was practically a "loss-leader" and that its intention was to create a project where the fans "trust the shit" out of her.[49]

Thorpe-Tracey also questions the degree to which artists are able to effectively engage large numbers of fans in crowd funded projects.[50] He argues that many campaigns are successful due to a small number of wealthy benefactors. Research conducted for this study with artists operating campaigns on a more modest scale to Palmer, supported Thorpe-Tracey's assertion where one artist attributed 35 percent of his total income to just 4 percent of his supporters.[51] On this modest scale, successful crowd funding can be very effective for artists to achieve almost any goal. Pledge Music, a platform specifically for music campaigns, and run on both a Direct-To-Fan and crowd-funding basis, operates with a large team of experienced music industry professionals to support artist campaigns. This support, alongside the specific music focus of the platform, prompts the artists to use "marketing and social interactions in more creative ways." This also reinforces the artist–fan relationship and creates an impact beyond the purely financial. However, on a sole financial basis, a small one-shot campaign can be invaluable, as one artist in this study explained: "we wanted an album that we could record and be able to sell at gigs, via websites etc. ... with no financial risk. We have all of this now and we are always in profit, sales-wise, as the whole project has been paid for."[52]

Individual artist subscription models

Subscription is another form of alternative revenue that is a deviation of crowd sourcing and direct sales, where an artist can offer a stream of their content (audio only, or various multimedia assets), which subscribers have access to in return for a regular financial contribution. This contribution is usually time-based, per month, although the Patreon service offers the option for subscribers to contribute per "thing."[53]

While the option for digital platforms to offer this option to artists is relatively new, it is similar to the model independent labels have been operating as a "singles club" for decades. In a traditional label singles club, a subscriber pays an upfront fee for a predetermined number of records to be released within a set timeframe.[54] The new digital subscription model differs, the volume and format of available music (or other media) is often less pre-defined, and the subscription is based more on an access-based model.[55] The advantage of these services is not just the regularly released records that would be available outside the service, but a variety of additional "added-value" content.[56]

Labels such as Domino Records are taking advantage of these new ways to engage with their fanbase by using the service Drip, a "membership platform"[57] that allows subscribers/members to download a combination of back catalog albums, new releases, and exclusive material every month.[58] With the rise of electronic dance music and a new culture of producing, distributing, and consuming music, it is notable that a number of labels featured on the service derive from artist producers, such as Diplo and Skrillex, releasing tracks, remixes, and a variety of alternative content to a non-traditional release schedule. This is one of the big advantages of the artist/label-centered subscription service, where artists have the freedom to create and release outside of the contractual obligation of fulfilling the requirement to produce within a traditional album cycle.

Artist Steve Lawson describes the subscription model as perfect for his needs: the ability to effectively remunerate the irregular release of small quantities of music by removing the "unit value" of the music, offering a high yield alternative to one-off works with a traditional high profit margin, such as albums.[59] The freedom of maintaining a regular income source through subscription, Lawson claims, allows more creative freedom and coupled with the ability to more regularly distribute work to your audience without detrimentally affecting the audience's desire for high-return products (such as albums), is definitely an advantage for many artists. While Lawson describes his subscription offering as his alternative to crowd funding,[60] Amanda Palmer has talked of how undertaking a successful crowd-funding campaign was part of building a trust relationship with her audience, to be able to effectively engage in a subscription model of funding through the site Patreon.[61]

Launched in 2013, Patreon is a platform that allows fans to support creative output by pledging a regular amount of money per month, or as Patreon defines it, per creation.[62] The service was founded by Jack Conte, one half of the act Pomplamoose, who grew a large fanbase by uploading videos from their home studio onto YouTube in 2009/10. Conte says he was moved to start Patreon to secure a more established income stream from fans, so he and other online creatives would be less dependent on volatile advertising revenue.[63]

Palmer joined Patreon in March 2015 stating that the platform provides a longer-term, more flexible solution for her creative needs than "flash/bang" crowd-funding campaigns, saying that "I don't want to get repetitive and exhaust the fanbase with 'HEY I'M MAKING YET ANOTHER RECORD, PRE-ORDER HERE. AGAIN!'"[64] While Conte acknowledges that Kickstarter or, one assumes, any alternative crowd-funding platform, is the best solution for larger projects,[65] evidence suggests that Patreon may be extremely effective in realizing the maximum financial benefits from Kelly's 1000 True Fans model.[66] Using Patreon's $5.79 average pledge, Musically approximates a "notional artist with 1000 'True Fans' ... who release a new song every fortnight ... their annual income could be around $150,000."[67]

The processes, creative freedoms and digital delivery from both Bandcamp and Patreon's current models go a long way to sidelining some of Chris Thorpe-Tracey's arguments against the crowd-funding model, and Palmer's quoted struggles in managing a million dollar album campaign. If you have an engaged audience, crowd funding now offers what seem sustainable opportunities in funding both one-off large projects, and more long-term career support.

A note about nuances of streaming, licensing, revenue, and audience engagement

As mentioned at the outset, the drive to take advantage of alternative revenue streams has come from the decline in global music revenue since the turn of the century, and increased cannibalization of download sales by streaming music services.[68] Many of the models mentioned here take advantage of the same technology that has caused this, but excel in placing it more directly in the creator's hands, and importantly focus on artist–fan communication.

It is important to view streaming as both a means of income and a tool of engagement, for any artist. While most of the platforms that facilitate the models previously discussed, such as Bandcamp and Pledge Music, take 10 to 15 percent commission,[69] streaming and digital sales platforms retain up to a third of all their income,[70] while other services such as digital aggregators (the intermediaries responsible for placing independent music on major streaming and download platforms) take additional percentages or flat fees from sales.[71] A potential driver for sales and engagement is simply a presence on these services however, as up to 10 percent of an artist's sales can be generated from within a music sales platform, and with the likes of Spotify and Apple building Direct-To-Fan tools within their platforms (Spotify Artists and Apple Connect), there may be a time when these services offer the direct communication with fans that is currently the preserve of Direct-To-Fan sales platforms.[72]

Spotify, Apple Music, Deezer and other streaming services operate on a "walled garden" basis, where users have to log in and provide personal data in order to listen to music. This is not the case for services such as YouTube and SoundCloud, which have advantages in building new audiences by offering a greater selection of tools to enable anyone to listen and importantly to share an artist's music. This comes at a financial compromise for the artist and rights holders, as YouTube is supported by advertising revenue and currently retains nearly half of its income generated through music streaming.[73] SoundCloud has achieved success in connecting electronic music communities but has also spent 2015 looking for a viable business model. This is because, at the time of writing, SoundCloud is being sued by the U.K. performance royalty collection society PRS For Music,[74] with the only rights holders receiving income through the service having licensed to its U.S. 'On SoundCloud' Service.[75]

Whether streaming is viable as a primary income source will likely be inconclusive for some time, especially while many of the licensing agreements for such services are subject to Non-Disclosure Agreements. The undisclosed equity stakes that labels and industry bodies are taking in services,[76] mean many are likely to remain under the suspicion of many independent artists.

Conclusion

The ability of the Internet to facilitate the low or no-cost distribution of music has enabled many unique options for artist funding that can be exploited to a maximum with a strong connection with your fan base. As Kelly states, "Direct fans are best," and artists need to nurture them.[77] The tools to do so often coincide with those that offer the most direct revenue, such as the ability to trust your audience and offer them the ability to Pay What You Want. Offering varying tiers of reward for this through crowd funding and subscription allows you to build your "True" or "Super" fans, while using the free tools available through streaming services and others to attract new converts.

Notes

1 The share of total revenues in the global music industry accounted for by recorded income has dropped from 60 percent in 2000 to just 36 percent in 2013—"60% growth in live revenue that has done most to offset the impact of declining music sales." Mark Mulligan, "The Great Music Industry Power Shift," June 4, 2014. https://musicindustryblog.wordpress.com/2014/06/04/the-great-music-industry-power-shift/ (accessed October 23, 2015).

2 David Byrne, *How Music Works* (Edinburgh: Canongate, 2012).

3 Kevin Kelly, "1,000 True Fans," March 4, 2008. http://kk.org/thetechnium/1000-true-fans/ (accessed October 23, 2015).

4 Midem, or Marché International du Disque et de l'Edition Musicale, describes itself as "the leading B2B event that gathers key players from the international music ecosystem" MIDEM, "MIDEM – The Event," http://www.midem.com/the-event/ (accessed February 28, 2016). With a heavy focus on digital and technological advancements within the music industries, it is an annual conference and showcase event in Cannes, France. The 2016 edition took place between June 3, 2016 and June 6, 2016.

5 Albin Serviant, "Interactivity: The Path to Fan Engagement ... and Sales," January 19, 2010. http://blog.midem.com/2010/01/interactivity-the-path-to-fan-engagement-and-music-sales/ (accessed October 23, 2015).

6 Ian Rogers, "Why Data Is the Future of the Music Biz," October 9, 2009. https://www.youtube.com/watch?v=uOv6iR5XX5A (accessed October 23, 2015)

7 Chris Anderton, Andrew Dubber, and Martin James, *Understanding The Music Industries* (London: Sage, 2013); Darren Hemmings, "Viral Marketing Presentation – 5th April 2012," April 5, 2012. https://vimeo.com/39830204 (accessed October 23, 2015).

8 Glenn Peoples, "Nielsen Study: Music Industry Could Add $450 Million to $2.6 Billion in Incremental Revenue With Premium Content," March 12, 2013. http://www.billboard.com/biz/articles/news/digital-and-mobile/1551730/nielsen-study-music-industry-could-add-450-million-to (accessed October 23, 2015).

9 Danny Quick, "How to Hack the Music Industry: The Audience Problem," September 1, 2015. https://medium.com/cuepoint/the-audience-problem-495947b0b2b7#.ra8q0af22 (accessed October 23, 2015).

10 Bandcamp is a Direct-To-Fan online music store launched in 2008 that also acts as a platform for artist promotion. Tracks are uploaded to Bandcamp by the rights holder and can be streamed for free on the website or where their apps have been embedded elsewhere online. The platform also offers fans the ability to purchase the music in a variety of different digital formats (MP3, FLAC, etc.) and offers a variable pricing model (Pay What You Want) as well as the ability to offer free downloads in exchange for the recipient's email address.

11 Topspin, or Topspin Media, is a Direct-To-Fan retail and marketing software for music makers, rights holders, and creators of other digital content. They "build software for artists to establish lasting and meaningful relationships with fans, communicate with them around the web, and sell far higher-value products in return." Topspin, "The Company," http://topspinmedia.com/about/ (accessed February 1, 2016). Beats Music (later sold to Apple and forming part of the Apple Music project) bought Topspin in March 2014, before selling its name and a majority of its business to Transom Capital Group, a partner in AEG's BandMerch/Cinder Block merchandising group. Chris Cooke, "Beats Sells Most of Topspin, to Be Merged in with BandMerch/Cinder Block," April 4, 2014. http://www.completemusicupdate.com/article/beats-sells-most-of-topspin-to-be-merged-in-with-bandmerchcinder-block/ (accessed October 23, 2015).

12 Music Glue is a UK based Direct-To-Fan platform which allows artists, labels, venues, promoters, festivals, and merchandisers to sell digital content, merchandise, and event tickets in multiple currencies and languages.

13 Next Big Sound is a provider of online music analytics and insights, tracking the popularity of artists through social media, streaming platforms, and radio around the world. The service was purchased by Pandora in May 2015; Stuart Dredge, "Pandora To Buy Music Analytics Firm Next Big Sound,"

May 19, 2015. http://musically.com/2015/05/19/pandora-buy-music-analytics-firm-next-big-sound/ (accessed October 23, 2015).

14 Rogers, "Why Data Is the Future of the Music Biz"; Stuart Dredge, "Amanda Palmer, Will.I.Am, Imogen Heap and Zoe Keating Talk Music Disruption," October 28, 2013. http://musically.com/2013/10/28/amanda-palmer-will-i-am-imogen-heap-zoe-keating-disrupters/ (accessed October 23, 2015).

15 Often referred to as a bundle.

16 Chris Austin and Lucy Blyth, "Rules for Chart Eligibility Albums," *Official Charts Company*, January 4, 2013. http://www.officialcharts.com/media/319098/official-uk-charts-album-chart-rules-april-2013.pdf (accessed October 23, 2015).

17 Tim Ingham, "How Self-Releasing Stereophonics Beat Sony In Intense Race To UK No.1," September 20, 2015. http://www.musicbusinessworldwide.com/how-self-releasing-stereophonics-beat-sony-in-intense-race-to-uk-no-1/ (accessed October 23, 2015).

18 Palmer Houchins, "How Wilco Used MailChimp Automation to Release Their New Album," July 28, 2015. https://blog.mailchimp.com/how-wilco-used-mailchimp-automation-to-release-its-new-album/ (accessed October 23, 2015).

19 Jaime Meline and Michael Render, "A Message from Run The Jewels," September 15, 2014. http://us9.campaign-archive1.com/?u=5d85f1f0b965282a961c32e96&id=cfbfa8fe1a&e=2f0b8444dd (accessed October 23, 2015).

20 Sylvester Jones, "Meow The Jewels," September 27, 2014. https://www.kickstarter.com/projects/1957344648/meow-the-jewels (accessed October 23, 2015).

21 Ryan Dombal, "Run The Jewels – Meow The Jewels," October 2, 2015. http://pitchfork.com/reviews/albums/21145-meow-the-jewels/ (accessed October 23, 2015).

22 Steve Lawson, "Tweet-Rant #2 : 23 Tweets About Bandcamp," August 1, 2015. http://www.stevelawson.net/2011/08/tweet-rant-2-23-tweets-about-bandcamp/ (accessed October 23, 2015).

23 Hope & Social, "Music," accessed October 1, 2015. http://www.hopeandsocial.co.uk/music/ (accessed October 23, 2015).

24 Lyn Gardner, "Pay-What-You-Decide Theatre: A Risk That's Worth Taking," December 10, 2014. http://www.theguardian.com/stage/theatreblog/2014/dec/10/pay-what-you-decide-theatre-arc-stockton (accessed October 23, 2015).

25 Annabel Turpin, "The Theatre Charter: An Arts Centre Perspective," August 4, 2014. http://futureartscentres.org.uk/uncategorized/the-theatre-charter-an-arts-centre-perspective (accessed October 23, 2015).

26 Annabel Turpin, "Here's What Happened When We Asked Audiences to Set Their Own Ticket Prices," July 8, 2015. http://www.theguardian.com/stage/theatreblog/2015/jul/08/audiences-ticket-prices-arc-stockton (accessed October 23, 2015).

27 Radiohead's previous three albums were *Kid A* (2000), *Amnesiac* (2001) and *Hail To The Thief* (2003): all reached No. 1 in the UK album charts and are certified platinum selling albums.

28 Music Ally, "Exclusive: Warner Chappell Reveals Radiohead's 'In Rainbows' Pot Of Gold," October 15, 2008. http://musically.com/2008/10/15/exclusive-warner-chappell-reveals-radioheads-in-rainbows-pot-of-gold/ (accessed October 23, 2015).

29 Lawson, "Tweet-Rant #2 : 23 Tweets About Bandcamp."

30 Marillion, "Anoraknophobia Pre-Order Press Release," April 1, 2001. http://www.marillion.com/news/newsitem.htm?id=5 (accessed October 23, 2015).

31 Tim Masters, "Marillion Fans to the Rescue," November 5, 2001. http://news.bbc.co.uk/1/hi/entertainment/music/1325340.stm (accessed October 23, 2015).

32 Peoples, "Nielsen Study: Music Industry Could Add $450 Million to $2.6 Billion in Incremental Revenue With Premium Content."

33 Kelly, "1,000 True Fans."

34 Fred Benenson, "Trends in Pricing and Duration," *Kickstarter*, September 21, 2010. https://www.kickstarter.com/blog/trends-in-pricing-and-duration (accessed October 23, 2015).

35 Pledge Music, "Launch," accessed February 1, 2016. https://www.pledgemusic.com/artists/sign_up (accessed October 23, 2015).

36 Kickstarter, "Stats," accessed October 1, 2015. https://www.kickstarter.com/help/stats (accessed October 23, 2015).

37 Bruce Houghton, "Amanda Palmer Made $19K In 10 Hours On Twitter," June 25, 2009. http://www.hypebot.com/hypebot/2009/06/amanda-palmer.html (accessed October 23, 2015).

38 Sara Thacher, "Olga Nunes on Making Transmedia Music," February 7, 2013. http://thachr.com/2013/olga-nunes-on-making-transmedia-music/ (accessed October 23, 2015).

39 Stuart Dredge, "Is Direct-To-Fan A Friend Or Foe For Record Labels?," April 30, 2014. http://musically.com/2014/04/30/direct-to-fan-labels-enter-shikari/ (accessed October 23, 2015).

40 Palmer offered rewards for up to ten people who pledged $10,000. Five would receive a "makeover/photoshoot full band invasion" and five would receive an "art-sitting & dinner" with Palmer. Of both rewards, only two people pledged for the latter, despite the project's huge success. Amanda Palmer, "Theatre Is Evil: The Album, Art Book and Tour," April 1, 2012. https://www.kickstarter.com/projects/amandapalmer/amanda-palmer-the-new-record-art-book-and-tour (accessed October 23, 2015).

41 Ibid.

42 Amanda Palmer, "Amanda Palmer: The Art of Asking," February 1, 2013. http://www.ted.com/talks/amanda_palmer_the_art_of_asking (accessed October 23, 2015).

43 Kate Torgovnick May, "Amanda Palmer on Expanding Her TED Talk into a Book and Getting a Lesson in Vulnerability from Brené Brown," November 19, 2014. http://blog.ted.com/amanda-palmer-on-expanding-her-ted-talk-into-a-book/ (accessed October 23, 2015).

44 Kickstarter, "Stats."

45 Chris Thorpe-Tracey, "The Case against Crowd-Funding Platforms," October 2, 2012. http://louderthanwar.com/the-case-crowd-funding-platforms/ (accessed October 23, 2015).

46 Zack O'Malley Greenburg, "Amanda Palmer Uncut: The Kickstarter Queen On Spotify, Patreon And Taylor Swift," April 16, 2015. http://www.forbes.com/sites/zackomalleygreenburg/2015/04/16/amanda-palmer-uncut-the-kickstarter-queen-on-spotify-patreon-and-taylor-swift/ (accessed October 23, 2015).

47 Joshua Clover, "Amanda Palmer's Accidental Experiment with Real Communism," *The New Yorker*, October 2, 2012. http://www.newyorker.com/culture/culture-desk/amanda-palmers-accidental-experiment-with-real-communism; Cord Jefferson, "Amanda Palmer's Million-Dollar Music Project and Kickstarter's Accountability Problem," September 19, 2012, accessed October 23, 2015. http://gawker.com/5944050/amanda-palmers-million-dollar-music-project-and-kickstarters-accountability-problem (accessed October 23, 2015).

48 Amanda Palmer, "Where All This Kickstarter Money Is Going By Amanda Fucking Palmer," May 22, 2012. http://blog.amandapalmer.net/20120522/ (accessed October 23, 2015).

49 Greenburg, "Amanda Palmer Uncut: The Kickstarter Queen On Spotify, Patreon And Taylor Swift."

50 Thorpe-Tracey, "The Case against Crowd-Funding Platforms."

51 Samuel Nicholls, "Fan Funding – Creative Impetus, Financial Stimulus & More. A Study of Bands Using the PledgeMusic Platform in the City of Leeds," Severn Pop Network: The Small Economies of the "New" Music Industry, University of Bristol, 2013). http://www.slideshare.net/whiskas9/bristol-presentation-3 (accessed October 23, 2015).

52 Ibid.

53 Patreon, "What Is Patreon?" https://patreon.zendesk.com/hc/en-us/articles/204606315-What-is-Patreon- (accessed February 1, 2016).

54 A traditional label running a single club would, for example release twelve monthly singles, released over the course of a year for a one-off upfront payment, for example Too Pure Records. Too Pure, "Too Pure," http://www.toopure.com/ (accessed February 1, 2016).

55 An access-based model is where the subscriber pays to access content, as opposed to receive permanent ownership. When the subscription ends, the subscriber ceases to have access to the content.

56 This could include a range of media including photographs and video, exclusive blog updates.

57 Drip, "What Is a Drip and How Does It Work?" http://drip.desk.com/customer/en/portal/articles/1822568-what-is-a-drip-and-how-does-it-work- (accessed October 23, 2015).

58 Shane Richmond, "Domino Drip Heralds the Subscription Record Label," August 30, 2012. http://www.telegraph.co.uk/technology/news/9507046/Domino-Drip-heralds-the-subscription-record-label.html (accessed October 23, 2015).

59 Steve Lawson, "The Future Is Here: Bandcamp Steve Lawson Subscription Launched!," October 23, 2014. http://www.stevelawson.net/2014/10/the-future-is-here-bandcamp-steve-lawson-subscription-launched/ (accessed October 23, 2015).

60 Steve Lawson, "Crowd-Funding My Next Solo Album (But Not How You'd Think ...)," July 5, 2015. http://www.stevelawson.net/2015/07/crowd-funding-my-next-solo-album/ (accessed October 23, 2015).

61 Greenburg, "Amanda Palmer Uncut: The Kickstarter Queen On Spotify, Patreon And Taylor Swift."

62 Patreon, "Become A Patreon Creator," https://www.patreon.com/become-a-patreon-creator (accessed October 23, 2015).

63 Jack Conte, "Digital Content Is Free. People Are Not," November 7, 2013. https://www.youtube.com/watch?v=s5Zaf0NKXvQ (accessed October 23, 2015).

64 Amanda Palmer, "Amanda Palmer Is Creating Art." https://www.patreon.com/amandapalmer (accessed October 23, 2015).

65 Stuart Dredge, "As Amanda Palmer Joins Patreon, CEO Jack Conte Tells Us Why (Interview)," March 3, 2015. http://musically.com/2015/03/03/amanda-palmer-joins-patreon/ (accessed October 23, 2015).

66 Kelly, "1,000 True Fans."

67 Stuart Dredge, "Analysis: What Are Musicians Making From Patreon?," February 16, 2015. http://musically.com/2015/02/16/what-are-musicians-making-from-patreon/ (accessed October 23, 2015).

68 IFPI, "IFPI Digital Music Report 2015," April 14, 2015. http://www.ifpi.org/downloads/Digital-Music-Report-2015.pdf (accessed October 23, 2015).

69 Bandcamp take a revenue share of 15 percent for digital goods, and 10 percent for physical merchandise, although the 15 percent digital fee drops to 10 percent if you sell $5,000 within a calendar year. Bandcamp, "Pricing," *Bandcamp*. https://bandcamp.com/pricing (accessed February 1, 2016). This does not include a percentage due to credit card processing or similar, e.g., Paypal. Pledge Music takes a consistent fee of 15 percent of all revenue taken, which includes a percentage towards processing fees. Pledge Music, "Launch."

70 Spotify, "How We Pay Royalties: An Overview." https://www.spotifyartists.com/spotify-explained/#how-we-pay-royalties-overview (accessed February 1, 2016).

71 Stuart Dredge, "Liveblog: Digital Music Transparency with Brian Message, Greg Pryor and Mike Skeet," June 17, 2014. http://musically.com/2014/06/17/digital-music-transparency-brian-message/ (accessed October 23, 2015); Stuart Dredge, "Music's Future: Stronger Artist/Fan Connections And Less 'Stupid Vanity Statistics,'" October 19, 2015, http://musically.com/2015/10/19/music-future-artist-fan-connections-lucy-blair/ (accessed October 23, 2015).

72 Benji Rogers, "Apple Connect: Direct-To-Fan Finally Gets The Stage It Deserves," June 11, 2015. http://www.musicbusinessworldwide.com/apple-connect-direct-to-fan-gets-the-stage-it-deserves/ (accessed October 23, 2015).

73 Tim Peterson, "YouTube to TV Networks: No More 'Sweetheart' Ad Deals for You!," October 31, 2013. http://adage.com/article/digital/youtube-tv-sweetheart-ad-deals/245019/ (accessed October 23, 2015).

74 PRS For Music, "PRS For Music Begins Legal Action Against Soundcloud," August 27, 2015. http://www.m-magazine.co.uk/news/prs-for-music-begins-legal-action-against-soundcloud/ (accessed October 23, 2015).

75 Alexander Ljung, "On SoundCloud Reaches 100 Premier Partners," March 2, 2015. https://blog.soundcloud.com/2015/03/02/on-soundcloud-reaches-100-partners/ (accessed October 23, 2015).

76 Tim Ingham, "Soundcloud Has Agreed Licensing Deal With Universal, Say Sources," August 17, 2015. http://www.musicbusinessworldwide.com/soundcloud-agreed-licensing-deal-universal-say-sources/ (accessed October 23, 2015).

77 Kelly, "1,000 True Fans."

CHAPTER 13

The portfolio career in practice: Key aspects of building and sustaining a songwriting and performance career in the digital era

Jo Collinson Scott and David Scott

The music industries are awash with stories about one-hit-wonders, inauspicious band break-ups, early deaths, and other variations on the theme of the unsustainable music career. Parents recoil at the suggestion that a child might want to study music at university: the prevailing notion is one of the fragility and ephemerality of success in the music industries, where that "success" depends on a singular career trajectory that results in large economic rewards. But this model of trajectory has since been joined by what has come to be referred to as the "portfolio career." Indeed, the authors of this chapter have built successful professional profiles that exemplify such a model: David's output as BBC broadcaster, lecturer, and leader of the band The Pearlfishers has spanned thirty years and has included collaborating with members of Belle and Sebastian, Deacon Blue, and Alex Chilton, as well as writing songs for well-known children's TV shows. Jo has worked for over fifteen years as a music researcher, multi-instrumentalist and songwriter, performing at venues such as the Carnegie Hall with artists including Vashti Bunyan and David Byrne, collaborating on songwriting for television, theater, and for bands such as Teenage Fanclub and Admiral Fallow. Both are active community music practitioners.

In this chapter, we will draw on these years of practical experience to suggest that sustainable careers in songwriting and performance *are*

FIGURES 13.1 *Jo Collinson Scott (aka Jo Mango) (photo credits Bob Rafferty and Sara Hill)*

FIGURES 13.2 *David Scott (photo credit Stefan Kassel)*

possible and will focus on two areas that we have identified as being key in this regard: evolving strong creative practices and sustaining enjoyment in them. These will be explored using Hugh Brown's helpful concept of "esteem"—focusing on the importance of building what we term "creative esteem" and maintaining musical "self-esteem."[1]

The digital era has brought enormous shifts in the music industries. In the first seventeen years of this century, the extent of technological innovation has been such that it has brought about what a number of theorists describe as a "new music economy."[2] Where previously there seemed to be a relatively simple singular career model for singer-songwriters in which record companies and publishers acting as gatekeepers to careers in music handed out salary-sized advances to the lucky few, an environment has developed in which a proliferation of opportunities exists for independent artists and entrepreneurs. These artists manage their own outputs to varying degrees and develop a wide range of different jobs related to music, combining these into a patchwork of roles that constitutes the "portfolio." Research into the working lives of musicians suggests that portfolio careers are increasingly common. For example, a study by the Musicians' Union in the United Kingdom showed that, in 2012, musicians very seldom earned money from a single music-related pursuit such as composing/writing or performing. It was also found to be the case that a very significant proportion of musicians worked in un-related or only partly music-related jobs alongside their musical activities.[3] Findings in the U.S.A. are broadly similar according to the U.S. Department of Labor's Bureau of Labor Statistics.[4] A detailed study in 2014 showed that only 11 percent of performers and songwriters surveyed spent "30 or more hours per week engaged in music-related activities ... and earn[ed] 80% or more of their income from music-related work." Such musicians were unusual enough among the general population of musicians to be classed as "success stories" by the researchers.

The use of the word "success" in this context is interesting to note. Much of the dialogue encountered around this issue seems to suggest that success in career terms for a musician is related to how many hours of their time spent on music directly results in monetary payment. It is the contention here that a long and rewarding career as a singer-songwriter does not necessarily hinge on receiving full-time economic remuneration from performing and recording solely as a singer-songwriter. There are a number of reasons why the work of a singer-songwriter might become unsustainable and certainly lack of income is one. However, there are others that are just as important. For example, many artists' careers come to an abrupt end despite their having a large degree of notoriety and access to major revenue streams. This might be because they lose the will or ability to write high quality songs, they suffer ill health, or they can't sustain the lifestyle that accompanies fame, for example. It is also the case that many singer-songwriters have long, extremely well respected and enjoyable careers in music where their songs and performances are highly critically acclaimed and influential, and yet they consistently work part-time jobs in other fields in order to fund the continued creation of their music. This is not to say that it doesn't matter whether musicians can make money from their music or not. Simply that the chosen focus here is a "career" as defined by the ability to satisfyingly and healthily create excellent music over a sustained period.

For many popular musicians this sustainable patchwork career exists within an understanding of music as a collaborative and community-based endeavor rather than a competitive, money-driven career path. Coulson describes such musicians as dismissive of "notions of individualistic competition in favor of co-operative networks and a commitment to music as a community, an art form, a source of identity and a way of life."[5] This has certainly been the case in terms of our own careers, in which we have both attempted to put music at the heart of our working lives by grounding ourselves in a range of musical communities and by augmenting our performing and songwriting activities with roles as community musicians, session musicians, composers for film and television, writers, researchers, lecturers, and radio producers. In fact, we see this breadth of experience as having been essential in the sustainability of our individual careers thus far—it has helped us to build the wide-ranging professional networks that are essential for creating opportunities, it has allowed us to develop a breadth of different musical skills and to generate a great range of musical materials from which to draw in our songwriting and performance activities.

Hugh Brown's understanding of the term "esteem" is helpful in contextualizing these thoughts.[6] In his study into independent music scenes, Brown uses this term to describe the value that is attached to a musician and their activities by fans, critics, business people, and peers (among others). Increasing and sustaining this esteem value is crucial for a musician's career, not least because it is this esteem that is converted into monetary value for the musician. Brown points out that being signed to a major record label would amount to an almost instant "infusion of esteem" from consumers. Musicians who build portfolio careers without the help of a major record label don't have this infusion of esteem and therefore must "develop [this] in less efficient (though potentially more rewarding) ways."[7] The slow and inefficient but ultimately creatively rewarding nature of the development of esteem across a range of music-related activities is the subject of the rest of this chapter.

There are three key esteem-related areas that can act as motivators for musicians in continuing their music making: monetized esteem (i.e., "I just want to earn a living from my music"), creative esteem (i.e., "I don't care about the money, I just want people to hear my music and respect it"), and self-esteem (i.e., "I just want to be happy with what I create and enjoy creating it"). Which of these is most important in the continuation of a career as a singer-songwriter varies from individual to individual, and they are of course all keenly interrelated. Since the means of monetizing esteem is a topic more fully covered elsewhere, this chapter aims to focus on generating creative esteem (i.e., the value attached to creative work and professional practice) and sustaining self-esteem (i.e., the enjoyment of music making). These considerations are particularly important for the increasing numbers of singer-songwriters who are totally self-managing, self-releasing, and self-publishing entrepreneurs, but it is equally relevant to those who are still largely independent but rely on a full team including manager, agent, publisher, and independent label for licensing recordings.

Generating esteem

An absolutely essential part of the building and sustaining of a portfolio career in the music industries is to cultivate esteem for creative work. This means generating esteem from peers, those who might hire or fund us, our fans, and the media. There are many ways in which this can be done, but the following are those considered to be the most important in this context: building networks, developing professional practices that facilitate the sustained creation of high quality creative output, and developing a high level of professionalism.

Building networks

Networking is a key contributor to the establishment of careers in the music industries via the way it facilitates the building of social capital using the currency of creative esteem and allows economic exchange.[8] Most musicians are only entrepreneurs by necessity rather than by choice, and therefore often have a hard time acknowledging or identifying that certain activities they undertake are indeed "networking" or "network building" activities.[9] However, most musicians are aware of the importance of meeting and keeping in contact with a wide range of people who might be able to offer creative opportunities or work. Whatever one calls this activity, it is clearly key in building up esteem and in gaining more opportunities to make more music and to be paid for it in different ways. Coulson has identified that the ad hoc nature of the work of freelance musicians means that building and sustaining networks of peers and industry contacts is a much less strategic affair for them than it is in some other entrepreneurial contexts. This is even more the case when considering that they often build networks across portfolios consisting of many different types of work. Popular musicians tend to make contacts with people they like and build their networks through friendship and in the context of community, rather than making contacts purely for the sake of exploitation. In this context, it is difficult to advise a set pattern of archiving, categorizing, prioritizing, and checking-in with specific key contacts. It seems that well-connected musicians simply try their best to keep in friendly contact with as wide a range of peers as possible in case any work comes up that might be sent their way through the network. It is a good discipline in quieter times, however, to send out a friendly e-mail to contacts you haven't seen in person in a while, just to enquire about news and keep channels open. Even where this doesn't result in any work or collaboration it may at least result in a chat over coffee and perhaps some sharing of advice or mutual support, which is in itself important.

With regard to building these networks in the first place, a good starting point is to try as much as possible to physically be at places where the type of music you want to make is happening, and make some friends. Go to as many gigs as you can, attend open mic nights or sessions, collaborate with other musicians on your billings, hang out in coffee shops where interesting music is advertised and get to know the staff, contact artists you have seen and whose music you have enjoyed to let them know this. Try not to say no to opportunities to collaborate or broaden your horizons. As Iain Rogers suggests in the title of his 2008 paper, "You've got to go to gigs to get gigs."[10]

Building networks of fans and supporters, as well as peers and industry contacts, is now vitally important to creative artists in a digital age of "participatory culture."[11] Seeing these groups as an intrinsic part of one's own communities of music making is increasingly important. There is a variety of types of support including emotional, financial, promotional, and a range of other in-kind benefits that can be engaged via social media and fan funding networks. This really does require *engagement* however. Audiences are ever more keenly attuned to nuances of exploitation or lack of authenticity in online relationships, and in order to give an artist their continued support and esteem they require real, authentic, and active contact with artists.[12] As is the case with peer networks, these contacts should be engaged with on the basis of social interaction and community building rather than purely with a view to commercial or financial gain. As Baym describes it, this may "entail a shift away from seeing the audience as revenue streams toward seeing them as relational partners engaged in shared enterprise."[13]

Sustaining creativity

Once these networks have been built and are engaged with sustained contact, it is important that the underlying creativity and quality of one's practice does not begin to suffer. After all, it is the quality of this practice on which esteem value via these networks is based. While this chapter is not designed to provide advice directly related to the craft of songwriting and performance there are nevertheless important aspects of professional practice without which such a decline can easily occur. In our experience, the critically and commercially disappointing artistic false step, which constitutes the music industry cliché of the "difficult third album," can be related not to a sudden dereliction of talent or desire on the part of the artist but to a simple change in circumstances and the increased demands of managers, promoters, and record companies. A sustained campaign of touring, radio, press, and online interviews usually correlates all too neatly with the time scale in which audience and industry expect the delivery of new material; the resulting squeeze can prove problematic for writers and performers used to extended periods in which to write, rewrite, hone, and rehearse. For the self-managing artist, too, the pressures of self-promotion, or fulfilling two or more jobs, can have the same negative effect over time. An important requirement of the portfolio career is the need to balance competing time demands in a way that allows creativity not only to be sustained but also to continually develop and improve.

One simple but helpful suggestion is to make routine the practice of collecting raw creative material—harmonic, melodic, or sonic ideas, titles and text fragments—to be stored and developed later. We have often observed songwriters throwing away magical moments of lyrical, melodic, or harmonic inspiration because pen, paper, and recording devices are either not at hand or forgotten about. But when these seed ideas are captured and simply cataloged and stored it is possible to build a pool of material that can provide a rich starting point for later projects, when time and the fabled "inspiration" are less abundant.[14]

For those who are primarily solo artists, challenging standard writing practices by looking to do more collaborative work and engaging in co-writing sessions with a diverse range of partners can also help provide fresh impetus and the introduction of new approaches and connections. Such activities inevitably generate esteem within the music community via the increasing of peer networks, exposure to new audiences, and expansion of one's own creative practices in new or different directions. Collaborative practices can also bring the introduction of an important outside editing voice that offers supportive criticism and a different perspective. We would argue that a positive reciprocal engagement with other musicians whether in song collaboration, the development of collaborative events, or simply sharing knowledge of music is the primary and most powerful form of professional networking. This being the case, it is important to put yourself in situations where such collaborative partnerships can be forged. This might be by attending open mic events or songwriting workshops, by using social media in order to connect with artists at a similar point in their career (or slightly further ahead) and suggesting a collaborative project, by developing side projects with a range of fellow musicians, or by contacting artists who are supporting you or being supported by you at an upcoming concert and suggesting a collaborative performance as part of the show.

Developing Professionalism

Another important part of building esteem value in peers and, more broadly, in networks of influential professionals comes through developing a series of essential professional skills. Zwaan, ter Bogt, and Raaijmaker's study into attributes of successful popular musicians in the Netherlands showed that more so than background, personality, and perception of talent, "the most important category of career success predictors is the professional context."[15] "Professional attitude," which was a characteristic described in interviews with key record industry decision-makers as common among successful musicians, was found to be significantly "positively related to career success" in the popular musicians studied, along with "networking" or "professional networks."[16] It is clear to us that not only is this certainly the case in the contexts that we work in, but that networking and professionalism are importantly linked: one way of developing powerful and sustainable networks lies in consistently demonstrating professional attitude, whether in the context of collaborative practice, solo performance, or other music-related work. Conversely, rumors of unprofessional practice will travel through wide networks of gatekeepers and can work against career opportunities and successes. Zwaan, ter Bogt, and Raaijmakers also suggest that musicians who have a professional support network, including managers, booking agents, etc., are more likely to become successful. Along with looking for certain levels of success and recognition, such industry agents see reliability and dependability in artists as a key indicator of potential for long-term career development.[17]

While there is perhaps a tendency among musicians to compartmentalize concepts of "professionalism" and "creativity"—to see the administrative moment as distinct from the creative moment—the adoption of professional behavior is vital in developing a structure that allows for sustained creative careers. At the most basic these relate to timekeeping, dependability, and the capacity to deliver; the well-worn music industry quip about the guitarist who operates on "rock and roll time" (at least an hour late for everything) or "dude time" (turns up when the hangover has become manageable) is a joke that wears thin with repeated experience and concomitantly dissipates in effect as the studio bill accumulates. The rock and roll myth, which champions transgressive and colorful behavior, is usually overstated in practice. The songwriter or performer who shows up on time, in good health, and prepared for the work ahead with plans and ideas, is immediately at an advantage over others. Flexibility is another attribute key to successfully building a reputation as the kind of writer or performer who is worthwhile employing across a range of musical activities. The musician who can accept challenges and develop skills while working within unfamiliar territory should find that in addition to getting the job done there is a dividend in terms of personal creative development.

Sustaining esteem

As we mentioned earlier, although the ability to generate esteem value and then to monetize it are two vital aspects of sustaining a career as a singer-songwriter, both will be of limited use if the singer-songwriter herself is too unwell or lacking motivation to continue writing and performing at all. In our experience of watching the career trajectories of our students and peers, too many extremely promising and exciting careers are cut short not because of lack of creative esteem or avenues for income, but because of disillusionment, interpersonal difficulties, ill health, or a lack of a balanced lifestyle.

Unfortunately, numerous studies have shown that being a professional popular musician can take a difficult toll, particularly in terms of the stress of job insecurity and related financial worries,[18] substance abuse rates,[19] or even rates of mortality.[20] Detailed studies by Cooper and Wills in 1988 and Dobson in 2010 have shown that popular musicians in particular suffer the effects of: high levels of self-criticism; performance anxiety; the stresses of job insecurity; the highs and lows of performing schedules; isolation from loved ones and from society in general because of challenging work schedules and cultures; the role of alcohol in work environments and in required professional sociability.[21] Although many of these issues flow from systemic causes that are not easily challenged, there are a number of small practical steps that are advisable in combating some of the more ubiquitous problems highlighted here. These are categorized under the headings of combating disillusionment and maintaining health.

Combating disillusionment

There are a number of pervasive romantic ideas regarding careers in the music industries that anachronistically continue to hold sway and can lead to damagingly unrealistic expectations. Most pervasive of all are ideas about "making it," which involve being spotted by a major record label and enjoying the fame and riches that are sure to follow. In the digital era, this expectation can exist in a more muted form—in aspirations to make a good living out of performing alone, or in the context of the bedroom YouTube video that accidentally goes viral. Lucy Green's 2002 study of popular musicians affirms the persistence of such ideas, and relates it to a "youthful aspiration" for fame: however; she found that those she interviewed who had reached a greater level of experience; "either dropped or had never espoused such ambitions and saw themselves more as craftspeople." She also found that, for all the musicians she studied, "enjoying and believing in what they were doing earned more acclaim than making money."[22]

Whatever the packaging, the myth remains—that success as a musician involves international notoriety and earning money from a singular practice. Taking a critical approach to such fantasies is crucial, as is surrounding oneself with people who do successfully work as self-employed musicians and measuring success along the more realistic scales that they represent. The ultimate goal should be to work toward a broad range of skills and activities out of which an exciting and sustainable workload can be built, feeding into increased expertise in creating music. A helpful activity in this regard is to keep a schedule of sketching out a three-year goal list, which is reviewed periodically. This avoids a pervasive sense of never achieving enough; there is usually a pleasant sense of surprise when looking back at how far one has come from the expectations of a few years ago.

Another cause of disillusionment can be the tendency to internalize critique. As Paul DiMaggio and Jason Toynbee both point out, in the cultural market there are no professional standards for judging the competence of one's work.[23] This means that media, peer, and audience critique is often the only way in which singer-songwriters feel they can measure the worth of their creations and performances. The result of this is often an insecure and fluctuating sense of self-esteem. This is made worse by the solitary nature of a freelance singer-songwriter's occupation (the people we work alongside are ever-changing and thus we often lack a set framework against which to measure performance) and the personal nature of the material that is produced for critique. A number of popular musicians in Dobson's study of young freelance musicians commented on this, with one adding:

> If you do write your own music, I think that's also a different thing from just playing other people's music ... you're very exposed and very open to criticism – you really kind of put yourself on the line, so you've got to be fairly strong-minded ... we're all kind of, with a lot of self-doubt, I suppose, in what we do.[24]

In order to try to mitigate some of this self-doubt we would suggest finding and relying on an A&R voice. In a model of the music industry dominated by major labels, specific staff-members would be charged with managing "Artists & Repertoire," which involved guiding the aesthetic quality of the work produced according to the market. Working independently of these structures often means this voice is missing and although, to many, avoiding outside meddling in the creative product is a prime goal of independence, there can be a cost to this loss in a sense of insecurity or uncertainty. In Jo's work, she relies on an experienced producer who worked with her on an early album and whose taste she trusts implicitly. In moments of self-doubt or shifting contexts of peer and audience approval, she makes a habit of sending him demos and listening to his positive critique above all others.

Finally, it is continually important to remember the reasons you wanted to make music in the first place. Studies have shown that prevalent motivations for popular musicians in creating and performing music include sense of community, social experience, catharsis, and self-expression.[25] Losing the passion that was a major motivation in creating music in times when there was less financial motivation to do so means that challenging times in one's career are less likely to be sustained. Remaining embedded within communities of artists is important in this respect, perhaps more so for the solo singer-songwriter who doesn't have the camaraderie of a band to fulfill this social function. Jo does this by returning as often as she can to the weekly open mic community in a Glasgow pub where she first began her career.

In terms of retaining the joy of self-expression and catharsis in one's music, there are further challenges in the tension between the desire for self-expression and the need to generate and monetize esteem. If, for example, satisfying one's need for self-expression might require a new musical direction that is alienating for one's audience, this needs to be balanced with the potential negative effects of that musical shift on esteem value and thus the ability to make money. One way to try to mitigate these tensions is to indulge in a range of side projects. These side projects can serve to fully meet the needs of self-expression and catharsis in a way that involves less pressure to monetize esteem. They can also be helpful in widening networks and building a range of musical experiences that will inevitably flow into new opportunities and creative practices.

Maintaining health

One of the hardest aspects of being a freelance worker of any kind is balancing workload. Most portfolio career activities for the self-employed musician are uncertain and widely varied, while income and expenditure can fluctuate wildly. This often creates a situation where stressful periods of over-work are followed by anxious periods with little income and uncertain prospects. Unfortunately, neither of the authors have much experience in overcoming this fluctuation: however, there are definite ways in which to attempt to overcome the resultant anxieties.

First: build a team if you need one. This is particularly the case with regard to aspects of your business that you feel least able to execute, as these are likely to cause the most personal stress if you undertake them alone. While an agent or a manager might limit aspects of creative control one has over certain activities, the percentage they take may ultimately be worthwhile if the stress of constantly hassling gig venues turns the music dream into a nightmare. Brown notes the importance of musicians "outsourcing the business functions through their networks as much as possible" in order to reduce what he describes as "significant angst" and "obvious impediments ... to the development of personal satisfaction."[26] Examples of how one might approach this are by commissioning fan-made videos, having social media followers administrate Facebook pages, recruiting a music student as an intern, and setting up various networks including contact exchanges as well as in-kind creative/business collaborations. All these activities should be thought about creatively—this makes them more satisfying and leads to distinctiveness. When doing such outsourcing, however, aspiring musicians should take care that they have learned every aspect of their business early on in their career in order to oversee this properly. A comprehensive understanding of income and outgoings, budgeting and revenue streams is important in safeguarding these and in developing a sense of creative control.

It is also important to value rest. Musicians can find themselves working every day for months on end unless rest is prioritized by building days off into the calendar. This is also the case for prioritizing time to take in the invaluable cultural stimuli that every songwriter needs to draw on in their work. Blocking out time for books, cinema, and gigs might seem unproductive, but seeing them as essential to your job is important in easing stress and sustaining physical and spiritual health. Ill health can obviously be related to such a lack of rest, but also can result from a lack of exercise and healthy diet, which are difficult to maintain around the unsociable hours of tour performances and studio schedules. Indeed numerous studies link rates of substance misuse and associated health problems to the freelance musicians' lifestyle.[27]

Staying healthy within demanding touring and recording cycles is particularly difficult: schedules are often over-full, meals can be rushed and limited in scope, and socialization happens in environments where networking involves alcohol consumption and ruining one's voice over loud music. This being said, there are numerous ways to stay healthy while on tour. Maintaining sociability needn't always involve over-indulgence; setting simple boundaries on drinking, researching healthy eating options ahead of time, and building in some exercise time are simple ways to keep healthy and, ultimately, retain creative control. Time spent endlessly hanging around can also be utilized for creative projects with a little imagination. When David was on tour, he often set himself a task to keep his mind at work—for example, making and sending a hand-made postcard with one of his drawings on it for every day of the tour. This activity kept him connected to a sense of home, practiced his creativity, and reduced the sense of purposelessness that—alternating with the highs of performance—can lead to the perceived need for self-medication with alcohol or other substances.

As with the advice above regarding reducing stress, the application of creativity and concerted effort to the problem of how to stay healthy within your career is of key importance. As ever, keeping a balance between the needs for creating and monetizing esteem with the requirement to sustain that esteem should be at the forefront of the mind in making these decisions, even on a day-by-day basis.

In conclusion then, any singer-songwriter whose goal is to enjoy a long and satisfying portfolio career in the digital age should focus on creating a holistic practice. The aim should be to weave the joy of music and creativity through every activity you undertake in order to continually develop and learn by widening the scope of the musical activities that constitute your career. This will involve professional attributes like flexibility, acceptance of challenge, and ability to collaborate. It will also involve being deeply involved in musical communities where collaboration with peers is commonplace and engagement with networks of fans and supporters is central to practice. Being constantly grounded in these musical communities and the fun and enjoyment they bring to the process of making music will be helpful in avoiding disillusionment, as will pushing aside ideas of singular career trajectories and measures of success based solely in economics.

Notes

1 Hugh Brown, "Valuing Independence: Esteem Value and its Role in the Independent Music Scene," *Popular Music and Society* 35 (2012): 519–39.

2 Patrik Wikstrom, *The Music Industry: Music in the Cloud* (Cambridge: Polity Press, 2009); Fabian Holt, "The Economy of Live Music in the Digital Age," *European Journal of Cultural Studies* 13 (2010): 243–61; Tim Anderson, *Popular Music in a Digital Music Economy: Problems and Practices for an Emerging Service Industry* (London: Routledge, 2013).

3 Musicians' Union, "The Working Musician," 2014. http://www.musiciansunion.org.uk/Files/Reports/Industry/The-Working-Musician-report (accessed August 5, 2015).

4 Bureau of Labor Statistics, "Occupational Outlook Handbook – Musicians

and Singers – 2014." http://www.bls.gov/ooh/entertainment-and-sports/musicians-and-singers.htm (accessed August 5, 2015).

5 Susan Coulson, "Collaborating in a Competitive World: Musicians' Working Lives and Understandings of Entrepreneurship," *Work, Employment and Society* 26 (2012): 257.

6 Brown, "Valuing Independence."

7 Ibid., 521.

8 E.g., Koos Zwaan and Tom ter Bogt, "Breaking Into the Popular Record Industry: An Insider's View on the Career Entry of Pop Musicians," *European Journal of Communications* 24 (2009): 89–101; Sheena Leek and Louise Canning, "The Role of Networking and Social Capital in Initiation of Relationships in Passion Based Service Networks," paper presented at the IMP Conference, Glasgow, Scotland, August 31–September 3, 2011; Coulson, "Collaborating in a Competitive World."

9 Coulson, "Collaborating in a Competitive World."

10 Ian Rogers, "'You've Got to Go to Gigs to Get Gigs': Indie Musicians, Eclecticism and the Brisbane Scene," *Continuum: Journal of Media and Cultural Studies* 22 (2008): 639–49.

11 Henry Jenkins, *Textual Poachers: Television Fans and Participatory Culture* (London: Routledge, 1992); Mark Deuze, "Participation, Remediation, Bricolage: Considering Principle Components of a Digital Culture," *The Information Society* 22 (2006): 63–75; Nancy Baym, "The Swedish Model: Balancing Marketing and Gifts in the Music Industry," *Popular Communication* 9 (2011): 22–38.

12 Ling Yang, "All for Love: The Corn Fandom, Prosumers, and the Chinese Way of Creating a Superstar," *International Journal of Cultural Studies* 12 (2009): 527–43; Francesco D'Amato, "Investors and Patrons, Gatekeepers and Social Capital: Representations and Experiences of Fans' Participation in Fan Funding," in *The Ashgate Research Companion to Fan Cultures*, eds. Stijn Reijnders, Koos Zwaan, and Linda Duits (Farnham: Ashgate, 2014), 135–48; Patryck Galuszka and Blanka Brzozowska, "Crowdfunding: Towards a Redefinition of the Artist's Role – the Case of MegaTotal," *International Journal of Cultural Studies* 4 (2015): 1–17, doi: 10.1177/1367877915586304 (accessed August 7, 2015).

13 Baym, "The Swedish Model," 25.

14 There is an array of accessible and powerful recording, text editing, and file-sharing apps for this, which are extremely helpful.

15 Koos Zwaan, Tom ter Bogt, and Quinten Raaijmakers, "So You Want to be a Rock 'n' Roll Star? Career Success of Pop Musicians in the Netherlands," *Poetics* 37 (2009): 261.

16 Zwaan and ter Bogt, "Breaking Into the Popular Record Industry," 257, 260.

17 Ibid.

18 Carey Cooper and Geoffrey Wills, "Popular Musicians Under Pressure," *Psychology of Music* 17 (1989): 22–6; Zwaan, ter Bogt, and Raajmakers, "So

You Want to Be a Rock 'n' Roll Star?" (2009); Bureau of Labor Statistics, "Occupational Outlook Handbook."

19 Susan Raeburn, John Hipple, William Delaney, and Kris Chesky, "Surveying Popular Musicians' Health Status Using Convenience Samples," *Medical Problems of Performing Artists* 18 (2003): 113–19; Melissa Dobson, "Insecurity, Professional Sociability, and Alcohol: Young Freelance Musicians' Perspectives on Work and Life in the Music Profession," *Psychology of Music* 39 (2010): 240–60; Kathleen Miller and Brian Quigley, "Sensation-Seeking, Performance Genres and Substance Use Among Musicians," *Psychology of Music* 40 (2011): 389–410.

20 Mark Bellis, Tom Hennell, Clare Lushey, Karen Hughes, Karen Tocque, and John Ashton, "Elvis to Eminem: Quantifying the Price of Fame Through Early Mortality of European and North American Rock and Pop Stars," *Journal of Epidemiology and Community Health* 61 (2007): 896–901.

21 Cooper and Wills, "Popular Musicians Under Pressure"; Dobson, "Insecurity, Professional Sociability, and Alcohol."

22 Lucy Green, *How Popular Musicians Learn: A Way Ahead for Music Education* (Aldershot: Ashgate, 2002), Kindle edition, Loc. 1376.

23 Paul DiMaggio, "Market Structure, the Creative Process and Popular Culture: Towards an Organizational Reinterpretation of Mass-Culture Theory," *Journal of Popular Culture* 11 (1977): 436–52, quoted in Jason Toynbee, *Making Popular Music: Musicians, Creativity and Institutions* (London: Hodder, 2000), 11.

24 Dobson, "Insecurity, Professional Sociability, and Alcohol," 246.

25 E.g., Sara Cohen, *Rock Culture in Liverpool: Popular Music in the Making* (Oxford: Oxford University Press, 1991); Holly Kruse, *Site and Sound: Understanding Independent Music Scenes* (New York: Peter Lang, 2003); Rogers, "You've Got to Go to Gigs to Get Gigs."

26 Brown, "Valuing Independence," 532.

27 Cooper and Wills, "Popular Musicians Under Pressure"; Bellis et al., "Elvis to Eminem"; Dobson, "Insecurity, Professional Sociability, and Alcohol"; Miller and Quigley, "Sensation-Seeking, Performance Genres and Substance Use."

CHAPTER 14

How to (almost) never play a bad gig again: A simple way to approach performing professionally

Emma Hooper (aka "Waitress for the Bees")

Having worked the professional music scene for almost twenty years now, I've performed and toured across Canada, the U.S.A., the U.K., Europe, and Japan both with my own acts and as a hired-gun viola player. Current creative projects include Waitress for the Bees, a solo project using viola, electronics, and vocals to write and perform songs about dinosaurs and insects that once landed me a Finnish knighthood, and the Stringbeans Quartet, a traditional string quartet playing non-traditional compositions, most often in venues where you wouldn't expect to find a string quartet. As a session player, I've played viola, violin, vocals, and a number of weird little instrument parts for a number of clients and projects including BBC Film and Television, Real World Studios, The Heavy, HBO Television, 2Kgames, Peter Gabriel, Newton Faulkner, and Toni Braxton.

So, it's with a fair bit of honest experience that I can say: we all play rubbish gigs, sometimes. It's inevitable. It's a learning experience. It's all part of being a real, live, professional performing musician. And my experience has certainly been no exception to this rule. I've played gigs for hecklers who only wanted jazz (I'm *not* jazz), gigs so far-flung and poorly paid that I've wound up way in the red, and gigs cancelled halfway through due to electrical fires or sinking venue-boats … . Sadly, there's not always a

FIGURE 14.1 *Emma Hooper (aka "Waitress for the Bees")*

way to completely avoid it; sometimes you just can't predict the disastrous turn an innocent-seeming booking will take.

But sometimes you can. After many, many years of ups and downs on the gigging circuit, I've stumbled across a formula that, when applied, has drastically cut down the number of not-worth-it gigs in my life. I call it the good-gig triangle, and it's really quite simple. In order for a gig to count as worthwhile, it has to satisfactorily offer at least two of the three sides of this "triangle" (fig. 14.2).

Economy is just another word for MONEY. We all feel a bit dirty worrying about and negotiating for money at gigs, but the sooner a performer can come to terms with that squeamishness the better. In my experience, promoters and bookers respect an artist who can talk candidly about finances, and they tend to value the music and performance of artists who value themselves. That is to say, people will often believe you're worth just what you tell them you are. (This could really be the topic of a whole other chapter, including a section called "Why you should never, ever, ever charge less than £5 for your album"... However, for now, we'll keep things brief and simple.) So, in short, "Economy" refers to how much money (after expenses) you're getting paid to play, plain and simple.

Opportunity refers to any potential benefits beyond money you might reap as a result of the gig. Examples might be a small-stage festival gig that gets you in with the promoter for a Glastonbury stage, or a gig at

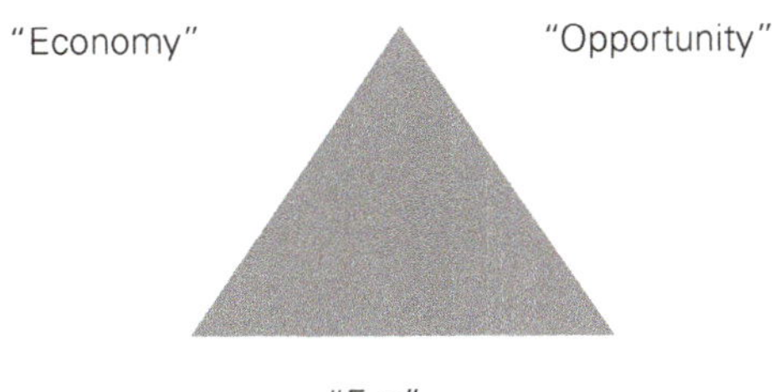

FIGURE 14.2 *The "good-gig" triangle*

an amazing venue you've always wanted to play, or the promise of high-quality sound or video footage.

Fun, meanwhile, is perhaps the most basic of the three triangle-sides, meaning just what it says on the tin: Will the gig be fun to play? Maybe it's just down the street from your house and two other of your favorite acts will be playing and there will be a cotton candy machine and balloons. That counts as fun. (For me at least.) Maybe you'll need to take three different buses with tons of equipment to a dark, smelly, and sticky venue where you'll have to wait around alone for three hours between sound-check and doors with no opportunity for dinner or even a free drink. That does not count as fun (for me ...).

Maybe the best thing about this formula is that it's flexible. For example, a gig that may have passed with flying colors back when you were starting out and £25 seemed like great money might not make the cut once you're a bit more established and it's not worth getting out of bed for less than £10,000. Or, the chance to trial your set in front of a real, live audience in a not-amazing venue might be a great opportunity if you're a new act, but might be more hassle than it's worth if you've just played the Olympics opening ceremonies the week before ... This formula leaves space for you to consider what's a good deal, what's a good opportunity, and what's good fun, for you and your music *right now*.

Seek two triangle-sides out of the three per gig, and I promise you'll drastically reduce your rubbish-gig count, and, at the same time, handle your music and time professionally. Sure, you'll still end up playing some terrible shows; you can't always know the kitchen's going to burn something and smoke everyone out, or that the address they gave you is actually forty miles from where Google tells you it is, or that the promoter will try to switch the terms on you at the last minute, but, for the most part, it will help, it will make a difference.

An added bonus is that it will also help you to consider and weigh what matters to you in terms of your music and how it's shared, skills that prove invaluable throughout your music career. And if you get £10,000, cotton candy, and the chance to share the stage with the queen (or a member of Queen) at the same time, well, that's good too.

PART FOUR

Case studies

CHAPTER 15

Vocal authorship: Marianne Faithfull and "Sister Morphine"

Alexandra Apolloni

What does it mean to write a song?

This seems like a simple question. When you write a song, you put pen to paper and work out the song's lyrics. You sketch out the outline of a melody or a chord progression. Then, you've written a song—right?

While this description might capture what it means to write a song on a basic level, when we think about what listeners expect of singer-songwriters, the question becomes more complex. We don't just expect a singer-songwriter to *write* a song with pen and paper and leave it at that. We expect them to *perform* those words and music in ways that infuse them with meaning. We want their performances to do more than tell the story: we want them to embody the story; to make it sound believable and true. A singer-songwriter performance is not simply a matter of taking some words and notes that someone wrote down and singing or playing them: instead, it's about creating meaning in those words and notes through the very act of performing them.

The way singer-songwriters convey meaning in performance often comes down to elements of music that cannot be captured by writing. Consider, for instance, what makes some of the best-known singer-songwriters stand out. Bob Dylan is known for the gravelly, nasal sound of his voice; Joni Mitchell for her ability to create—or perhaps become—different characters as she sings; Tracy Chapman for rich and hushed vocal timbres that affect intimacy with her audiences. These singers use their voices as songwriting tools that convey the meaning of their music. A sad song might be enhanced if the singer can perform with weariness or fatigue. A joyful song could be enhanced by lightness in a performer's voice. Beyond voice, a performer can use her entire body to create meaning. She could look out into the audience and make meaningful eye contact, or she might play her instrument with visible passion, anger, or tenderness. A performer's every gesture can become part of the act of songwriting.[1]

In the case of singer-songwriters, then, the act of *writing* a song is so much more than just putting pen to paper. However, despite the fact that music is created through this active, performative process, copyright laws in the United States and the United Kingdom don't necessarily recognize or protect these processes.[2] In the eyes of the law, the person who "owns" a song, so to speak, is the person who holds the *rights* to a song: the rights holder receives royalty payments when a song is played or performed. Sometimes, that person might be the songwriter. But in many cases, even when a songwriter receives credit for writing a song, they might not own the rights to a song; depending on the terms of their contracts with management, record, and publishing firms, songwriters often sign their rights over to publishing companies.[3]

If songwriting is more than just "writing," but if the law only recognizes a narrow definition of songwriting, what is the singer-songwriter to do to? In this essay, I explore this tension by investigating the case of one specific song by one particular singer-songwriter: "Sister Morphine," co-written and recorded by Marianne Faithfull. As we'll see, it's a song with a disputed authorial history. But Faithfull's performances of a song reveal how a singer-songwriter can assert authority over a song, even if they aren't legally recognized as its writer.

Marianne Faithfull was seventeen in 1964 when she got her first record deal. She became one of the musical and style icons of the 1960s British pop and rock scene. Her career has been challenging, and her image has shifted considerably over the years. In the mid-1960s, Faithfull was a folk-pop ingénue with an innocent but sexy image. In those early years, Faithfull's managers modeled her image after that of the singer-songwriters of the 1950s and 1960s folk revival. The release of her first hit, the Mick Jagger/Keith Richards-penned ballad "As Tears Go By," coincided with early records by artists like Joan Baez and Joni Mitchell. These folk songbirds had naturalistic images: they dressed unpretentiously, and their voices often sounded untrained. In interviews, they spoke with candor and honesty. Faithfull's manager, Andrew Loog Oldham, hoped to capitalize on this trend by crafting Faithfull's "bohemian" image.

By the end of the decade, Faithfull had fallen in with the Rolling Stones, and had left her husband and young son to pursue a short-lived relationship with Mick Jagger. In the years that followed, she was plagued by scandal, and was derided as more of a groupie than a musician. In the 1970s, after years of drug addiction and homelessness, she re-emerged with the punk-inspired album *Broken English*, and since then has transformed herself into one of the most respected singer-songwriters of the twentieth century.

Faithfull struggled to be taken seriously for many years before attaining her current stature. Like many young women in the music industry, she had little control and agency over her early career. The media was particularly hostile toward her in the late 1960s and 1970s, and much of the conversation around her had a decidedly sexist bent.[4] While the Stones were able to easily bounce back from scandal, the music industry and public opinion weren't kind to young women who strayed from the path of righteousness. For Faithfull, transforming herself into a singer-songwriter worthy of respect was all the more challenging because she was navigating a rock scene that was frequently hostile to women. It was in that context that Faithfull used her singing voice to assert authorship over her songs: a particularly powerful gesture given the ways in which women musicians are so frequently denied control and authority over their music and careers.

Listening for Faithfull's authorial voice

From the outset of her career, Faithfull wanted to assert her artistic voice. In 1964, for instance, she agreed to record a pop album—but only if her record company also agreed to let her make a folk music album. She also began writing songs in the 1960s, collaborating with many of the musicians in her circle, including the likes of the Rolling Stones. In 1969, Faithfull collaborated with Jagger and Richards to write "Sister Morphine." The harrowing song is narrated from the point of view of an accident victim begging a nurse for painkillers. Faithfull recorded the first version of the song that year, as the b-side to her single "Something Better." Soon after its release, though, "Sister Morphine" was quickly pulled from the shelves by Decca Records, who balked at the song's lurid subject matter, and at the connections it suggested to rumors of Faithfull's drug use. In 1971, the Rolling Stones released a version of the song on the album *Sticky Fingers*, and, for many years, that version was the best known.

The question of "Sister Morphine's" authorship remains in dispute. Faithfull claims responsibility for writing its lyrics. In 2013, she told the *Guardian* that the song was inspired by Lou Reed's "Heroin," and by the poems of Baudelaire.[5] While Richards has corroborated Faithfull's claim, Jagger questions it. In 1995, he told *Rolling Stone* that Faithfull "wrote a couple of lines; she always says she wrote everything, though. I can't even tell you which ones. She's always complaining she doesn't get enough money from it. Now she says she should have got it all."[6] Until 1994, Faithfull did not have an official songwriting credit for her work on "Sister Morphine," but reported that Allen Klein, the Stones' manager and publisher, sent her regular royalty checks.[7] When *Sticky Fingers* was re-issued in 1994, the liner notes finally included Faithfull as a songwriter.[8]

Despite this disputed authorship, many fans and critics were quick to assume that "Sister Morphine" was Faithfull's handiwork, and was autobiographical—largely because the song's references to addiction and drug use resonated with the stories of Faithfull's own downward spiral into addiction. In 1979, for instance, critic Kris Needs reviewed Faithfull's album *Broken English* and lauded the songs in which she sang about "experience, her life." "The only time she's done that before was on 'Sister Morphine'," he writes, "one of the most graphic, harrowing songs ever." Faithfull has gone back and forth on the autobiographical nature of the song. She told her biographer, David Dalton, that "I'm much too clever to want to write about myself all the time. It would bore me to death. 'Sister Morphine' was written before I ever took morphine. It's a story I made up, as I have been saying for years." However, Faithfull had also been saying, for years, that her aptitude at performing the song was because it was inspired by her lived experience. In the 1989 concert film *Blazing Away*, she says that "Sister Morphine" "was written out of my direct experience. And it's my direct experience that can get me through it. I know I can sing 'Sister Morphine.' I wrote it, it belongs to me, and it's part of my stuff."[9]

Why would Faithfull both deny that the song is about her, and yet also claim that its power comes from the way that her life influenced it? The answer to this question lies in what audiences expect of singer-songwriters: truth, honesty, and authenticity. In the singer-songwriter genre, a performer's ability to convey truth is what marks them as successful and gives them power and authority. Faithfull's artistic power and authority were undermined throughout her career, but particularly in the dispute over "Sister Morphine's" authorship. By identifying with the song, Faithfull was claiming that she was due respect as a performer because of the way in which she channeled her lived experience in song. And even though she came to disavow any autobiographical element to the *story* of "Sister Morphine," the way she has *sung* the song insists on an autobiographical thread. Faithfull's voice has experienced pronounced changes over the years—she's gone from singing with a flexible, girlish soprano, to a deep, gravelly contralto. These shifts in her voice—which now sounds raspy, harsh, and even damaged compared to the voice of her younger self—makes it sound as though her experiences of trauma affected her body and her instrument, and imbue every song she performs with an autobiographical ethos. In essence, Marianne Faithfull uses her voice in such a way that listeners assume that they can hear her experiences.

Three "Sister Morphines": 1969, 1979, and 1989

Considering three different versions of "Sister Morphine" shows how Faithfull has used her voice to claim authority as a singer-songwriter. In her first recording of "Sister Morphine" in 1969, Faithfull's voice is high and light, with a warbling vibrato. Her singing sounds fragile and almost ghostly; the line "tell me, Sister Morphine" little more than a whisper. Listening retrospectively, given that Faithfull would experience both physical and emotional trauma in the years immediately following the track's release, this vocal quality suggests her own precarious position. Her voice is almost overwhelmed by the accompanying guitars, as though Faithfull is being obscured.[10]

In 1979, Faithfull re-emerged with *Broken English,* a punk-inspired departure from her earlier records, and she recorded a re-imagined "Sister Morphine." This version of the song is markedly different from the one made in 1969.[11] Instruments take a back seat to Faithfull's strident, pointed vocal delivery. While she sings in the same key as in 1969, and while the warble in her voice is equally pronounced, she now sings with force. "Tell me, Sister Morphine," is not a plea, but a command. Rather than whispering the words, she now uses her voice to depict the trauma that the song recounts. When she sings "the scream of the ambulance," her voice rises shrilly as if to depict a siren; on "can't you see, Sister Morphine? I'm just trying to score," the reverb around her voice suggests that she's isolated and alone—perhaps reflecting Faithfull's own isolating experience of addiction. *Broken English* was framed as a comeback, after years of addiction and trauma, that represented the work of an older and wiser artist. The version of "Sister Morphine" included on the record takes advantage of the way that knowledge of Faithfull's biography would inform how listeners interpreted the song. Faithfull took a song that may or may not be autobiographical and, through performance, firmly asserted its connection to her lived experience.

As Norma Coates has argued, it wasn't until Faithfull began drawing on her experiences of trauma in ways that bolstered perceptions of her artistic authenticity that she was taken seriously as an artist.[12] A recent review in the *Telegraph* provides evidence of this assessment. Critic Neil McCormick evokes both the misogyny frequently directed at young women involved in rock culture, and the romantic myth that pain fuels creativity, when he writes that Faithfull's "longevity seems extraordinary when you consider what a lightweight she first appeared, flimsy muse of Mick Jagger, sacrificial virgin on the altar of another band's mythos. Ravaged by heroin and enlarged by life experience, she has grown into an artist of substance."[13] The confessional 1979 version of "Sister Morphine" is a manifestation of this narrative: it distances Faithfull from the youthful, folk-pop ingénue image of her youth, and constructs her as a singer-songwriter whose lived experience grants her authority.

In 1989, Faithfull performed "Sister Morphine" as part of a live concert film, *Blazing Away*, and, to this day, she continues to perform the number during her live shows. As mentioned previously, she introduced the 1989 performance by describing how the song was inspired by her "direct experience."[14] In her introduction, she also ties the song to her suicide attempts, which occurred in 1969 and 1970, *after* "Sister Morphine" was written and released. She says, "when I sing it, I actually have a visual in my head and I see it like bits from my own sort of movie in my mind. I hear the ambulance whenever I sing the line about the ambulance. I have this sort of feeling and this picture of being driven to hospital, but I obviously couldn't hear it because I was unconscious."[15] While the fact that "Sister Morphine" was written *before* her suicide attempts means that it's impossible that they inspired the *writing* of the song, Faithfull indicates that they clearly inspire her *performances* of the song. Moreover, her listeners and fans would have brought their awareness of her past to bear on their hearing of "Sister Morphine." By claiming this autobiographical connection, Faithfull is staking her claim on the song—regardless of who legally, officially claimed authorship over it. As previously stated, she has commented, "I wrote it, it belongs to me, it's part of my stuff."[16]

Faithfull's voice on the 1989 performance and on subsequent performances affirms that "Sister Morphine" can, in fact, be hers, as she sings in such a way as to highlight the connection to her lived experience. Years of drug abuse and chronic bouts of laryngitis had permanently contributed to the changes her voice. The resulting sound was rougher, rawer, and deeper. While she came by this voice due to unfortunate circumstance, she also embraces it. As on *Broken English*, her vocal sound mimics the pain the protagonist of "Sister Morphine" is experiencing, sounding particularly raw and harsh on lines such as "what am I doing in this place, why does the doctor have no face?" Faithfull's voice is also the centerpiece of the musical arrangement. While her backing musicians take turns on solos, they seem to fade out and back away at her bidding, and remain subdued while she sings. The staging also frames Faithfull as authority figure. She's dressed in a bulky leather jacket that makes her look like a larger-than-life, looming presence, and, for much of the performance, she is illuminated while all else is in shadow.

The vocal quality that Faithfull used in 1989 continues to be her trademark and has only become more pronounced with time. On her recent albums, such as 2011's *Horses and High Heels*, her voice is close-miked so that you can hear every breath and every rasp, leading one critic to describe it as "a choir of cracked knuckles."[17] While her sound is not an affectation, by any means, she uses it and brings it out in a very particular way: to remind us of her difficult history, of a path from teen pop star to fallen angel to wise and world-weary singer-songwriter. Her voice creates that character, and gives her authority when she sings dark and difficult songs. Despite having gone without a songwriting credit for so long, Faithfull's voice gives her authority over the words and melodies of "Sister Morphine," letting her claim ownership over it in the ears of her listeners.

FIGURE 15.1 *Marianne Faithfull on the set of Thank Your Lucky Stars, 1965: http://www.gettyimages.com/detail/news-photo/marianne-faithfull-poses-on-the-set-of-thank-your-lucky-news-photo/96410651*

FIGURE 15.2 *Marianne Faithfull performing at The Dominion Theatre, London, U.K., on June 8, 1982: http://www.gettyimages.com/detail/news-photo/marianne-faithfull-performing-at-the-dominion-theatre-news-photo/487119621?esource=social_TW_gallery*

FIGURE 15.3 *Marianne Faithfull performs at Carre on May 13, 1990: http://www.gettyimages.com/detail/news-photo/marianne-faithfull-vocal-performs-at-carre-on-13th-may-1990-news-photo/462994885*

What can singer-songwriters learn from the story of Marianne Faithfull and "Sister Morphine"? On one level, this is a story about the importance of making sure that the contracts you sign protect your interests and authorial rights. On another level, this is a story that demonstrates that authorship takes place through performance. While "Sister Morphine" was not necessarily an autobiographical song, Faithfull's performances make it seem as though it is about her, enabling her to assert authority and perform authenticity, enabling her to transform, as critic Stephen Deusner put it, into a performer with "interpretive authority."[18] Skilled singer-songwriters can achieve this effect with songs that they've written, as well as with songs that others have written. A skilled singer-songwriter can take any song, and by using their voice strategically, personalize it and write it anew each time that they sing it.

Notes

1 There is a wealth of literature on performance as act of musical creation. Useful starting points include Philip Auslander, "Musical Personae," *TDR: The Drama Review* 50 (1) (2006): 100–19; Nicholas Cook, *Beyond the Score: Music as Performance* (Oxford: Oxford University Press, 2014); Nicholas Cook and Richard Pettengill, eds., *Taking It to the Bridge: Music as Performance* (Ann Arbor: University of Michigan Press, 2013). For more on Faithfull's performances of identity, see Norma Coates, "Whose Tears Go By? Marianne Faithfull at the Dawn and Twilight of Rock Culture," in *She's so Fine: Reflections on Whiteness, Femininity, Adolescence and Class in 1960s Music* (Farnham: Ashgate, 2010), 183–202.

2 For a discussion of the implications of intellectual property law for songwriters and composers, see Roger Wallis, "Copyright and the Composer," in *Music and Copyright*, eds. Lee Marshall and Simon Frith (New York: Routledge, 2013), 103–22.

3 See Jason Toynbee, "Musicians," in *Music and Copyright*, eds. Lee Marshall and Simon Frith (New York: Routledge, 2013), 123–38.

4 See Coates, "Whose Tears Go By," for discussion of this coverage. As Coates notes, media coverage of drug charges brought against the Rolling Stones in 1967 following a police raid, in which Faithfull was supposedly discovered nude and wrapped in a fur rug, was preoccupied with Faithfull's apparent sexual deviance. Coates writes: "The effort by the establishment to reinforce class and gender norms and conventions focused on young women, not on young men ... To these ends, a fourth person was put on trial in the Stones' drug case, this time in the court of public opinion. The day after [Keith] Richards's trial, the headline in the times was not about his sentence. Instead it screamed, "Young woman 'wearing only fur rug' at guitarist's party." (194)

5 Dave Simpson, "Marianne Faithfull: 'I Don't Think I Had Any Choice but to

Be Decadent'," *Guardian*, January 10, 2013. http://www.theguardian.com/culture/2013/jan/10/marianne-faithfull-decadent-mick-jagger (accessed August 31, 2015)

6 Jann Wenner, "Jagger Remembers," *Rolling Stone*, December 14, 1995.

7 Marianne Faithfull, *Faithfull: An Autobiography* (London: Little Brown, 1994), 217.

8 The Rolling Stones, *Sticky Fingers,* recorded 1971, Virgin 7243-8-39525-2-6, 1994, compact disc.

9 Marianne Faithfull, vocal performance of "Sister Morphine," *Blazing Away*, directed by Lawrence Jordan, recorded November 25–26, 1989 (Island Visual Arts, 1990), VHS.

10 Marianne Faithfull, vocal performance of "Sister Morphine," on "Something Better," Decca F-12889, 1969, 45rpm disc.

11 Marianne Faithfull, vocal performance of "Sister Morphine," on *Broken English*, recorded 1979, deluxe edition, Island Records 371 173-2, 2013, compact disc.

12 Coates, "Whose Tears Go By," 202.

13 Neil McCormick, "Marianne Faithfull, Give My Love To London, Review: 'Unbalanced,'" *Telegraph,* October 2, 2014. http://www.telegraph.co.uk/culture/music/cdreviews/11135910/Marianne-Faithfull-Give-My-Love-To-London-review-unbalanced.html (accessed August 31, 2015)

14 *Blazing Away.*

15 Ibid.

16 Ibid.

17 Jason Heller, "Review: Marianne Faithfull, Horses and High Heels," *The A.V. Club*, June 28, 2011. http://www.avclub.com/articles/marianne-faithfull-horses-and-high-heels,58157/ (accessed August 31, 2015)

18 Stephen Deusner, "Review: Marianne Faithfull, Horses and High Heels," *Paste*, June 27, 2011. http://www.pastemagazine.com/articles/2011/06/marianne-faithful-horses-and-high-heels.html (accessed August 31, 2015)

CHAPTER 16

Indie folk's bowerbirds: Nostalgia and contemporary singer-songwriters

Claire Coleman

Nostalgia for an imagined, selectively constructed past is a defining influence on singer-songwriters operating in the indie folk genre. The prominent place of the nostalgic past in popular culture is periodically discussed and sometimes decried by both academics and music critics.[1] However, the prevalence of retro and vintage aesthetics in popular cultural industries indicts academics to further thorough, grounded examinations of the ramifications of this trend. Work produced by contemporary singer-songwriters is inherently nostalgic, trading heavily in conventions and archetypes drawn from the folk revival and folk-rock of the late 1960s and which have significantly influenced the modern genre. These conventions may establish an artist as a "craftsperson"[2] who creates work perceived to be of "great distinction for their poetic and 'meaningful'" composition.[3] Since the 1960s, singer-songwriters have been known to utilize "lyrical introspection, confessional songwriting, gentle musical arrangements and an understated performance style."[4] In drawing upon these genre norms, modern singer-songwriters invoke the powerful constructions of authenticity that are associated with these modes of musical communication. By making more extensive use of past aural, visual, thematic, and rhetorical elements, singer-songwriters may go beyond convention and imaginatively reconstruct a nostalgic version of the past.

With this heritage at their disposal, indie folk singer-songwriters act in a manner that can be likened to the habits of bowerbirds. Bowerbirds are known for building treasure-filled nests referred to as "bowers" from found objects. Gathered according to what a particular bowerbird deems attractive, bowers often comprise unexpected items collected from the local habitat and thus may equally utilize coins, colored glass, or pieces of plastic in addition to natural objects such as leaves, flowers, feathers, stones, and seashells. The invented verb "bowerbirding" used throughout this chapter likens indie folk singer-songwriters' creative process to the bowerbird's deliberate, taste-based collecting of desirable items, highlighting the unique nature of the culminating product. Indie folk singer-songwriters often produce works that display similarly eclectic, sometimes astonishing, juxtapositions of elements from the past and the present, resulting in musical works that are distinct and idiosyncratic. The myriad ways indie folk singer-songwriters' bowerbird heritage and innovation, re-figuring and re-using outmoded sounds, images, ideas, and conventions alongside contemporary techniques in the creation of new work, insert reconstructed nostalgic pasts into the current moment as substitutes for reality and as objects of longing. In their nostalgic departure from the present, singer-songwriters betray ambivalence, even anxiety, about certain aspects of contemporary life and exist in a state of temporal rupture on the boundaries of past, present, and future.

This chapter will examine bowerbirding of elements from the past and the present in work by three contemporary musicians operating in the indie folk genre: Justin Vernon (best known as his alter ego, Bon Iver), Joanna Newsom, and Sufjan Stevens. These three prominent North American singer-songwriters are useful subjects for an analysis of nostalgic bowerbirding due to the similarities and differences their work demonstrates. Vernon, Newsom, and Stevens have all been active in the same time period, with international careers spanning approximately a decade from the mid-2000s until the present day. Justin Vernon's debut as Bon Iver was 2007's *For Emma, Forever Ago*, a barren and solitary album which quickly transitioned from an initial small-scale independent release to wider international distribution. *For Emma* charted internationally and was followed in 2011 with the expansive, self-titled *Bon Iver*, which won the Grammy for Best Alternative Music Album in 2012. Bon Iver was named Best New Artist in the same awards. In 2009 and 2013 Vernon released albums with band Volcano Choir that were also critically well received both in the U.S. and abroad. Joanna Newsom's career thus far demonstrates a similar trajectory from obscurity to relative eminence, including a significant cinematic appearance in 2014 film *Inherent Vice*. Her first broadly distributed album *The Milk-Eyed Mender*, released in 2004, achieved notoriety as much for the divisive nature of her singing as for its unusual use of solo harp to accompany the album's twelve folk-pop songs. Her second album, 2006's *Ys*, bore a decisive mellowing of her vocals alongside the expansion of her instrumental range to include a symphony orchestra with her, alongside her signature harp, but remained unconventional due to its use of long song forms that do not adhere to simple verse–chorus structures. Her most recent albums, *Have One On Me* (2010) and *Divers* (2015), blend the stylistic extremes articulated in her early work and convey a distinct artistic maturity in her more controlled vocal tone and her highly polished songwriting. Sufjan Stevens rose to international prominence with 2003's *Michigan*, the first offering of the "50 states project" in which he promised an album for each state in North America. Although only one further album was released in this project, 2005's *Illinois*, Stevens's other albums, *Seven Swans* (2004), *The Age of Adz* (2010), and *Carrie and Lowell* (2015), were critically well received and displayed varied musical influences ranging from traditional folk to electronica. An adept arranger, Stevens's work characteristically includes decorative textural flourishes from woodwind, brass, and string instruments. The variations within and between the works of these three artists offer a reasonably representative sample of indie folk's general tendencies. Noting the major nostalgic themes that emerge through their bowerbirding of past and present indie and folk music conventions, the following analysis will reveal sites of environmental, social, and spiritual anxiety for which the nostalgically reconstructed past attempts to compensate.

Nostalgic reimagining: Bowerbirding indie and folk

The bowerbirding process of creating a new work that cobbles together past and present conventions from a range of styles and systems is necessarily nostalgic, highlighting and foregrounding favored elements from music and culture of the past while discarding those that are undesirable or of little interest. Cultural historian Raphael Samuel calls this "retrochic," which he likens to "salvage" or "beach-combing,"[5] suggesting that "[m]usically it draws its energies from the juxtaposition and assimilation of wildly dissonant lexicons ... and calls on centuries of songwriting, as well as echoes and half echoes of its own more recent past."[6] He further argues that constructing retrochic works is an active and engaged process that magnifies the significance of the relics it bowerbirds, stating:

> Retrochic trades on inversion, discovering hitherto unnoticed beauties in the flotsam and jetsam of everyday life; elevating yesterday's cast-offs into antique clothes and vintage wear; and treating the out-of-date and anachronistic – or imitations of them – as though they were the latest thing.[7]

Samuel notes two key aspects of the bowerbirding process. First, he highlights its irreverence, in its frequent combining of highly divergent sounds and styles based purely on the singer-songwriter's personal tastes. The resultant work is unique to the performer, but in Samuel's reckoning it also "draws its energy" from this convergence of varied elements. Second, Samuel observes the very visible and obvious place of the past in this music. Although music from any genre is inevitably influenced by its predecessors in some way, hybrid genres like indie folk make reference to sounds, styles, and aesthetics from the past in a shameless manner that at its best appropriates and references, and at its worst duplicates and counterfeits.

While Samuel characterizes the retrochic process as an active and engaged adoration of objects and artifacts, art historian Hal Foster observes the same blending process in contemporary art and architecture but finds its irreverence problematic for its dismissal of the potential conflict of different relics' contexts.[8] Indeed, indie folk singer-songwriters operate in a completely new technological landscape than their predecessors. The digitization of music creation, production, and distribution allows greater scope for artists to work entirely independently, and democratizes audiences' access to a wide range of listening opportunities. Foster's concerns are to some extent valid in indie folk; bowerbirding does place disparate, often surprising, combinations of past artifacts into an entirely new cultural and musical context. However, indie folk also acknowledges its heritage, trading in the original genre context Foster prizes. In particular the use of singer-songwriter conventions from folk music, such as confessional, introspective lyrics and performance styles, and from indie music, such as the DIY aesthetic (now enabled digitally), associates contemporary singer-songwriters with a long heritage of performers and imparts newly minted songs with the authority and distinction accorded their forebears. Indie folk's bowerbirding is an active and engaged process of individuation that relies on elements drawn from its indie and folk roots, refashioned for a new context.

Indie folk singer-songwriters have two divergent schools of musical style and convention at their disposal: indie, which is more commonly associated with a rock aesthetic, and folk, which here includes supposedly "pure" traditional folk music as well as the dominant folk-rock genres popular from the late 1960s. Indie music of the 1980s and early 1990s defined itself by its independence from major labels, which were perceived to exert a homogenizing force on their artists in service of commercial interests.[9] The indie underground's DIY aesthetic and distribution via fan networks during this period was seen to allow more scope for artistic license.[10] Contemporary indie folk, while not explicitly anti-major label, continues a tradition which prizes artistic idiosyncrasy over widespread commercial success.[11] Indie folk's use of home and lo-fi recording technologies further represents the heritage and ideological underpinnings inherited from indie. Despite advances in technology meaning home recordings are often highly polished products which may bear little auditory resemblance to their lo-fi forebears, there remains a profound difference in the artistic freedom DIY recording is presumed to provide by comparison to studio-based productions. Drawing on the techniques and ideologies of indie music associates contemporary singer-songwriters with independent artists of the past, privileging creativity over marketability.

The folk heritage of indie folk also relies on a perceived authenticity defined "in opposition to commercial pop."[12] Indie folk draws on music from both the traditional folk canon and the folk-rock movement of the mid-to-late 1960s. In both cases a performer's supposed authenticity, perceived to be linked to either their accurate renditions of orally transmitted, communally owned, traditional tunes, or their performances bearing markers of "soulbaring and poetic vision,"[13] was crucial. A fundamentally imaginary folk heritage, described by rock critic Simon Reynolds as "the unsettled wildness of early America; a self-reliant existence, outside society and remote from urban centres,"[14] underpins the ideology of folk's authenticity. Indie folk uses this heritage of constructed authenticity by drawing upon acoustic or understated sounds, a homemade or amateur aesthetic that connects it with DIY in indie,[15] and intimate lyrics often conveying folk archetypes. The various constructions at work in indie folk in no way diminish in authority when they are understood to be constructions.[16] Authenticity, folk archetypes, and the imagined past are conventionally constructed communicative elements of indie folk singer-songwriters' nostalgic discourse, serving to emphasize desired aspects of the past.

Nostalgia and cultural anxiety

Nostalgia highlights cultural anxieties about the present by adoring and longing for aspects of the past that may be perceived as under some kind of threat. Sociologist Fred Davis highlights the unconscious nature of this activity, stating: "the nostalgic evocation of some past state of affairs always occurs in the context of present fears, discontents, anxieties or uncertainties even though these may not be in the forefront of the person's awareness."[17] This unawareness is crucial for the analysis to follow. It is not the position of this chapter that indie folk singer-songwriters deliberately, consciously use their craft as a vehicle for communicating cultural anxieties. Rather, it argues that as indie folk singer-songwriters go about their ordinary business of songwriting, recording, and performing, they bowerbird elements from the past and present in a way which constructs a particular, nostalgic version of the past. The things, specific and general, about which they are nostalgic hint at complementary absences or dissatisfactions in contemporary culture, which in the following analytical examples occur around the statuses of the natural world, the home, and the sacred. The process of reimagining the past occurs partly as a means of overwriting these potentially problematic aspects of the present.

The analysis to follow will consider three significant thematic areas which appear in the work of all three selected singer-songwriters, but in the interests of brevity each theme will be paired with one performer. Bon Iver's debut album will be used to elaborate the position of *nature* archetypes in indie folk, musically, and rhetorically outlining a precious and inspiring nature space under threat. Longing for *home*, absent in time as well as space, is manifested through the proliferation of the homemade and DIY aesthetic with its privileging of perceived amateurism, as will be demonstrated through an analysis of Joanna Newsom's work. Finally, uncertainties surrounding the *sacred* in contemporary life are considered in the context of Sufjan Stevens's songwriting practice, with its flexible and selective theological, cultural, and memorial references. Using these three themes as the nexus for the examination also provides a thorough overview of singer-songwriter practice within broader culture, considering songwriters versus their environment in *nature,* versus society in *home*, and versus the spiritual in *sacred*. By examining the ways these indie folk singer-songwriters communicate nostalgia by bowerbirding elements from the past and present, the particular cultural uncertainties relevant to the performers, and by extension their audiences, may be extrapolated.

Bon Iver: Nostalgia for nature's primacy

A nostalgic tale is circulated about Bon Iver's debut album, *For Emma, Forever Ago* (2007), which situates the record firmly in the bitter and unforgiving landscape of winter in the Wisconsin forest. Initially told through the album's press release and later through other media, the story is inseparable from the album itself. It informs the ways audiences and critics receive the album, and communicates the ideological importance of natural world narratives for singer-songwriters in indie folk. According to the tale, Justin Vernon was in personal and professional meltdown prior to the recording of what became *For Emma*. In emotional, physical, and financial strife, Vernon repaired to his family's isolated cabin in the Wisconsin woods to recuperate. The time however also proved creatively productive. With the thaw in the weather Vernon completed a transformation, returning from the cabin under the moniker Bon Iver, a deliberate misspelling of the French *bon hiver* or "good winter," and bearing the tracks that were later released as *For Emma* that were said to comprise "[all] his personal trouble, lack of perspective, heartache, longing, love, loss and guilt … suddenly purged into the form of a song."[18]

This narrative nostalgically romanticizes the impact of nature spaces on singer-songwriters, employing tropes of Edenic return identified by environmental historian Carolyn Merchant as "the most important mythology humans have developed to make sense of their relationship to the earth."[19] The *For Emma* narrative constructs a perfect nature space entirely separate from the human, where Reynolds's "self-reliant existence"[20] can be pursued and where social pressures are not keenly felt. Vernon is linked with bohemian archetypes that imagine nature as a site of authentic creativity, in contrast with stereotypes casting the urban as dominated by capitalism, commercialism, and artificiality. This portrayal is idealistic more than it is realistic, decorating Vernon's actual experience with bowerbirded mythology associated with reclaiming a lost natural Paradise. A closer examination of Vernon's retreat shows that the cabin was reasonably comfortable, and close enough to the nearest town that he received a number of visitors over the winter, many of whom participated in the recording of *For Emma*. On a complex level this story draws upon constructions of the natural world as a nurturing and healing Edenic space that bolsters creativity by providing singer-songwriters with a retreat from the distractions of civilization, and hints at anxiety that these two spaces exist in conflict.

The imagined, natural, wintry landscape of *For Emma*'s accompanying narrative is further conveyed through the album's distinctive musical and lyrical elements. These portray a romanticized construction of a natural order in which winter, while cold and melancholy, always gives way to the growth and renewal of spring. Occasional references to the winter are scattered throughout the lyrics on *For Emma*; "Blindsided," "For Emma," and "re:stacks" all explicitly mention snow or freezing, using nature as a metaphor for the emotional state of the songs' protagonists and communicating stasis, discordance, termination, and immuration. The album's irregular soundscape elements illustrate this nostalgic landscape. "Flume" utilizes an E-Bow's mechanical clatter alongside warm tape splices and synthesizer to create a spare and barren sonic space. The slow introduction of consonant and dissonant, indistinct layered vocals on "Lump Sum" is used to spacious and eerie effect. Vernon's peculiar use of falsetto here and throughout the album positions the primary melodic material in his upper register, lending the vocals a delicate and fragile crispness, while the addition of further layered vocals with considerable reverb swaddle the melody, as if against the cold, so it retains a sense of frailty without becoming insubstantial. Whether these auditory effects denote the presence of winter for some or for many listeners, the careful balance of wintry bleakness against spring's renewal on *For Emma* draws on nostalgic archetypal representations of nature.

In aspects of creation and substance, *For Emma* portrays nature as providing an escape from civilization, an alternative to commercialism and predictability through cyclical renewal. Bon Iver's idiosyncratic sonic elicitation of winter elaborates the album's thematic examination, creating an enclosed, contained space and giving primacy to the natural world's beautiful and brutal character. Nature is constructed as simultaneously creatively inspiring and fundamentally other. Ambivalence is suggested toward the dominance of the urban and supposedly civilized. These conceptions of nature's purpose and character offer neither strictly credible nor factual accounts. *For Emma*'s nostalgic interpretations of stereotypes and archetypes of nature, and its function in culture, both communicate with and capitalize upon cultural anxiety surrounding perceived urban dominance and the diminishing of nature spaces. Although nature is positioned opposing civilization, certain aspects of society are also presented as objects of longing by singer-songwriters in indie folk.

Joanna Newsom: Home, intimacy, domesticity

Indie folk singer-songwriters' work uses intimacy and domestic space to convey longing for home. Discussing immigrants' experiences of displacement, cultural theorist Svetlana Boym suggests nostalgia for home often manifests as longing for familiarity and intimacy. She notes that the absent immigrant's homeland undergoes changes over time, becoming both physically and temporally distant and eventually existing only in the past and in the immigrant's nostalgic memories. Immigrants and natives alike may experience this nostalgia for an extinct home. Boym observes a less location-specific longing for home emerging with the knowledge of impossible return,[21] stating:

> To feel at home is to know that things are in their places and so are you; it is a state of mind that doesn't depend on actual location. The object of longing, then, is not really a place called home but this sense of intimacy with the world; it is not the past in general but that imaginary moment when we had time and didn't know the temptation of nostalgia.[22]

Nostalgia for home by indie folk singer-songwriters is partly observable in their use of DIY aesthetics. Occasional amateur aspects of performance, references to the folk tradition's prioritization of the local, and homemade visual and aural markers situate works that display these tendencies within domestic and intimate home spaces. Indie folk singer-songwriters' use of DIY aesthetics creates intimacy, and then attempts to close the distance between the present and the nostalgically longed-for home of the past.

Although indie folk albums are not summarily recorded in the home rather than the studio, Encarnacao observes that many of these albums still carry "connotations of domesticity."[23] In the case of Joanna Newsom's 2004 debut, *The Milk-Eyed Mender*, Encarnacao argues that although the album sounds "professionally recorded ... the performative elements and minimal instrumentation of the tracks impart an intimacy that suggests a private space."[24] Listeners are given access to this intimate space through the album's visual and auditory invitations. The album art on *Mender* conveys nostalgic intimacy by its overtly homemade look. Combining untidy embroidery with photographs and loose-woven hessian textures, the artwork is a loving collage of found and hand-made objects which visually articulates the bowerbirding process at work. In later albums this visual homecrafting is not as conspicuous, but the precious treatment of the domestic remains. The cover of 2010's *Have One On Me*, for example, features a photograph of Newsom elegantly camouflaged in the midst of an extensive collection of meubles and ornamental household objects.[25] Newsom's figure is absorbed and shrouded within her bower, surrounded by carefully selected and arranged domestic objects. The inside CD sleeves include a series of black-and-white photographs of her arranging her hair that offers covert access to private moments. In the exterior and interior images of *Have One On Me* she is at home in the intimate spaces depicted, situating the works she creates also within the private space. Using these distinctly homemade and intimate characteristics in a publicly available artistic product allows listeners access to domestic space.

The albums' aural production techniques affirm this positioning of Newsom and her work within imagined domestic space. In particular, Newsom's critically divisive vocals have an amateurish element to them which runs counter to other complex and meticulously worked aspects of the album's songwriting. Described variously by reviewers as "a ragged, childlike voice, sent to us from the gods in heaven"[26] or as having the potential to "compel certain listeners to want to throw her CDs out the window,"[27] her vocal "incomparable mish-mash of warbles, squeaks and pops"[28] aligns her work with folk traditions that conflate authenticity with simplicity of production. In interviews she explains her idiosyncratic singing, particularly apparent on her early albums, as the result of inexperience, describing her voice as untrained and her singing as influenced by the Appalachian folk tradition.[29] Associating her work with folk's oral transmission and amateur production values further situates Newsom's music within intimate spaces of domestic production. She describes her songwriting process in highly domestic terms, stating: "I have little objects and every once in a while I take them out of my pockets, lay them all in a row and I like the way they look next to each other, so that's a song!"[30] Her works often depict her own home or family with longing, as is the case for tracks "Emily" or "In California." The domestic references in her work are sometimes specific to her hometown or childhood, and other times draw on collective and cultural memory. Newsom depicts real and imagined domestic space in a manner which elides intimacy and folk conventions, conveying nostalgic longing for belonging.

Newsom conveys the intimate and the domestic through use of DIY aesthetics and links to folk heritage. This desire for home spaces is primarily informed by nostalgic longing for the past, as argued convincingly when Lowenthal states, "the past is tangible and secure; people think of it as fixed, unalterable, indelibly recorded ... We are at home in it because it is our home – the past is where we came from."[31] Using general markers such as homemade styling, amateur production values, and folk references, Newsom conjures collectively recognized and owned intimacy and domesticity. When conveying intimacy, indie folk singer-songwriters recreate a home from which they are separated by physical and temporal distance. The imaginative re-construction of an extinct home space that does not rely on reality fills the space between desire and fulfillment of nostalgic longing for home. In addition to the longing for home discussed here, references to folk heritage and mythology may also convey spiritual nostalgia.

Sufjan Stevens and the nostalgic sacred

At the heart of Sufjan Stevens's musically varied and highly idiosyncratic oeuvre lies a thematic fascination with Christian traditions, in particular apocalyptic narratives. Literary philosopher George Steiner suggests attraction to sacred and secular spiritual mythologies pervades Western culture due to a "decline of religious certitude"[32] leading to a social "hunger for myths, for total explanation: we are starving for guaranteed prophecy."[33] This tendency, which Steiner calls "nostalgia for the absolute," does not require the wholesale adoption or appropriation of a belief system and may instead involve bowerbirding particular rites or assertions from various doctrinal sources to construct a personally and culturally palatable spiritual framework. Cultural commentator David Brooks borrows the term "flexidoxy" from Rabbi Gershon Winkler to describe the educated class's desired religious system; one which offers "a hybrid mixture of freedom and flexibility on the one hand, and the longing for rigor and orthodoxy on the other."[34] Sufjan Stevens's work bowerbirds a conception of the Christian God as humanity's powerful and mystical supernatural creator-judge, an idea often conveyed in gospel-style folk music of the first half of the twentieth century, with more recent sounds and technologies. In doing so Stevens subverts conventional models of Christianity and Christian music production of the late twentieth and early twenty-first centuries, hybridizing present musical technologies with past ideologies and doctrines.

Stevens's communication of the sacred is impacted by his music's sound, which is highly technical and very polished while still adhering to some folk and indie conventions. His work eschews amateurism, while still bearing strong connections to indie music's DIY culture in the sense that Stevens is involved in nearly every element of a project's completion and execution, including composing, arranging, performing, recording, engineering, and styling most of his albums. Stevens openly acknowledges his music's connection to folk, describing himself in a recent interview as "fundamentally a narrative folk singer, first and foremost."[35] This songwriting identity dominates his work's expression of the sacred, from the banjo-laden prophetic hymns of 2004's *Seven Swans* to the delicate and desolate interrogation of the afterlife on *Carrie and Lowell* in 2015. Folk's confessional narratives pervade even where Stevens's albums deviate sonically from folk's conventional acoustic instrumentation and intimate expression, as occurs on 2010's electronically influenced *Age of Adz*. These departures from the common amateurism of folk and indie demonstrate the bowerbirding process in Stevens's work. Stevens uses contemporary sounds and production techniques while simultaneously communicating conceptions of God drawn from earlier musical and doctrinal periods.

Stevens's work draws significantly on the representation of the sacred found in various traditional folk songs without adopting their sound or performance style. Useful examples of this heritage are found on the second volume of Harry Smith's *Anthology of American Folk Music*. Although the *Anthology* is a slightly problematic resource if mistaken for an ethnographic or anthropological collection of field recordings, which it is not, Smith's work of creative curation nevertheless provides several examples which represent this aspect of Stevens's musical heritage. Nominally titled "Social Music," the *Anthology*'s second volume contains traditional folk tracks performed by various Reverends and church singing groups that collectively foreground God's supernatural power and inscrutability. Apocalyptic prophecy and the coming judgment are seamlessly amalgamated with everyday human concerns. For example, Rev. Sister Mary Nelson's performance, "Judgement," warns a disbelieving public of God's impending judgment, drawing on images from the biblical book of Revelation. Repentence and judgment are examined in similar, though modernized, terms by Stevens in tracks such as "Get Real, Get Right," "Seven Swans," and "The Tranfiguration." Where Stevens calls on God for help in times of calamity, as he does in "Oh God, Where Are You Now?" or "John My Beloved," his work recalls traditional folk hymns that seek God's intercession found in the *Anthology*, like "Since I Laid My Burdens Down" or "Shine On Me." Stevens's tracks actively rebel against modern conceptions of God in Christian music, drawing nostalgically on representations of God's omnipotence conveyed in traditional gospel folk songs.

Stevens's work is nostalgic in the sense that it possesses a kind of antiheritage, conveyed through his conscious disassociation with the Christian Contemporary Music (CCM) market and forms of Liberal Protestantism dominant in the second half of the twentieth century. CCM emerged from the Jesus People movement which began in North America in the mid-1960s.[36] Approximately concurrent with the folk revival, the Jesus

People actively sought to create a dialogue and connection between their Christian faith and the period's youth culture.[37] As a result, the music produced by the Jesus People bears many musical and stylistic similarities to that of the folk revival and later folk-rock, but unlike its secular contemporaries it explicitly communicated Christian morals and ideology. The Jesus People movement reflected a growing trend in the Western evangelical church toward Liberal Protestantism, which has pervaded since this time. Reaching its zenith in the 1970s and 1980s, when Stevens was growing up, Liberal Protestantism sought to make Christianity more approachable by finding correlations between contemporary culture and traditional church doctrine, and reshaping Christianity in culturally meaningful forms.[38] By the 1990s, the Liberal Protestant model and the example set by the Jesus People had spawned a "formidable [entertainment] industry"[39] focused on the production and dissemination of music made by Christians and communicating the gospel message as they perceive it, one of "redemption, reconciliation and renewal."[40] Stevens is openly dubious about CCM, categorizing it as "'devotional artifice' and 'didactic crap'"[41] and questioning its authenticity, stating: "Christian music (as a genre) exists exclusively within a few insulated floors ... of some corporate construction in Nashville, Tennessee. Otherwise, there's no such thing as Christian music."[42] Further to these categorical attempts to create separation between his work and CCM, Stevens's music's utilization of earlier doctrines conveys suspicion of more recent Christian culture. His strong interest in the prophetic supernatural elicits the Christian church's neo-orthodoxy trend of the 1930s, which emphasized God's otherness.[43]

Highlighting supernatural elements of Christian theology such as prophecy, miracles, divine intervention, and apocalypse, Stevens communicates ambivalence to biblical interpretations that downplay God's divinity in promoting His accessibility. Leapfrogging over forms of Christian thought and creative practice that dominated the last fifty years, Stevens's work suggests disdain for conceptions of the sacred in contemporary culture and nostalgically longs for past doctrine and practice.

Conclusion: The past as future

The presence of the past in music created by singer-songwriters in indie folk is unavoidable. The past is referenced where singer-songwriters draw upon the conventions of their musical forebears from indie or folk traditions, aligning themselves with supposedly anti-commercial ideologies and establishing themselves as primarily interested in what is perceived as authentic songcraft and artistic expression. The past is palpable through the bowerbirding process, by which singer-songwriters may select desirable sounds, aesthetics, and themes from bygone times, irreverently combining them with present-day elements and creating unique and idiosyncratic works that conjure the past while remaining firmly contemporary articles. The past is evoked where cultural archetypes are drawn upon to reconstruct imagined versions of the past, conveying nostalgia for aspects of collective and individual heritage. Although singer-songwriters such as those examined here generally communicate their musical and cultural inheritance in an unconscious and unintended manner, a nostalgic past is nevertheless constructed in the ways it is referenced and manifested in indie folk music.

Bowerbirding certain, specifically selected, aspects of musical and cultural heritage communicates nostalgia for the imagined past, uncertainties about the present, and desires for the future. Through the adoring representation of the wintry landscape and rhetoric surrounding *For Emma, Forever Ago*, Bon Iver communicates nostalgia for nature as a primary and uncontrollable force. Complementary anxieties about the status of the natural world in the present, and longing for a future in which the separation of human and environmental spheres remain intact, are implied. Joanna Newsom's use of DIY aesthetics to create intimate-sounding music conveys a desire for the restoration of domestic "home" spaces of the past. In the knowledge of impossible return to a past that is absent in time as well as space, intimacy and domesticity are made to stand in for the longed-for home in the present and future. Imagining the future involves a return to the sacred past in Sufjan Stevens's work. Drawing on conceptions of God as absolute deity conveyed in gospel folk song, and eschewing Christian doctrine and culture of the latter half of the twentieth century, Stevens's music nostalgically foregrounds God's power and mystery. In each case, the form in which singer-songwriters imaginatively construct the past implies the shape of the desired present and future. The past's presence in indie folk is not casual, but rather plays particular roles in communicating individual and collective desires.

Acknowledgments

Many thanks to Dr. Peter Elliott of Perth Bible College for assistance with matters pertaining to church history and bible translations, and to Dr. Diana Blom, Dr. Kate Fagan, and Mr. John Encarnacao for their editorial suggestions and endless patience.

Notes

1 See, for example, Stephanie Coontz in *The Way We Never Were: American Families and the Nostalgia Trap* 2nd edn (New York: Basic Books, 2000), 22;

David Lowenthal in *The Past is a Foreign Country* (Cambridge: Cambridge University Press, 1985), 69; Raphael Samuel in *Theatres of Memory Vol. 1: Past and Present in Contemporary Culture* (London, New York: Verso, 1994), 17; and Simon Reynolds's *Retromania* (New York: Faber and Faber, 2011), xx.

2 Robert Strachan and Marion Leonard, "Singer-songwriter," in *Continuum Encyclopedia of Popular Music and the World*, eds. John Shepherd and David Horn (New York: Continuum, 2003), 199.

3 Gillian Mitchell, *North American Folk Music Revival: Nation and Identity in the United States and Canada, 1945–1980* (Farnham, Burlington: Ashgate, 2007), 137.

4 Strachan and Leonard, "Singer-songwriter," 198.

5 Samuel, *Theatres of Memory*, 111–12.

6 Ibid. 90.

7 Ibid. 85.

8 Hal Foster, *Recodings: Art, Spectacle, Cultural Politics* (Washington: Bay Press, 1985), 30.

9 See Michael Azerrad, *Our Band Could Be Your Life: Scenes from the American Indie Underground 1981–1991* (New York: Back Bay Books, 2001), 5; and Ryan Hibbett, "What is Indie Rock?" *Popular Music and Society* 28 (1) (February 2005): 58.

10 Ibid.

11 John Encarnacao, *Punk Aesthetics and New Folk: Way Down the Old Plank Road* (Farnham: Ashgate, 2013), 75.

12 Simon Frith, "'The magic that can set you free': The Ideology of Folk and the Myth of Rock," *Popular Music*, 1 (1981): 162.

13 Ibid., 164.

14 Reynolds, *Retromania*, 344.

15 Encarnacao, *Punk Aesthetics*, 215.

16 Ibid., 27.

17 Fred Davis, "Nostalgia, Identity and the Current Nostalgia Wave," *Journal of Popular Culture* 11 (2) (Fall 1977): 420.

18 "Bon Iver: *For Emma, Forever Ago*," media release, Jagjaguwar, 2008. http://www.jagjaguwar.com/onesheet.php?cat=jag115 (accessed August 15, 2015).

19 Carolyn Merchant, *Reinventing Eden: The Fate of Nature in Western Culture* (London: Routledge, 2003), 2.

20 Reynolds, *Retromania*, 344.

21 Svetlana Boym, *The Future of Nostalgia* (New York: Basic Books, 2001), xiii–xv.

22 Ibid., 251.

23 Encarnacao, *Punk Aesthetics*, 200.

24 Ibid.

25 According to Jody Rosen this photo was taken in Newsom's home among her own belongings. See "Joanna Newsom, the Changeling," *New York Times*, March 3, 2010. http://www.nytimes.com/2010/03/07/magazine/07Newsom-t.html?pagewanted=all&_r=0 (accessed February 25, 2014).

26 Sally Pryor, "Joanna Newsom: The Milk-Eyed Mender," August 16, 2004. http://www.noripcord.com/reviews/music/joanna-newsom/the-milk-eyed-mender (accessed August 15, 2015).

27 Erik Davis, "Nearer the Heart of Things," *Arthur Magazine* 25 (Winter 2006). http://arthurmag.com/2006/12/23/nearer-the-heart-of-things-erik-davis-on-joanna-newsom-from-arthur-no-25winter-02006/ (accessed June 3, 2013).

28 Amanda Petrusich, "Invisible Jukebox," *The Wire*, Issue 314 (April 2010): 27.

29 Erik Davis, "Nearer the Heart of Things."

30 Ibid.

31 Lowenthal, *The Past is a Foreign Country*, 4.

32 George Steiner, *Nostalgia for the Absolute* (Toronto: CBC Publications, 1974), 5.

33 Ibid, 6.

34 David Brooks, *Bobos In Paradise: The New Upper Class and How They Got There* (New York: Simon and Schuster Paperbacks, 2000) 224.

35 Dave Eggers, "Sufjan Stevens talks to Dave Eggers: 'I was recording songs as a means of grieving'," *Guardian*, March 27, 2015. http://www.theguardian.com/music/2015/mar/26/sufjan-stevens-dave-eggers-carrie-lowell-i-was-recording-songs-means-of-grieving (accessed April 15, 2015).

36 Omotayo O. Banjo and Kesha Morant Williams, "A House Divided? Christian Music in Black and White," *Journal of Media and Religion* 10 (3) (2011): 117.

37 David Roark, "How Sufjan Stevens Subverts the Stigma of Christian Music," *The Atlantic*, March 29, 2015. http://www.theatlantic.com/entertainment/archive/2015/03/sufjan-stevens-and-a-better-way-to-write-music-about-faith/388802/ (accessed August 30, 2015).

38 Alister McGrath, *Historical Theology: An Introduction to the History of Christian Thought*, 2nd edn (Chichester: Wiley-Blackwell, 2013), 196.

39 Banjo and Williams, "A House Divided," 117.

40 Ibid.

41 Roark, "Stevens Subverts Christian Music."

42 Ibid.

43 McGrath, *Historical Theology*, 199–200.

CHAPTER 17

Play the Bluebird to the Bitter End: Open mics in Nashville, NYC, and Shanghai

Juliane Jones

In Paris at P'tit Bonheur La Chance, at Yuyintang in Shanghai, in London at Green Note, in Nashville at the Bluebird Cafe, in NYC at the Bitter End—the host calls my name, I plug in my guitar and approach the mic. I am surrounded by open-minded listeners and courageous artists: a seasoned songwriter who came to test new material, a theater major visiting to see if she could make a living as an artist, a music school university student perfecting her craft, a ten-year-old aspiring songwriter, a tourist passerby drawn in by the sound of guitars. This is an open mic—almost anything can happen.

An open mic is a live show of individual performances, run by a host, that usually takes place on a regular basis (weekly or monthly) at a music venue or coffeehouse. Open mics may include poetry reading, instrumental music, and comedy acts; here, we focus on open mics for singer-songwriters. The open mic participatory format has roots in the folk music hootenanny, a celebratory gathering where audience members often joined in.[1] Weekly hootenannies took place in Greenwich Village in the 1960s at iconic venues that have long since closed, like Gerde's Folk City and the Gaslight. Open mics vary in *format* and *feel* depending on the venue, host, and the city's musical culture. Sometimes there is a lottery system to determine the order of performers; other times there is a signup sheet. The atmosphere of the event may be that of an amateur community gathering, nurturing performance training ground, or competitive showcase environment. Because open mics rely on a mixture of regular and visiting musician-participants passing through a city to record or check out an urban music scene, and anyone can sign up, performances vary widely. There are open mics for singer-songwriters around the world, but the term "open mic" is generally not translated from English, and remains associated with freedom of expression and Western popular music.[2]

Open mics feature singer-songwriters who perform a repertoire of songs to which notions of personal authenticity—that is, appearing genuine to the self and thus also to the audience—have consistently been attached.[3] In performance, singer-songwriters generate personal authenticity through the illusion of unmediated communication with typically acoustic music and intimate lyrics. The concept of the authentic singer-songwriter is associated with 1960s and 1970s songwriters like Carole King, Joni Mitchell, and Bob Dylan, who were inspired by the American Folk Music Revival, but wrote personal songs rather than only performing traditional repertoire.[4] While personal authenticity remains a trademark of the singer-songwriter genre, the genre has broadened.[5] In the 1980s, the anti-folk movement—characterized by subversive lyrics set to acoustic music—began at the after-hours venue The Fort on the Lower East Side in Manhattan. Although intimate lyrics and acoustic guitar are still common in the genre, today's songwriters may use diverse instrumentation such as ukulele, types of zither, or kalimba, may have an alter ego or depict a fictional character, and interact with their audience beyond the venue: through the evolving micro-communities, blogs, and video channels on the Internet.

Open mics take place in cities around the world. In NYC alone, there are two or three well-known open mics every night of the week. I focus on two open mics, the Bluebird Cafe in Nashville, TN, and the Bitter End in Greenwich Village, NYC, because they serve as meccas for international songwriters, and demonstrate the interactions between local, regional, and global visions of popular song. These open mics have an aura that attracts songwriters on journeys akin to a pilgrimage. The aura draws people in through a confluence of shifting authenticities—shared conceptions that make an experience seem genuine. The particular authenticities, like the history of the venue and its place in the songwriter tradition, vary between open mics.[6] First, I will discuss these two clubs to investigate the underlying forces at open mics and the role these events play in the evolving music industry ecosystem.[7] Then I will examine Shanghai's rock venue Yuyintang to consider how the Western open mic relates to global cultural flows in its exported and localized manifestations on stages around the world.

The Bluebird Cafe in Nashville, Tennessee

FIGURE 17.1 *The Bluebird Cafe, 2011 (Photo by Juliane Jones)*

> *On a sweltering summer day, the line stretches long outside. It's an hour and a half before the 6pm Monday night open mic is scheduled to begin, but the visitors and Nashville natives hoping to "play the Bluebird" have already arrived. A CBS camera crew combs the line looking for models that fit the stereotype of "Music City." They stop at a young man with shoulder-length hair and aviator sunglasses sitting beside me. Brendan has flown in from California. He is a janitor by day and songwriter by night. A CBS reporter asks him: "Where are you from? What are you hoping to accomplish tonight? What are you going to do if your number isn't picked?" Brendan explains that he hopes to be discovered tonight and, in jest, to score some drugs. If he's not picked, he'll stick around for next Monday's open mic. Maybe he'll even move here …*

It's not just the 90 degrees temperature heating up the Bluebird. What exactly is this aura that draws 100 or so songwriters, myself included, from all over the United States and Canada to stand in line for hours before an open mic?

At the Bluebird, artists and listeners feel a reverence for the physical venue and the tradition of Writer's Nights, the possibility of a personal transformation of the performer, and anticipate an emphasis on self-expression revealed in lyric categories. These are all shades of authenticity that are constantly shifting according to who is authenticating. Listeners may be drawn to the site by different combinations of authenticities. I understand this convergence of authenticities as generating an *aura* around the Bluebird—the energy that stems from the thrill of live performance situated in the club's history and tradition. The aura that one experiences at the Bluebird is generated by the transformative, one-song moment of the open mic, the first tier of the Writer's Night system. At this charged moment, the songwriter has one chance to show who s/he is. The songwriter stands on a famous stage, shares an intimate story under the spotlight, could be transformed into a star, and symbolically joins the tradition of Nashville songwriters.

> *Most of the songwriters standing in line with me won't draw a high enough number to play, but they wait in line practicing and mentally preparing to perform their song if afforded the chance. I flew in for a four song recording session at a local studio and to play out my songs during the evenings.*[8] *The girls behind me drove from Iowa City, and Eric, standing next to me, is a Nashville native. I draw the number forty-seven. That's not high enough to get a slot in tonight's roster. Out of about sixty songwriters tonight, only the first twenty-five will get to play—so I take a stamp that will bump me to the first ten next time, should I choose to come back on another Monday.*[9]

The lottery format is the first step in creating a competitive atmosphere: less than half of the musicians in line draw a high enough number to perform. The discussions in the line about potentially being discovered build hype around the event. The Bluebird is no longer that "small-town" venue where talent was organically nurtured in the days Garth Brooks rolled into town looking for work. Now the venue has been bought by the Nashville Songwriters Association International to secure its lineage. It is also the stage where artists return to experience real country music on the ABC hit TV show *Nashville* that premiered in October 2012. (On the set of *Nashville,* they have created a replica of the Bluebird cafe.) Yet even in the more commercialized setting, artists hone their skills and network at the open mic.

> *Entering the Bluebird, I see a modestly decorated listening room: wooden tables and chairs, pew-like benches on the sides, plastic tablecloths, and a carpeted stage with a few chairs, mic stands, and amplifiers. Album covers of stars who have performed there line the walls. A large photograph of Taylor Swift is positioned behind the stage.*

FIGURES 17.2 AND 17.3 *Inside the Bluebird Cafe, 2011 (Photos by Juliane Jones)*

The Bluebird stakes its authenticity as a venue on being an unassuming listening room that preserves the tradition of songs performed acoustically by their original creators. Although the Bluebird is not projecting a country image of the barn dance or back porch, nor the honkey-tonk neon lights,[10] the modest decor and ban of backing tracks creates an environment that simulates spontaneous music in a family environment.

Songwriters' and listeners' shared reverence for the venue is rooted in the history of country music in Nashville and the model of the Grand Ole Opry. The Bluebird's projection of itself as authentic through its down-home image and rules for performance is reinforced by songwriters' reflexive comments about the venue when on stage. At the Grand Ole Opry House east of downtown Nashville, a six-foot circle of dark oak that was cut from the former stage at Ryman Auditorium, where the Opry was housed from 1943 to 1974, is inlaid into the center of the new stage.[11] Throughout the history of the Opry, performers have reveled in the memory of playing on the same stage as former country legends such as Hank Williams (1923–53), Patsy Cline (1932–63), and Johnny Cash (1932–2003). At the open mic, there is a similar reverence for the past based on the notion of stage as shrine. One songwriter at the open mic proclaimed after his performance: "If I die and go to heaven tonight, at least I'll know I played on this stage."

Promise of transformation and personal expression

The Bluebird has historically been a gateway to record deals. Songwriters know this was the stage where Garth Brooks, Faith Hill, and Taylor Swift among others started off their careers. Reinforcing a shared belief in the promise of transformation, songwriters' lyrics express the desire for reinvention of the self and/or possibility to become a star. In "Dreamer," fourteen-year-old Codi Lester sings about this, narrating her own journey from South Carolina to Nashville.

> *So what do you do when your dreams are bigger than you / Do you stare and act like you don't care if they never come true / What do you say to people trying to hate / You just smile and walk on by because you've got faith / So what do you do when your dreams are bigger than you.*[12]

At the Bluebird, the moments on stage are intensified by the risk a songwriter takes in sharing intimate lyrics in front of an audience. The most performed songs depict being *in love* and *hurting love. In love* songs typically characterize love as sublime or unexplainable and often use metaphors of travel, games, and photographs. *Hurting love* songs often express regret and nostalgia for lost love, commonly with metaphors of burning. Fewer songs are not explicitly about love, but there are typically at least some in the following lyric categories: Songs of *revelry* usually depict a male narrator in a bar scene, drinking and picking up women. Songs about *church* depict the small-town community. Other common song themes include family relationships, faith in God, travel, revenge, comedy, soul searching, and death. Songwriters who play the Bluebird generally know the categories established by Nashville hit-songwriters, and attempt to fit within them.

On the Monday night open mic, each songwriter plays one song. In some acts the stage is a cathartic space for expressing sadness and personal loss; in others it is a safe space to sing about a violent, illegal act; in others it is a space for re-invention of the self; for others it is a space where the sacred and secular merge in song; and in many others, it is a place to chase dreams.

> *A duo of two men in their early 20s narrate their struggle as songwriters in Nashville. They have Taylor guitars and one has a harmonica. They sing: "It's a matter of timing of rhythm and rhyming, playing my own country hits / but it's one wrong decision from head on collision / that will send me to calling it quits." I am led through familiar sites such as downtown Nashville, and the duo references playing the Bluebird. This song exemplifies the common subject of songwriters singing about the struggle along their musical journey.*

At this open mic, there are five teenage girls hoping to be signed by a label. Sixteen-year-old Hanna sings her hook: "I'm sorry that I'm not sorry, but you picked the wrong girl," a classic break-up song in pop-country style. Eleven-year-old Katy sings a piece about loneliness and the struggle to be her inner self. Mickey, twenty, sings a lost love song, "Go After Your Girl." The girls at this open mic generally portray themselves as sensitive and sentimental, and emphasize their young age. In the Nashville music industry, the younger you are the better chance you have at becoming the next Nashville sweetheart. The emphasis on youth is particularly directed toward women; the stage, however, becomes a site for violence and revelry for many of the young men. "Mr. B" fiercely strums his Martin guitar as he sings "On the Run."

> *There's nothing left for me in this damn town / except a bottle on the floor*
> *Every last bridge I built I burnt it down / and slammed shut every door*
> *The bitter bastard in this busted mirror / clutches a broken bloody fist*
> *It's time to leave, there's nothing left round here / It's just another for the list*
>
> *Another battle with the blues, another brawl another bruise*
> *Somewhere there's someone going to lose*

I know I'm not the only one to trigger a loaded gun
I'm on the run, I'm on the run

Another songwriter sings "Sweet Love and Whisky." In this song, he picks up a girl at a bar and takes her home in his truck. The refrain is: "I'm a wild child country style bad to the bone / She's a redneck heart attack taking my soul / Fellows kick back tilt your head to the blond / She said sweet love and whisky, yeah gets you going." The male songwriters portray themselves as reckless and wild, whereas the women characterize themselves as youthful and nostalgic for lost love. Why do songwriters reinforce gender stereotypes even in their original lyrics? Many songwriters assume they will not succeed if they play too far out of the accepted musical and lyrical boundaries set up by precedent in the music industry.

The open mic finishes without a conclusion. In these acts, I have travelled to landscapes of Paris, Nashville, LA, and Santa Fe, as well as to psychological landscapes of loneliness, longing, fear of death, and violence. Many of the songs used imagery from Nashville and the surrounding countryside, but one song took me to the depths of being trapped in a caved-in mine, while another brought me to the heights of flying to the moon and jumping off of buildings. I feel mentally exhausted after hearing these songs—some polished and some still in process.

At the Bluebird, songwriters generate the illusion of authenticity in songs with intimate and risky lyrics usually about love or conviction to portraying a character. If the singer-songwriters were playing on the street or at another famous venue, their performance would not carry the same meaning. The aura of the Bluebird comes from the thrill of live performance embedded in a unique history and tradition where transformation to stardom seems possible.

The Bitter End in Greenwich Village, NYC

I close my eyes and imagine the "different village" that Bob Dylan described of 1960s lower Manhattan where snow piled up in the streets, where "Nobody had nothing / There was nothing to get / Instead of being drawn for money you were drawn for other people / ..."[13] *When I step into the Bitter End where Dylan played in the early 1960s, it feels like entering a museum for that lost village he described of smoky late-night bars where troubadors flocked. Even as the Bitter End of 2015 commemorates its past with a mural of legends like Bob Dylan, Joni Mitchell, and Stevie Wonder who performed there—it has a distinct*

FIGURE 17.4 *The Bitter End, 2015 (Photo by Juliane Jones)*

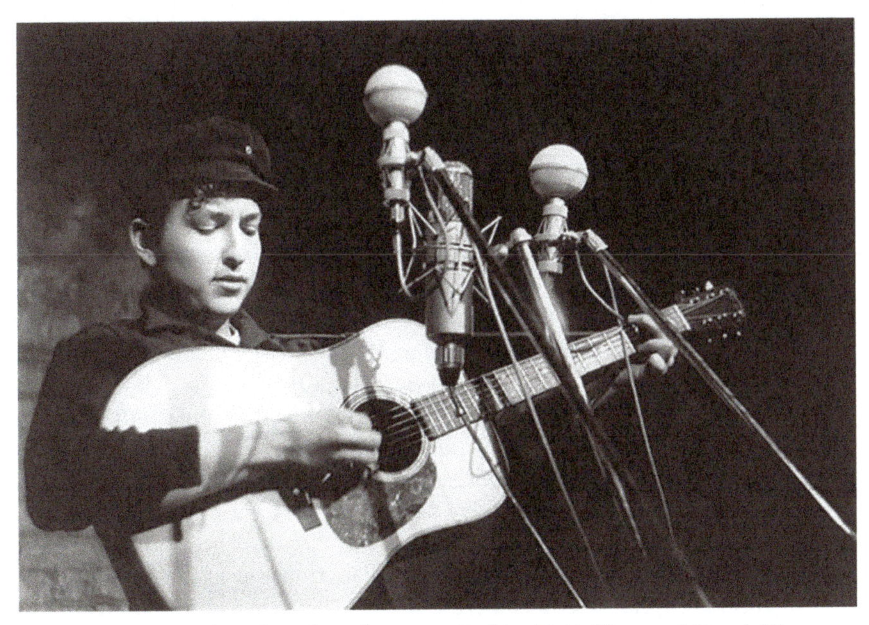

FIGURE 17.5 *Bob Dylan plays the Bitter End in 1961 (Sigmund Goode/Getty Images)*

> *aura in the present. The Saturday afternoon open mic is a mecca for international songwriters with diverse visions of American music. The designer stores in today's Greenwich Village may undermine the bohemian feel of that different village, but the Bitter End still functions as an epicenter in the global flow of singer-songwriter culture. Before I've finished looking around, a group of songwriters invites me to sit down. On this afternoon, I've met a mix of artists from Paris, Singapore, Tokyo, and the local boroughs.*[14]

At the Bitter End, there is an aura created by the nostalgia for the American songwriting tradition of the 1960s and 1970s and the diverse visions of American popular music inspired by that history. Artists come to the Bitter End to experience one of the original platforms for the folk movement—icons like Pete Seeger and Peter, Paul and Mary performed there—as well as early rhythm & blues and rock 'n' roll acts. Since Fred Weintraub opened the Bitter End in 1961, it has been known for bringing songwriters together, originally through the Tuesday night hootenannies.[15] At those "hoot nights"—often used by record labels to tap new talent—performers had to audition in the day for a slot in the evening.[16] In today's commercialized downtown Manhattan, the Bitter End open mic still plays a vital role in the NYC and global songwriter scene by facilitating interaction between local and international songwriters, among visions of American popular music of the past and present, as a place for self-reinvention, and as a social activist platform.

Evan Kremin currently hosts the Bitter End open mic, on Saturday afternoons from 1 to 6 p.m. Paul Rizzo, the current owner, and Kremin began the open mic in June 2014. I listened, conducted formal and informal interviews with performers, and played original songs there from January to August 2015. Outside on Bleecker Street, songwriters gather about half an hour before to sign up in the order they arrive. The format is each performer may play two pieces and take home a recording of his/her set for ten dollars. For local songwriters (those who live within the five boroughs), it's a place to return each week and see how new material resonates with the audience, to network with other artists, and to promote future gigs in NYC. For international songwriters, the Bitter End is a landing pad that allows them to immediately engage with the NYC music community. International artists often look to play as many gigs as they can in a short time in NYC. Other than open mics, they play the subway, on the streets in front of famous venues that they've seen in movies, and at organized gigs at small venues in the Lower East Side, Greenwich Village, and Brooklyn.

In addition to connecting with the audience through autobiographical and/or intimate lyrics, there is a trend for traveling artists to connect with the audience through adopting an alter ego imbued with their aspirations and idealized identity. Artists who theatrically construct their identity often have a background in performance arts. The trend of alter egos among traveling musicians may reflect different motivations: the alienating impact of traveling alone as a musician, the assumption that a foreign name could not lead to international success, and/or the freedom in the anonymity of a moniker.

> *A French Soul/Rock 'n' Roll artist from the suburbs of Paris with the moniker SINGE, shakes his legs like Elvis Presley, singing "Je Te Hais" in French over a 12 bar blues progression with a melody and bass line clearly inspired by Elvis's "Hound Dog" (1956). SINGE is on a tour of musical monuments in the US with gigs and open mics planned in between. His first stop is the Bitter End. Next stop is Ryman Auditorium in Nashville.*[17]

In response to my question about his alter ego, SINGE reflects: "It's actually just me, this other side of me that grew up after my parents gave me my first name. Choices you make in your life define who you are and SINGE defines me better than Charlie at this point. SINGE means monkey. It is an animal that's highly symbolic in many different ways. I let people make up their own idea of what it means, if it does mean something at all."[18] From

FIGURE 17.6 *SINGE performs at the Bitter End open mic, 2015 (Photo by Juliane Jones)*

meeting SINGE and watching him perform, I see that SINGE is the courageous side of Charlie: the fearless artist traveling through America.

Another character that I've met recently is Binx the Bee, a young singer-songwriter who recently moved to Greenwich Village to pursue modeling and songwriting careers. When she performs, she dresses in a black and yellow bumblebee-like bikini. She started a band in South Africa when she was ten and chose the African honey bee to represent her. Her animal alter ego has similarities to her personality: like Binx, bees are good omens and communicate through dance and music. But the bee is also an idealized characterization of herself—if Binx could have a super power, it would be to fly. Binx uses the bee to stand out from other artists and connect with the audience by reminding them of her South African roots.

Inspired by the Bitter End's history as the oldest rock venue in NYC, international and local artists at the open mic appropriate early American pop music into their own musical and cultural idioms, blurring previously constructed, though historically ambiguous, sonic and social relationships.

Dru Chen sings "Turnaround," a song imploring his girlfriend to come back: "It's up to you what you do / Not what I say, can't make you stay / But anytime that you find / You'll be changing your mind / It's okay,

FIGURE 17.7 *Dru Chen performs at the Bitter End open mic, 2015 (Photo by Juliane Jones)*

don't delay / Turnaround, turnaround." Chen creates a groove on his guitar with the careful placement of sixteenth notes that melodically recall his falsetto vocal; he's swaying, almost dancing during his guitar solos. The audience is feeling it, too, and cheers during his falsetto passages.[19]

Born in Melbourne, Australia, and raised in Singapore, Chen is inspired by the visceral falsetto shrieks and guitar riffs over harmonic vamps of early funk artists like James Brown. While Chen's music is inspired by funk and soul, he personalizes the narrative content. American soul music was originally the music of racial rebellion that expressed the black nationalism of the mid-1960s, articulated in the early Memphis soul sound of Aretha Franklin, James Brown, and Otis Redding.[20] Like Chen's re-invention of funk, it is common to see visiting artists appropriate the prominence of the vocal line, blues harmonies, and soul guitar riffs into their music. Open mic performers are similarly in dialogue with early rock 'n' roll. We saw SINGE re-invent the music and lyrics of Elvis's "Hound Dog," itself an appropriation of a popular African-American tune recorded by "Big Mama" Willie Mae Thornton in 1952.[21]

At the Saturday afternoon open mic in June 2015, Ian Andrew takes the stage. Originally from Miami, he now works full-time as a songwriter, traveling between Miami, Nashville, NYC, and LA. For Ian, there is a distinction between an artist and a songwriter: "I always notice when I watch good songwriters play, there's a lack of ego." That's the direction Ian has taken in his social activist anthem song, "Believe In Me," that he intends for the organization Black Lives Matter. Andrew sings on an acoustic guitar over a rock progression (chorus): "Say to the world, I'll be ok / We all got our problems and you'll find your way / From the bottom of my heart I understand / If you need my help just take my hand / Cause you know I love you / If you want me to be happy, let me be me / If you don't believe in yourself, believe in me / When you got nobody else, I know where you're coming from / and I know where we are / Believe in me / Believe in me."

Andrew's song is a call for mutual understanding and empathy between young African-Americans and white police officers in the wake of the racially motivated homicides and subsequent failure to bring an indictment in the killings of Eric Garner (1970–2014), Michael Brown (1996–2014), and Trayvon Martin (1995–2012). The song reassures all that, with understanding, we can reconcile seemingly irreconcilable race relations.

Andrew writes the verses from the perspective of a young African-American male. While the chorus begins with the African-American youth's voice, it shifts to a more inclusive perspective with the use of "we" and an ambiguous "you," emphasizing the reconciliatory goal of the song. He aims for "Believe In Me" to raise funds and attention like the 1985 charity ballad sung by multiple stars, "We are The World," did for African famine relief.

Through Andrew's social activism, he engages with The Bitter End's history as a venue that was a platform for protest songs in the Civil Rights Movement. His piece resonates with Dylan's songs on racial injustice: "Blowin' in the Wind" (1962), "Only a Pawn in Their Game" (1964), and "Hurricane" (1976). All these pieces musically articulate equal rights and peace through narrative lyrics accompanied by acoustic guitar and harmonica.

The Bitter End open mic has a vintage rock atmosphere from the old photos and concert tickets on the walls to the song choice of the performers. It's common to hear an artist perform one original tune and then a cover of a famous singer-songwriter's hit (e.g., Billy Joel). There's a supportive, collective feel because the audience is mostly songwriters. The audience sometimes joins in singing with a performer or hums along when a local songwriter improves on the same tune from last week. International artists tend to be more influenced by vintage rock, while local artists are often more engaged with recent and contemporary American songwriters. The past is what draws songwriters in, but they leave with a stronger network and performance skills. The Bitter End functions as a time capsule bringing us back to that different village where artists share stories and plan gigs together, and as a safe space to test new songs and voice opinions.

Occupying the Open Mic: Yuyintang in Shanghai

A local student band takes the stage in a Shanghai rock venue in an old factory with graffiti walls, populated by university students, traveling musicians, and foreigners smoking cigarettes and drinking. The Shanghai club, which opened in 2004, has an eerie resemblance to the old CBGB in Greenwich Village, with similar punk aesthetics. The door guard assures me that this is an open mic, but there is no signup sheet or strict format. If you want to play, you have to tell the sound engineer at the back of the room. The system doesn't always work smoothly. Tonight, the student band called IF holds the stage for seven songs. A few guitarists passing through Shanghai clutch their instruments, waiting. IF plays American vintage covers sung in English and a few originals in Chinese.

Yuyintang open mic may be viewed as an appropriated concept or technology (not so different from the trajectories of gramophones, phonographs, and current media technologies) that facilitates a complex process of cultural production in which Chinese and Western musical cultures

FIGURE 17.8 *Yuyintang rock club in Shanghai, China, 2015 (Photos by Juliane Jones).*

interact.[22] Yuyintang open mic serves as a nascent space for forging a unique modernity, reflecting Shanghai's historical cosmopolitanism, the counterculture aesthetics of 1980s Chinese rock, and the retro-futuristic modernism of the city of Shanghai.

Like the 1920s–1930s Shanghai of the golden age that served as a gathering place for Europeans, Japanese, and Chinese migrants, contemporary Shanghai draws musicians and audience members from all over the world. At this open mic there is a jazz guitarist from Japan, myself, a cross-cultural popular musician based in NYC, and another guitarist from Beijing, among traveling musicians and tourists in the audience. The heterogeneous mix of performers participating in the unstructured event intensifies the emergent creative energy in the room.

Yuyintang presents the rock aesthetics of cultural opposition: it is underground in an unrenovated factory within the futuristic city of Shanghai, a city that celebrates modernity through its brilliant and vertical skyline. Shanghai is known as the site of Chinese jazz that flourished during the city's golden age, but Yuyintang is mainly a rock club. Chinese popular song has been hybrid from its beginnings in the early twentieth century. Its multiple and evolving genres of Mandarin pop have developed from mixtures of American jazz, rock, Hollywood orchestration, Tin Pan Alley, and Chinese folk music.[23] Among the diverse influences on Mandarin pop, many contemporary Chinese bands are still affected by the Chinese rock 'n' roll movement, established by pioneering rock musicians like Cui Jian, whose songs evoked the sense of disillusionment of 1980s Chinese youth. *IF* echo this sentiment with their songs that pose societal questions.

> *IF open with a cover of "Californication," the 1999 Red Hot Chili Peppers song that critiques the exportation of superficial Hollywood culture. IF ironically critique superficiality as they sing in Shanghai, a city also highly concerned with image. They also identify with the U.S. rock band and the dream of ultimate freedom symbolized by California. IF's originals follow the band's name, putting into question pressing social dilemmas. One song in Chinese asks: "Do you really like your life?" which is to say they don't. IF respond to the social pressures of getting into a top university and the fierce job competition in the rapidly growing Chinese economy. The young woman playing the Roland keyboard and the lead guitarist take turns singing lead vocals and talking to the audience. She sings a cover of "Shut Up and Let Me Go" by the popular contemporary British dance-punk duo The Ting Tings. Through the lyrics, she brings to attention the importance of individual liberty through taking a stand in a relationship. After the punk rock cover, IF finish with a soft version of "Hey Jude" by the Beatles. IF relate the classic tune to their own situation: when faced with the social pressures from the rigidity of the education system, "don't carry the world upon your shoulders."*

Occupying the stage for a full set, *IF* turn the open mic associated with individual expression in the West into a space for collective questioning. What are the meanings of pleasure, freedom, and the individual in a city where time and space are collapsing? Underground and shielded from the symbols of high-speed urban change, the open mic provides a space for locals and transient musicians to escape and pose question that may not be broached above ground.

Shanghai is often interpreted as a retro-futuristic city because of its visually provocative architecture, built since the early 1990s, that re-stages tradition and history. The emergence of newness within Shanghai's exploratory cityscape draws attention to process and anticipation of the future.[24] The retro-futurism and hunger for the future that characterizes Shanghai is also evoked at Yuyintang open mic. Through *IF's* musical sampling of British, American, and Chinese pop rock interlaced with original tunes, they are not merely imitating, but seizing the stage to negotiate their own version of modernity. *IF* draw on themes of nostalgia in Chinese and Western vintage pop, and exoticism and idealism in their covers of American West Coast pop to explore, question, and assert the place of youth in contemporary Chinese society.

Conclusion

Open mics across the world are a space for artists to experiment, a crossroads for traveling musicians, and an intersection of visions of popular music. Open mics are not just a format, but sites of cultural production that challenge space, time, stereotypes, and our conceptions of popular song. Thinking back to the rolling hills in Nashville, Tennessee, Nashville may be viewed as the original site of the open mic, where performers use the one-song moment to express themselves and inscribe their names on a piece of history. In NYC, songwriters try on a new identity through an alter ego, and the singer-songwriter develops through the open mic as an intersectional space. Shanghai provides a nascent space where the open mic is counterculture in a way that it no longer is in Nashville or NYC. Yuyintang draws on the counterculture spirit of the open mic and adapts it to a society that places greater emphasis on the collective within an environment of drastic social and economic change. Some view open mics as only the first step in the music industry ecosystem, but in reality they are places where all levels of musicians hone their craft and are exposed to new musical styles and ideas. Open mics across the world are manifestations of the current local musical culture and its relationship to global cultural flows.

Advice from fellow songwriters

- Register your live sets to get paid: http://www.bmi.com/special/bmi_live (accessed October 28, 2016).
- Play out! If you can strip down an orchestrated song to a melody and simple accompaniment, you'll see what's working and what can be improved.
- If you can relate to an audience that didn't come to see you, you'll

be even better at your own shows when people come specifically to see you.

- Value other musicians in your community. When you're starting out as a songwriter, you'll see attendance at your local shows increase if you network at open mics.
- There is not one road to artistic or commercial "success" in the music industry. You are an inventor. Make your own path.

Notes

1 The term hootenanny was propagated by folk groups and the entertainment industry after Pete Seeger (1919–2014) brought it back to Greenwich Village clubs from his travels in the Pacific Northwest in 1941 with Woody Guthrie (1912–67). Seeger writes: "And it was in Seattle that Woody and I came across the term 'hootenanny.' We liked the sound of the word. I inquired as to its origins and was told 'hootenanny' came from Indiana, that it was an old country word for 'party.' ... Woody and I took the word 'hootenanny' back to New York with us and used it for our rent parties" Pete Seeger with Robert Santelli, "Hobo's Lullaby," in Robert Santelli and Emily Davison, eds. *Hard Travelin: The Life and Legacy of Woody Guthrie* (Hanover: Wesleyan University Press, 1999), 29.

2 By Western popular music, I am referring to common song structures including verse–chorus–bridge forms, triadic harmonies, and 4/4 and 3/4 meters. The format of an open mic live show is more popular in democratic countries, suggesting that it is associated with individualism and freedom of speech. Open mics only became popular in Beijing and Shanghai in the early 2000s at venues frequented by foreigners. In Asia and continental Europe, the term open mic is almost always not translated, and songs with English lyrics are often performed.

3 For an analysis of personal authenticity, see Allan Moore, "Authenticity as Authentication." *Popular Music* 21 (2) (2002): 209–23.

4 The American Folk Music Revival was a movement that began in the 1940s that involved the performance of traditional songs and dances. See Dave Laing, "Folk Music Revival," *Grove Music Online*, *Oxford Music Online*, Oxford University Press. http://www.oxfordmusiconline.com.ezproxy.library.ubc.ca/subscriber/article/grove/music/46854 (accessed August 11, 2015).

5 I am using David Brackett's definition for genre: "Genres are a group of stylistic tendencies, codes, conventions, and expectations that become meaningful in relation to one another at a particular moment in time." David Brackett, "(In Search of) Musical Meaning: Genres, Categories and Crossover," in *Popular Music. Studies: International Perspectives*, eds. David Hesmondhalgh and Keith Negus. London: Arnold, 2002), 67. For more

on the concept of the authentic songwriter reflected in the press see Robert Windeler, "Carole King: 'You Can Get to Know Me through My Music,'" in *The Pop, Rock, and Soul Reader,* ed. David Brackett (New York: Oxford University Press, 2009), 350–61.

6 In research on singer-songwriters within popular music studies, scholars have debated the notion of the construction of authenticity—how the performer creates a sincere connection with the audience—in relation to textuality—how the performer evokes a literary and musical narrative—in songs. In popular music studies, scholars have interpreted authenticity as primality, where something or someone is authentic if it can be traced back to an initiatory source, purity of practice, and honesty to experience, amongst other critiques and definitions. While there are multiple interpretations of authenticity in popular music, the crucial point is that authenticity is relativistic and maintains a paradoxical nature, while it functions differently according to genre. Like many genres in popular music that simultaneously depend on and deconstruct authenticity, in the singer-songwriter genre performers manifest a paradoxical relationship to mass culture and commercial music. See Timothy Taylor, *Global Pop: World Music, World Markets* (New York: Routledge, 1997) and Philip Bohlman, *The Study of Folk Music in the Modern World* (Bloomington, IN: Indiana University Press, 1988).

7 The music industry is in a state of flux. While I am writing this, the music industry is shifting towards streaming services like Spotify and Apple Music.

8 "Play out" is a term that producers and songwriters use in the music industry. It means to publicly perform songs.

9 Because of the increasing notoriety of the open mic, on June 1, 2015, the Bluebird changed its sign-in policy for open mic to phone-in. Now the venue accepts the first twenty-five callers starting at 11 a.m. on Mondays.

10 Joli Jensen, *The Nashville Sound: Authenticity, Commercialization, and Country Music* (Nashville: Vanderbilt University Press, 1998), 9.

11 "History of the Opry," Grand Ole Opry. http://www.opry.com/history (accessed July 22, 2015).

12 https://open.spotify.com/album/4gcFp5nTvCa7DD4Jwqfo1j (accessed July 22, 2015)

13 Bob Dylan, liner notes to *In the Wind*, Peter, Paul and Mary, Warner Bros. Records, CD, 1963.

14 On the album jacket to Peter, Paul and Mary's 1963 LP *In The Wind*, Dylan described his earliest days in New York City.

15 Paul Colby (1917–2014) managed the Bitter End in the 1960s and bought a small bar next door that he renamed "The Other End." When Paul bought the main space in 1974, he joined the venues together, and renamed it "Paul Colby's The Bitter End." It was co-owned by Kenny Gorka (1947–2015) and Paul Rizzo, and is currently owned by Paul Rizzo.

16 See Paul Colby's *The Bitter End: Hanging Out at America's Nightclub* (New York: Cooper Square Press, 2002), in particular, Chapter 4, "What's A Hootenanny?"

17 SINGE's live acoustic album is entitled *À Poils*. http://singe-fr.bandcamp.com/releases (accessed August 11, 2015).

18 SINGE, e-mail message to author, June 9, 2015.

19 http://druchen.bandcamp.com/track/turnaround-2 (accessed August 11, 2015).

20 Phyl Garland, *The Sound of Soul: The Story of Black Music* (Chicago: H. Regnery Co., 1969), 2–11; and Brian Ward, *Just My Soul Responding: Rhythm and Blues, Black Consciousness, and Race Relations* (Berkeley: University of California Press, 1998), 183.

21 Garland, *The Sound of Soul,* 17.

22 YouTube, Google, and SoundCloud are currently banned in China. Students still access some foreign websites, but the circulation of ideas and music is restricted by the Chinese government. When a foreign band tours China, they must first submit a translation of all lyrics and a 45 minute video of a live performance to obtain a permit.

23 It is beyond the scope of this chapter to analyze in detail the evolving popular music genres in China. Rock music used to be distinguished from government-sanctioned music, but has increasingly moved into the mainstream media. For more on Chinese popular music see Andrew F. Jones, *Yellow Music Media Culture and Colonial Modernity in the Chinese Jazz Age* (Durham: Duke University Press, 2001).

24 For an insightful explanation of the rebirth of modernity in twenty-first-century Shanghai see Anna Greenspan, *Shanghai Future: Modernity Remade* (New York: Oxford University Press, 2014).

BIBLIOGRAPHY

Aldredge, Marcus. "Singer-songwriters and open mics." In *The Cambridge Companion to the Singer-songwriter*, edited by Katherine Williams and Justin A. Williams, 278–90. Cambridge: Cambridge University Press, 2016.

Anderson, Tim. *Popular Music in a Digital Music Economy: Problems and Practices for an Emerging Service Industry*. London: Routledge, 2013.

Anderton, Chris, Andrew Dubber, and Martin James. *Understanding The Music Industries*. London: Sage, 2013.

Ankeny, Jason. "Joni Mitchell." *AllMusic*. http://www.allmusic.com/artist/joni-mitchell-mn0000270491 (accessed February 5, 2016).

Auner, Joseph. "'Sing It for Me': Posthuman Ventriloquism in Recent Popular Music." *Journal of the Royal Musical Association* 128 (2003): 98–122.

Barber, Simon. "'Will You Love Me Tomorrow': The Brill Building and the Creative Labor of the Professional Songwriter." In *The Cambridge Companion to the Singer-Songwriter*, edited by Katherine Williams and Justin A. Williams. Cambridge: Cambridge University Press, 2016.

Barber, Simon, and Brian O'Connor. *Sodajerker On Songwriting*, podcast audio, MP3, 2011–2015, http://www.sodajerker.com/podcast (accessed October 5, 2016)

Barker, Hugh, and Yuval Taylor. *Faking It: The Quest for Authenticity in Popular Music*. New York: W. W. Norton & Co., 2007.

Barlindhaug, Gaute. "Analog sound in the age of digital tools. The story of the failure of digital technology." In *A document (re)turn: Contributions from a research field in transition*, edited by R. Skare, N. Windfeld Lund, and Andreas Vårheim, 73–93. Frankfurt am Main: Peter Lang, 2007. http://munin.uit.no/bitstream/handle/10037/971/paper.pdf?sequence=1 (accessed August 11, 2015).

Barthes, Roland. *Writing Degree Zero*. Translated by Annette Lavers and Colin Smith. London: Jonathan Cape, 1967.

Bell, Adam, Ethan Hein, and Jarrod Ratcliffe. "Beyond Skeuomorphism: The Evolution of Music Production Software Interface Metaphors." *Journal on the Art of Record Production* 9 (2015). http://arpjournal.com/beyond-skeuomorphism-the-evolution-of-music-production-software-user-interface-metaphors-2/ (accessed August 11, 2015).

Bennett, Dawn. "Rethinking Success: Music in Higher Education." *The International Journal of the Humanities*, 5 (2012): 181–7.

Bennett, Joe. "Collaborative songwriting – the ontology of negotiated creativity in popular music studio practice." *Journal on the Art of Record Production* 5 (2011): ISSN: 1754–9892. http://arpjournal.com/875/collaborative-songwriting-—the-ontology-of-negotiated-creativity-in-popular-music-studio-practice (accessed August 11, 2015).

Bennett, Joe. "Constraint, Collaboration and Creativity in Popular Songwriting Team." In *The Act of Musical Composition: Studies in the Creative Process*, edited by Dave Collins, 139–69. Farnham: Ashgate, 2012.

Biddle, Ian. "'The Singsong of Undead Labor': Gender Nostalgia and the Vocal Fantasy of Intimacy in the 'New' Male Singer/Songwriter." In *Oh Boy!: Masculinities and Popular Music*, edited by Freya Jarman-Ivens, 125–44. New York and London: Routledge, 2007.

Bidini, Dave. *Writing Gordon Lightfoot: The man, the music, and the world in 1972*. Toronto: McClelland & Stewart Ltd, 2011.

Blume, Jason. *Six Steps to Songwriting Success*. New York: Billboard, 2008.

Bohlman, Philip V. "Pilgrimage, Politics, and the Musical Remapping of the New Europe." *Ethnomusicology* 40 (3), Special Issue: Music and Religion (Autumn 1996): 375–412.

Bohlman, Philip V. *The Study of Folk Music in the Modern World*. Bloomington: Indiana University Press, 1988.

Bourriaud, Nicholas. *Postproduction*. New York: Lukas & Sternberg, 2010.

Bowman, David. *fa fa fa fa fa fa: The Adventures of Talking Heads in the 20th Century*. London: Bloomsbury, 2002.

Brackett, David. "(In Search of) Musical Meaning: Genres, Categories, and Crossover." In *Popular Music Studies*, edited by David Hesmondhalgh and Keith Negus, 65–83. London: Arnold, and New York: Oxford University Press, 2002.

Brown, Andrew. *Computers in Music Education: Amplifying Musicality*. New York: Routledge, 2007.

Burgess, Richard James. *The Art of Music Production: the Theory and Practice*. 4th edn Oxford: Oxford University Press, 2013.

Burgess, Richard James. *The History of Music Production*. Oxford: Oxford University Press, 2013.

Burns, Gary. "A typology of 'hooks' in popular records." *Popular Music* 6 (1) (1987): 1–20.

Burns, Lori, Alyssa Woods, and Marc Lafrance. "Sampling and Storytelling: Kanye West's Vocal and Sonic Narratives." In *The Cambridge Companion to the Singer-Songwriter*, edited by Katherine Williams and Justin A. Williams, 159–70. Cambridge: Cambridge University Press, 2016.

Butler, Mark J. *Unlocking the Groove: Rhythm, Meter, and Musical Design in Electronic Dance Music*. Bloomington: Indiana University Press, 2006.

Byrne, David. *How Music Works*. Edinburgh: Canongate, 2012.

Cascone, Kim. "The Aesthetics of Failure: 'Post-Digital' Tendencies in Contemporary Computer Music." *Computer Music Journal* 24 (4) (2000): 12–18.

Cauty, Jimmy, and Bill Drummond. *The Manual: How to Have a Number One Hit the Easy Way*. KLF Publications, 1988. http://freshonthenet.co.uk/the-manual-by-the-klf/ (accessed September 28, 2015).

Citron, Stephen. *Songwriting: A Complete Guide to the Craft* (revised and updated edition). New York: Limelight Editions, 2008.

Cloonan, Martin. "What is popular music studies? Some observations," *British Journal of Music Education* 22 (1) (2005): 1–17.

Cloonan, Martin, and Lauren Hulstedt, *Taking Notes: Mapping and Teaching Popular Music in Higher Education*, York: Higher Education Academy, 2012.

Cohen, Ronald. *A history of folk music festivals in the United States: Feasts of musical celebration*. Lanham, Toronto, and Plymouth: The Scarecrow Press Ltd., 2008.

Cohen, Sara. *Rock Culture in Liverpool: Popular Music in the Making*. Oxford: Oxford University Press, 1991.

Colby, Paul, and Martin Fitzpatrick. *The Bitter End: Hanging Out at America's Nightclub*. New York: Cooper Square Press, 2002.

Conte, Jack. "Digital Content Is Free. People Are Not." November 7, 2013. https://www.youtube.com/watch?v=s5Zaf0NKXvQ (accessed August 11, 2015).

Conte, Jack. "5 Reasons Why SMBC Killed It on Patreon." December 18, 2013. https://www.youtube.com/watch?v=X10kp77UJHE (accessed August 11, 2015).

Conte, Jack. "Patreon Raised $15 Million." June 23, 2014. https://www.youtube.com/watch?v=Q5vAdw3WY9Q (accessed August 11, 2015).

Conte, Jack. "Pomplamoose 2014 Tour Profits (or Lack Thereof)," November 24, 2014. https://medium.com/@jackconte/pomplamoose-2014-tour-profits-67435851ba37#.n84y4iz9y (accessed August 11, 2015).

Cooper, Cary L., and Geoffrey I. D. Wills. "Popular Musicians Under Pressure." *Psychology of Music* 17 (1989): 22–6.

Coryat, Karl, and Nicholas Dobson. *The Frustrated Songwriter's Handbook*. San Francisco: Backbeat Books, 2006.

Coulson, Susan. "Collaborating in a Competitive World: Musicians' Working Lives and Understandings of Entrepreneurship." *Work, Employment and Society* 26 (2012): 246–61.

Cousins, Mark, and Russ Hepworth-Sawyer. *Practical Mastering: A Guide to Mastering in the Modern Studio*. Oxford: Focal Press, 2013.

Cramer, Florian. "What is Post-digital?" *APRJA* 3:1 (2014). http://www.aprja.net/?page_id=1291 (accessed October 9, 2015).

Crawford, Richard, and Larry Hamberlin. *An Introduction to America's Music*. 2nd edn New York: W. W. Norton & Co., 2013.

D'Amato, Francesco. "Investors and Patrons, Gatekeepers and Social Capital: Representations and Experiences of Fans' Participation in Fan Funding." In *The Ashgate Research Companion to Fan Cultures*, edited by D. S. Reijnders, D. K. Zwaan and D. L. Duits, 135–48. Farnham: Ashgate, 2014.

Dibben, Nicola. "Vocal Performance and the Projection of Emotional Authenticity." In *The Ashgate Research Companion to Popular Musicology*, edited by Derek B. Scott, 317–33. Farnham and Burlington: Ashgate, 2009.

Dobson, Melissa C. "Insecurity, Professional Sociability, and Alcohol: Young Freelance Musicians' Perspectives on Work and Life in the Music Profession." *Psychology of Music* 39 (2010): 240–60.

Dylan, Bob. Liner notes to *In the Wind*. Peter, Paul and Mary. Warner Bros. Records. CD. 1963.

Egan, Sean. *The Guys Who Wrote 'Em*. London: Askill Publishing, 2004.

Eno, Brian. "Studio as Compositional Tool." In *Audio Culture: Readings in Modern Music*, edited by Christopher Cox and Daniel Warner. London: Continuum, 2007.

Eshun, Kodwo. *More Brilliant than the Sun: Adventures in Sonic Fiction*. London: Quartet Books, 1999.

Filene, Benjamin. *Romancing the folk: Public memory and American roots music*. Chapel Hill and London: The University of North Carolina Press, 2000.

Fitzgerald, Jon. "When the Brill building met Lennon–McCartney: Continuity and Change in the Early Evolution of the Mainstream Pop Song." *Popular Music and Society* 19 (1) (1995): 59–77.

Flanagan, Bill. *Written in My Soul: Conversations with Rock's Great Songwriters*. Chicago: Contemporary Books, 1987.

Fleet, Paul, "'I've Heard There was a Secret Chord': Do we Need to Teach Music Notation in UK Popular Music Studies?" In *The Routledge Research Companion to Popular Music Education*, edited by Gareth Dylan Smith, Zack Moir, Matt Brennan, Shara Rambarran, and Phil Kirkman, 166–76. London: Routledge, 2016.

"Four Tet." *Sound on Sound*, July 2003 http://www.soundonsound.com/sos/jul03/articles/fourtet.asp (accessed August 11, 2015).

Frith, Simon. "'The magic that can set you free': The ideology of the folk and the myth of the rock community." *Popular Music* 1 (1981): 159–68.

Frith, Simon. *Performing Rites: On the Value of Popular Music*. Cambridge, MA: Harvard University Press, 1996.

Garcia, Luis-Manuel. "On and On: Repetition as Process and Pleasure in Electronic Dance Music." *Music Theory Online* 11 (4) (October 2005). http://www.mtosmt.org/issues/mto.05.11.4/mto.05.11.4.garcia.html (accessed October 19, 2015).

Gardner, Lyn. "Pay-What-You-Decide Theatre: A Risk That's Worth Taking," December 10, 2014. http://www.theguardian.com/stage/theatreblog/2014/dec/10/pay-what-you-decide-theatre-arc-stockton (accessed August 11, 2015).

Gaunt, Helena, and Ioulia Papageorgi. "Music in universities and conservatoires." In *Music Education in the 21st Century in the United Kingdom: Achievement, analysis and aspirations*, edited by Susan Hallam and Andrea Creech. London: The Institute of Education, University of London, 2010.

Gilbert, Jeremy, and Ewan Pearson. *Discographies: Dance Music, Culture and the Politics of Sound*. London: Routledge, 1999.

Gilroy, Paul. *The Black Atlantic: Modernity and Double Consciousness*. London: Verso, 1993.

Gordon, Jeremy. "Joanna Newsom: 'Spotify Is the Banana of the Music Industry. It Just Gives Off a Fume,'" October 16, 2015 http://pitchfork.com/news/61661-joanna-newsom-spotify-is-the-banana-of-the-music-industry-it-just-gives-off-a-fume/ (accessed February 8, 2016).

Green, Lucy. *How Popular Musicians Learn: A Way Ahead for Music Education*. Aldershot: Ashgate Publishing Ltd., 2002.

Greenburg, Zack O'Malley. "Amanda Palmer Uncut: The Kickstarter Queen On Spotify, Patreon And Taylor Swift," April 16, 2015 http://www.forbes.com/sites/zackomalleygreenburg/2015/04/16/amanda-palmer-uncut-the-kickstarter-queen-on-spotify-patreon-and-taylor-swift/ (accessed August 11, 2015).

Harding, Phil. *PWL from the Factory Floor*. Welwyn: WB Publishing, 2009.

Hass, Richard W., Robert W. Weisberg, and Jimmy Choi. "Quantitative

case-studies in musical composition: the development of creativity in popular-songwriting teams." *Psychology of Music* 38 (4) (2010): 463–79.
Hebdige, Dick. *Cut 'n' Mix: Culture, Identity and Caribbean Music*. London: Comedia, 1987.
Heiser, Marshall. "SMiLE: Brian Wilson's Musical Mosaic." *Journal on the Art of Record Production* 7 (2012) http://arpjournal.com/smile-brian-wilson's-musical-mosaic/ (accessed September 28, 2015).
Henriques, Julian. *Sonic Bodies: Reggae Soundsystems, Performance Techniques and Ways of Knowing*. London: Continuum, 2011.
Hillhouse, Andrew. "Touring as social practice: Transnational festivals, personalized networks, and new folk music sensibilities." PhD diss., University of Toronto, 2013.
Hirschhorn, Joel. *The Complete Idiot's Guide to Songwriting*. Indianapolis: Pearson, 2001.
Hoefnagels, Anna. "Children's folk music in Canada: Histories, Performers, Canons." *Musicultures* 37 (2010): 14–31.
Hopper, Jessica. "Grimes Comes Clean: Synth-Pop Provocateur on Her Big Year." *Spin*, December 6, 2012. http://www.spin.com/articles/grimes-interview-2012-big-year (accessed June 24, 2015).
Jacobson, Tyler. "David Gray: *White Ladder*." *Hybrid Magazine*. http://www.hybridmagazine.com/reviews/1100/dgray.shtml (accessed August 11, 2015).
Jensen, Joli. *The Nashville Sound: Authenticity, Commercialization, and Country Music*. Nashville: Vanderbilt University Press, 1998.
Jones, Michael L. *The Music Industries: From Conception to Consumption*. London: Palgrave Macmillan, 2012.
Kaschub, Michele, and Janice Smith. *Minds on Music: Composition for Creative and Critical Thinking*. Maryland: Rowman and Littlefield Education, 2009.
Katz, Bob. *Mastering Audio: the Art and the Science*. 3rd edn Oxford: Focal Press, 2014.
Katz, Mark. *Capturing Sound: How Technology Has Changed Music*. Berkeley: University of California Press, 2010.
Katz, Mark. *Groove Music: The Art and Culture of the Hip-hop DJ*. Oxford: Oxford University Press, 2012.
Kelly, Kevin. "1,000 True Fans," March 4, 2008. http://kk.org/thetechnium/1000-true-fans/ (accessed August 11, 2015).
Khanna, Vish. "Interview with Sufjan Stevens: An excerpt." *Kreative Kontrol*, October 12, 2009. http://vishkhanna.com/2009/10/12/sufjan-stevens-interview-an-excerpt/ (accessed September 27, 2015).
Kimpel, Dan. *Electrify My Soul: Songwriters and the Spiritual Source*. Boston: Thomson, 2008.
Kruse, Holly. *Site and Sound: Understanding Independent Music Scenes*. New York: Peter Lang, 2003.
Laing, Dave. "Folk Music Revival." *Grove Music Online. Oxford Music Online*. Oxford University Press. http://www.oxfordmusiconline.com.ezproxy.library.ubc.ca/subscriber/article/grove/music/46854 (accessed July 20, 2015).
Lankford, Ronald D., Jr. *Women Singer-Songwriters in Rock: A Populist Rebellion in the 1990s*. Lanham, Toronto, and Plymouth: The Scarecrow Press, 2010.

Lebler, Don, Rosie Burt-Perkins, and Gemma Carey. "What the students bring: examining the attributes of commencing conservatoire students." *International Journal of Music Education* 27 (3) (2009): 232–49.

Lebler, Don, and Naomi Hodges. "Popular Music Pedagogy: Dual Perspectives on DIY Musicianship." In *The Routledge Research Companion to Popular Music Education*, edited by Gareth Dylan Smith, Zack Moir, Matt Brennan, Shara Rambarran and Phil Kirkman, 272–84. London: Routledge, 2016.

Long, Paul, and Simon Barber. "Voicing passion: The emotional economy of songwriting." *European Journal of Cultural Studies* 18 (2) (2015): 142–57.

Macnie, Jim. "Joni Mitchell: Biography." *Rolling Stone*. http://www.rollingstone.com/music/artists/joni-mitchell/biography (accessed February 5, 2016).

McCormick, Neil. "James Blake: pop, but not as we know it." *Telegraph*, February 16, 2011. http://www.telegraph.co.uk/culture/music/rockandpopmusic/8329194/James-Blake-pop-but-not-as-we-know-it.html (accessed August 11, 2015).

McDonald, Chris. "'From both sides now?': Ethnomusicology, folklore and the rise of the Canadian singer-songwriter." In *Folk music, traditional music, ethnomusicology: Canadian perspectives, past and present,* edited by Anna Hoefnagels and Gordon E. Smith, 50–60. Toronto: Cambridge Scholars Publishing, 2007.

McIntyre, Phillip. "Creativity and Cultural Production: A Study of Contemporary Western Popular Music Songwriting." *Creativity Research Journal* 20 (1) (2008): 40–52.

McIntyre, Phillip. "Rethinking the creative process: The systems model of creativity applied to popular songwriting." *Journal of Music, Technology and Education* 4 (1) (2011): 77–90.

McLaughlin, Sean. "Mediations, Institutions and Post-Compulsory Popular Music Education." In *The Routledge Research Companion to Popular Music Education*, edited by Gareth Dylan Smith, Zack Moir, Matt Brennan, Shara Rambarran and Phil Kirkman, 114–26. London: Routledge, 2016.

Mantie, Roger. "A comparison of 'popular music pedagogy' discourses". *Journal of Research in Music Education* 61 (3) (2013): 334–52.

Marrington, Mark. "Experiencing musical composition in the DAW: the software interface as mediator of the musical idea." *Journal on the Art of Record Production* 5 (2011). http://arpjournal.com/experiencing-musical-composition-in-the-daw-the-software-interface-as-mediator-of-the-musical-idea-2/ (accessed August 11, 2015).

Massey, Howard. *Behind The Glass: Top Record Producers Tell How They Craft The Hits*. Milwaukee: Backbeat Books, 2000.

Mercer, Michelle. *Will You Take Me as I Am: Joni Mitchell's* Blue *Period*. New York: Free Press, 2009.

Miller, Paul D. *Sound Unbound: Sampling Digital Music and Culture*. London: MIT Press, 2008.

Milner, Greg. *Perfecting Sound Forever*. London: Granta Books, 2010.

Mitchell, Gillian. *The North American folk music revival: Nation and identity in the United States and Canada, 1945–1980*. Aldershot: Ashgate Publishing Ltd., 2007.

Moir, Zack, and Haftor Medbøe, "Reframing popular music composition as performance-centred practice." *Journal of Music, Technology & Education* 8 (2) (2015): 147–61.

Moir, Zack. "Popular Music Making and Young People: leisure, education, and industry." In *The Oxford Handbook of Music Making and Leisure*, edited by Roger Mantie and Gareth Dylan Smith, 223–40. Oxford: Oxford University Press, 2016.

Moliné, Keith. "Tongue Twister." *The Wire* 267 (May 2006): 42–7.

Mooney, James. "Frameworks and affordances: Understanding the tools of music-making." *Journal of Music, Technology and Education* 3/2&3 (2010): 141–54.

Moore, Allan. "Authenticity as Authentication." *Popular Music* 21 (2002): 209–23.

Moylan, William. *Understanding and Crafting the Mix: The Art of Recording*. 3rd edn Oxford: Focal Press, 2014.

Mulligan, Mark. "The Great Music Industry Power Shift," June 4, 2014 https://musicindustryblog.wordpress.com/2014/06/04/the-great-music-industry-power-shift/ (accessed August 11, 2015).

Neal, Jocelyn R. "Narrative paradigms, musical signifiers, and form as function in country music." *Music Theory Spectrum* 29 (1) (2007): 41–72.

Negus, Keith. "Narrative Time and the Popular Song." *Popular Music and Society* 35, no. 4 (2012): 483–500.

Negus, Keith, and Pete Astor. "Songwriters and song lyrics: architecture, ambiguity and repetition." *Popular Music* 34 (2) (2015): 226–44.

Nicholls, Samuel. "Fan Funding – Creative Impetus, Financial Stimulus & More. A Study of Bands Using the PledgeMusic Platform in the City of Leeds." University of Bristol, 2013 http://www.slideshare.net/whiskas9/bristol-presentation-3 (accessed August 11, 2015).

Oswinski, Bobby. *The Recording Engineer's Handbook*. 2nd edn Independence: Delmar, 2009.

Palmer, Amanda. "Theatre Is Evil: The Album, Art Book and Tour," April 1, 2012. https://www.kickstarter.com/projects/amandapalmer/amanda-palmer-the-new-record-art-book-and-tour (accessed August 11, 2015).

Palmer, Amanda. "Where All This Kickstarter Money Is Going By Amanda Fucking Palmer," May 22, 2012. http://blog.amandapalmer.net/20120522/ (accessed August 11, 2015).

Palmer, Amanda. "Amanda Palmer: The Art of Asking," February 1, 2013. http://www.ted.com/talks/amanda_palmer_the_art_of_asking (accessed August 11, 2015).

Palmer, Amanda. "Amanda Palmer Is Creating Art." https://www.patreon.com/amandapalmer (accessed October 1, 2015).

Parkinson, Tom, "Values of Higher Popular Music Education: Perspectives from the UK." Unpublished PhD Thesis. University of Reading, 2014.

Parkinson, Tom, and Gareth Dylan Smith. "Towards an epistemology of authenticity in higher popular music education." *Action, Criticism, and Theory for Music Education* 14 (1) (2015): 93–127.

Pattison, Pat. *Songwriting without Boundaries: Lyric Writing Exercises for Finding Your Voice*. Canada: Writer's Digest, 2012.

Pegg, Ann, Jeff Waldock, Sonia Hendy-Isaac, and Ruth Lawton, *Pedagogy for Employability*. York: Higher Education Academy, 2012.

Posen, Sheldon. "The beginnings of the children's (folk) music industry in Canada: An Overview." *Canadian Folk Music Journal/Revue de musique folklorique canadienne* 21 (1993): 19–30.

Prior, Nick. "Software Sequencers and Cyborg Singers: Popular Music in the Digital Hypermodern." *New Formations* 66 (2009): 81–99.

Rachel, Daniel. *Isle of Noises: Conversations with Great British Songwriters*. London: Picador, 2013.

Ramone, Phil, and Christopher L. Granata. *Making Records: The Scenes Behind the Music*. New York: Hyperion Books, 2007.

Reynolds, Simon. *Energy Flash*. London: Faber and Faber, 2013.

Rietveld, Hillegonda C. *This is our House: House Music, Cultural Spaces and Technologies*. Aldershot: Ashgate, 1998.

Rodgers, Jeffrey Pepper, ed. *Songwriting and the Guitar (Acoustic Guitar Guides)*. San Anselmo, CA: String Letter Publishing, 2000.

Rogers, Ian. "'You've Got to Go to Gigs to Get Gigs': Indie Musicians, Eclecticism and the Brisbane Scene." *Continuum: Journal of Media and Cultural Studies* 22 (2008): 639–49.

Rose, Tricia. *Black Noise: Rap Music and Black Culture in Contemporary America*. Hanover: Wesleyan University Press, 1994.

Sarath, Ed., David Myers, John Chattah, Lee Higgins, Victoria Lindsay Levine, David Rudge, and Timothy Rice, *Transforming Music Study from its Foundations: A Manifesto for Progressive Change in the Undergraduate Preparation of Music Majors*. College Music Society, 2014.

Savage, Steve. *The Art of Digital Audio Recording: A Practical Guide for Home and Studio*. New York: Oxford University Press, 2011.

Savage, Steve. *Mixing and Mastering in the Box*. New York: Oxford University Press, 2014.

Schloss, Joseph G. *Making Beats: The Art of Sample-based Hip-hop*. Middletown: Wesleyan University Press, 2004.

Seeger, Pete, with Robert Santelli. "Hobo's Lullaby." In *Hard Travelin': The Life and Legacy of Woody Guthrie,* edited by Robert Santelli and Emily Davidson, 22–33. Hanover: Wesleyan University Press/University Press of New England, 1999.

Serviant, Albin. "Interactivity: The Path to Fan Engagement ... and Sales," January 19, 2010. http://blog.midem.com/2010/01/interactivity-the-path-to-fan-engagement-and-music-sales/ (accessed August 11, 2015).

Shuker, Roy. *Popular Music: The Key Concepts*. 2nd edn London and New York: Routledge, 2005.

Shumway, David R. "The Emergence of the Singer-Songwriter." In *The Cambridge Companion to the Singer-Songwriter*, edited by Katherine Williams and Justin A. Williams, 11–20. Cambridge: Cambridge University Press, 2016.

Simos, Mark. *Songwriting Strategies: A 360° Approach*. Boston: Berklee Press/Hal Leonard, 2014.

Smith, Gareth Dylan. "Seeking 'success' in popular music," *Music Education Research International* 6 (2013): 26–37.

Smith, Gareth Dylan. "Popular music in higher education," *Advanced Musical Performance: Investigations in Higher Education Learning*, edited by Ioulia Papageorgi and Graham Welch, 33–48. Farnham: Ashgate, 2014.

Smith, Gareth Dylan. "Neoliberalism and symbolic violence in higher music education." In *Giving voice to democracy: Diversity and social justice in the music classroom*, edited by Lisa C. DeLorenzo, 65–84. New York: Routledge, 2015.

Smith, Gareth Dylan, Zack Moir, Matt Brennan, Shara Rambarran, and Phil Kirkman. "Popular Music Education (R)evolution." In *The Routledge Research Companion to Popular Music Education*, edited by Gareth Dylan Smith, Zack Moir, Matt Brennan, Shara Rambarran, and Phil Kirkman, 5–13. London: Routledge, 2016.

Smith, Larry David. *Elvis Costello, Joni Mitchell, and the Torch Song Tradition.* Westport and London: Praeger, 2004.

Spicer, Mark. "(Ac)cumulative forms in Pop-Rock Music." *Twentieth Century Music* 1 (2004): 29–64. http://dx.doi.org/DOI:10.1017/S1478572204000052 (accessed August 11, 2015).

Taylor, Timothy. *Global Pop: World Music, World Markets.* New York: Routledge, 1997.

Théberge, Paul. *Any Sound You Can Imagine: Making Music/Consuming Technology.* Middletown: Wesleyan University Press, 1997.

Thorpe-Tracey, Chris. "The Case against Crowd-Funding Platforms," October 2, 2012. http://louderthanwar.com/the-case-crowd-funding-platforms/

Thornton, Sarah. *Club Cultures: Music, Media and Subcultural Capital.* Hanover and London: University Press of New England, 1996.

Till, Rupert. "Popular Music Education: A step into the light." In *The Routledge Research Companion to Popular Music Education*, edited by Gareth Dylan Smith, Zack Moir, Matt Brennan, Shara Rambarran, and Phil Kirkman, 14–30. London: Routledge, 2016.

Toft, Robert. *Hits and Misses: Crafting top 40 singles, 1963–71.* London: Continuum, 2011.

Toulson, Rob. "Mixing can be simple, you just have to think one step ahead." *Sound On Sound Magazine*, March 2010.

Toynbee, Jason. *Making Popular Music: Musicians, Creativity and Institutions.* London: Arnold, 2000.

Tsai, Sija. "Public policy and the Mariposa Folk Festival: Shared ideals in the 1960s and 1970s." *Musicultures* 38 (2011): 147–58.

Tsai, Sija. "Surface sketches of a wandering festival." *Canadian Folk Music/ Musique Folklorique Canadienne* 45 (1) (2011): 8–14.

Tsai, Sija. "Mariposa Folk Festival: The sounds, sights and costs of a 50-year road trip." PhD diss., York University, 2013.

Väkevä, Lauri. "Garage Band or GarageBand®? Remixing musical futures." *British Journal of Music Education* 27 (1) (2010): 59–70.

Ward, Brian. *Just My Soul Responding: Rhythm and Blues, Black Consciousness, and Race Relations.* Berkeley: University of California Press, 1998.

Webb, Jimmy. *Tunesmith: Inside the Art of Songwriting.* New York: Hyperion, 1998.

Webster, Peter Richard. "Construction of Music Learning." In *MENC Handbook of Research on Music Learning,* edited by Richard Colwell and Peter Richard Webster, Vol. 1, 35–83. New York: Oxford University Press, 2011.

Westerlund, Heidi. "Garage rock bands: A future model for developing musical expertise?" *International Journal for Music Education* 24 (2) (2006) 119–25.

Wheeler, Duncan, and Lucy O'Brien. "The Cultural and Gender Politics of Enunciation: Locating the Singer-Songwriter within and beyond Male Anglo-American Contexts." *Journal of World Popular Music* 1 (2014): 228–48.

Wiggins, Jackie, Deborah VanderLinde Blair, S. Alex Ruthmann, and Joseph L. Shively, "A heart to heart about music education practice." *The Mountain Lake Reader* (Spring 2006): 82–91.

Wikstrom, Patrick. *The Music Industry: Music in the Cloud.* Cambridge: Polity Press, 2009.

Williams, Chris. "The Soulquarians at Electric Lady: An Oral History." *Red Bull Music Academy Daily*, June 1, 2015. http://daily.redbullmusicacademy.com/2015/06/the-soulquarians-at-electric-lady (accessed October 4, 2015).

Williams, Justin, and Ross Wilson. "Music and Crowdfunded Websites: Digital Patronage and Artist–Fan Interactivity." In *The Oxford Handbook of Music and Virtuality,* edited by Sheila Whiteley and Shara Rambarran, 593–612. London: Oxford University Press, 2016.

Williams, Katherine, and Justin A. Williams, eds. *The Cambridge Companion to the Singer-Songwriter.* Cambridge: Cambridge University Press, 2016.

Windeler, Robert. "Carole King: 'You Can Get to Know Me through My Music.'" In *The Pop, Rock, and Soul Reader*, edited by David Brackett, 350–61. New York: Oxford University Press, 2009.

Wise, Tim. "Singer-Songwriter." In *Continuum Encyclopedia of Popular Music of the World*, Vol. 8, edited by David Horn, 430–4. New York: Continuum, 2012.

Zagorski-Thomas, Simon. "The Stadium in Your Bedroom: Functional Staging, Authenticity and the Audience-Led Aesthetic in Record Production." *Popular Music* 29 (2010): 251–66.

Zollo, Paul. *Songwriters on Songwriting*. New York: Da Capo, 2003.

Zwaan, Koos, and Tom F. M. ter Bogt. "Breaking Into the Popular Record Industry: An Insider's View on the Career Entry of Pop Musicians." *European Journal of Communications* 24 (2009): 89–101.

INDEX